MAKE
GOOD
TROUBLE

BRIANA PEGADO

MAKE
GOOD
TROUBLE

A PRACTICAL GUIDE
TO THE ENERGETICS
OF DISRUPTION

WATKINS
1893

This edition first published in the UK and USA in 2024 by
Watkins, an imprint of Watkins Media Limited
Unit 11, Shepperton House
89-93 Shepperton Road
London
N1 3DF

enquiries@watkinspublishing.com

Design and typography copyright © Watkins Media Limited 2024

Text copyright © Briana Pegado 2024

Briana Pegado has asserted her right under the Copyright, Designs and
Patents Act 1988 to be identified as the author of this work.

1 2 3 4 5 6 7 8 9 10

Typeset by JCS Publishing Services Ltd

Printed and bound in The United Kingdom

A CIP record for this book is available from the British Library

ISBN: 978-1-78678-787-3 (Paperback)
ISBN: 978-1-78678-788-0 (eBook)

www.watkinspublishing.com

To the little one (within each of us)
who always remembers …

CONTENTS

PREFACE

It is Samhain as I write these words sitting at my kitchen table, feeling the breeze of the changing seasons. Neighbours far and close have already starting shooting fireworks into the darkness in preparation for Bonfire Night. I hear them crackling in the wind, as if the sky is waiting in excited and nervous anticipation of the crack of a firework cutting through the air. The atmosphere is tense. Not only because the veils between worlds are thin on this Witches' New Year, but because even more significant changes are in the air, high up in the cosmos. The beginning of Mars retrograde yesterday – 30 October 2022 – signals an energetic shift. The light flickers in my kitchen and I adjust the dimmer switch, which cuts through the buzzing that hums in the background if I forget to turn the light all the way up. An ancestor has perhaps affected the lighting level a few moments before I started to write these words, to signal their support and love. At least, this is how I interpret it.

I have spent the day in quiet ritual. Taking my time, taking rest when I need it. Also, clearing away: bundles of cardboard and a half-full bin bag from the kitchen, glass into the recycling, compost into the compost bin off the busy street in Glasgow where my flat sits. All the while, it felt deeply intuitive to welcome in this New Year with cleanliness, signalling to the cosmos that it is time to be out with the old and in with the new, to usher in new energies in this season of quiet reflection, and waiting.

I ate my meals slowly and methodically, remembering the jokes, sounds, and mannerisms of those dearly departed. My grandmother loved mustard, and I picked up a jar of wholegrain to eat with my homemade gluten-free sausage rolls – something I never saw her eat, but the act of taking them out of the oven and burning myself in the process reminded me of her "asbestos hands", as food writer Nigella Lawson would have called them.

My grandmother's hands were tough, but she was soft on the inside, a trait she demonstrated through the devotion she put into feeding me, a little one with an insatiable appetite. She would place candied mint leaves, covered in sprinkles of hard sugar, half a stick of gum or a Life Saver into the palm of my hands at significant moments. It was like she always knew when I was getting impatient or wanted a reminder of her presence in the queue at the local pharmacy or during a long car ride.

There was also my father, who spent hours in the kitchen marinading, seasoning, and taking delicious things out of the oven. He was often to be found scaling fish, or cleaning carcasses to prepare them for a delicious meal.

These family rituals of those who have passed on, which shaped my childhood, now rest only in my memory and in the curvature of my thumbnails or the shape of my thighs where they hit my hip and resemble my father's and my grandmother's.

Now the light switch dims again, bringing that irritating, thrumming sound back to the otherwise quiet kitchen. The only other noises are the click of the oven timer and the occasional sound of a car driving by, cutting through the air in a way that reminds me of the gentle but fierce pulse of waves in a seashell. Though we know that this is only the sound of the blood flow in our own eardrums, this undulating noise also suggests a tension, a moment suspended and something to come. The light's buzz ceases once more as it flickers, then steadies. What signal am I being sent? Perhaps the cosmos is suggesting that the Mars retrograde ushers in a two-and-a-half-month-long period of tension . . .

According to the LA-based queer intersectional feminist astrologer Chani Nicholas, this period of Mars retrograde invites us to revisit, explore, and dive into our relationship with "power", "agency", "anger", "bitterness", "rage", and "how we use it". It is asking us for "accountability for the ways we cause harm and how harm lives within us".[1] I am a firm believer in the idea that we all have the capacity to harm and cause harm, intentionally and unintentionally. Our lack of awareness of the impact we have on others and our lack of understanding of our own power both contribute to the harm we cause. It is not a question of whether this happens but how.

Following on from this assertion, it is also a question of knowing when it is necessary to disrupt rather than cause harm. How our disruptions are received and the context in which we cause disruption are things outside our control; what we do have agency and control over, however, is how we communicate our disruption and the intention behind it, which Chani suggests is an important aspect of this retrograde period. We then have more of a chance to manage how it is received or how it lands. And there is no greater time to explore the energetics of disruption, and all of the messy conditions, feelings, and impacts disruption causes, than during a Mars retrograde.

Moreover, this Samhain falls exactly halfway through eclipse season. Two eclipses – a partial solar eclipse in Scorpio that took place on 25 October in the South Node and a lunar eclipse in Taurus set to take place on 8 November in the North Node – usher in a period of release and growth.[2] Similar to the process of death, rebirth, and transformation, eclipses were often feared by ancient indigenous communities because of their obscuring of the light of the sun and the moon. This moment of blockage suggests that we rest and avoid taking too much action; yet it also suggests reflection, because our light, the light of our inner sun, is also obscured. More importantly, the general energy is muddled. We are not sure or completely aware of the facts and full meaning of what is taking place around us. We are walking in the twilight. The sensible thing to do here is to pause before we act, until we have more information. This moment of obscurity is transitional, like the crossing between the states of life and death; we can sit with this moment of pause before change.

Change signifies the end of one thing and the start of another. The first eclipse, in Scorpio, took place in a zodiac sign that embodies transformation through the process of death and rebirth. Uncertainty draws out our fear of the unknown, and the uneasiness of creating something new that has not yet arrived or does not yet exist. Chani Nicholas and other astrologers talk about the liminality of change, the in-between space of nothingness before something occurs, arises, appears, and begins. Like the in-between space of the thinning veil between worlds on All Hallows' Eve that allows us to connect with the souls of ancestors dearly departed, or like the humming of track lighting filling the air and sonically illustrating a feeling of tension before release – this tension is a key. It is a precursor to an act of disruption akin to the crack of fireworks in an otherwise calm, undisturbed space.

And it is like my own times of confusion, of the explosive and revelatory impact I have had on situations by sharing insights, facts, secrets, and truths that seemed obvious to me in the situations in which I've found myself, but which sometimes seemed prophetic to the people that I revealed this information to. I have found myself moving from space to space, situation to situation, workplace to workplace, close friendship to close friendship without really understanding what was happening. I asked myself if it was me. And it surely was, but it was not until I studied the dynamics of these situations – like a post-mortem analysis – that I began to understand and to work intentionally with energetics of disruption that I will be sharing with you in this book.

INTRODUCTION

Now, I'm unsure why you have picked up this book. Are you? We live in a world that is already incredibly disruptive. We are more connected than we have ever been and more knowledgeable, given the supercomputer level of information available at our fingertips thanks to smartphones and tablets. We know more about disasters, wars, conflicts, and developments in countries halfway across the world than we know about the happenings in the lives of our next-door neighbours. We work at a pace out of step with the rhythms we've moved in for centuries.

Technology, data, and artificial intelligence are continuing to develop at a rate that is transforming our existence and pushing us to ask important questions about how we might live in the near future. We find ourselves in one of the most significant moments of change in human history; but it is not just about change – it is an age of disruption. So what better time to understand what disruption means and how we can nurture a more intimate relationship with it than ever before?

The secret to disruption is that its quality is informed by its component parts. Disruption is a choice. It is a change in movement and direction. It is an energy that we can channel however we like; that is, once we understand how it works and why it is fundamental to our very being. A disruptor – anyone who chooses to disrupt or brings on disruption in any given situation – can facilitate change so radical that it becomes foundational. Understanding the elementary components of disruption in order to foster good disruption, disruption that facilitates a change in circumstances – rights a wrong, helps you communicate your boundaries, or initiates a fundamental shift in the perceptions of others – is a skill that requires clever execution. There is probably no better way for us to explore how to make good trouble than by understanding one of the original examples of a troublemaker, embodied by the archetype of the Fool in the Tarot, for ultimately the path of tomfoolery can lead to great wisdom. This book will take us through the meaning of disruption and the energetics of disruption by using key archetypes and symbols from the Tarot, astrology, mythology, and wisdom traditions.

As will become clear, making good trouble is about differentiating between making trouble for its own sake and its inverse: trouble that allows us to act in our integrity, to respond with our inner authority. Making good trouble is about making trouble that does not compromise your health but instead allows you to "habitually cause trouble", to become a troublemaker sustainably. Because, good God, do we need habitual troublemakers. This book will provide a framework for, and definitions of, how to understand the energetics of disruption and stand in your integrity: how to make good trouble.

What is Disruption?

Being a troublemaker brings with it an air of needless conflict and destruction. It is almost as if "making trouble" is simply a moniker or a badge of honour. But what is a troublemaker truly? According to the *Oxford English Dictionary*, one definition of a troublemaker is a person who "habitually causes difficulty or problems, especially by inciting others to defy those in authority". This being so, what does it take for someone to habitually cause trouble and how might this be received? How might troublemaking relate to making good trouble through acts of disruption?

Disruption involves interrupting anything that is moving in a certain direction and which remains unchallenged, unquestioned, and is accepted as being normal or "just the way things are". It can be as simple as asking a question, stating the obvious, interrupting the assumption that how things stand is how they should continue, or wearing something different that disrupts the usual way of dressing. It could mean standing up for someone who experiences abuse walking down the street. It can be daring to try something new at work, at school, at home, and with your friends. Even if you believe that you are not usually someone who is able to speak up, I guarantee that you are disruptive in other ways. You may be disruptive because of how you think, how you see the world, and how you treat the people closest to you. Disruption is not only about the big challenges like mass protests or major movements; it is also about how we disrupt our thinking by questioning the assumptions we make about how our lives are supposed to be and, in turn, how we live among others.

Yet disrupting and disruption can be explosive, when, for example, speaking our truth may result in disorientation, confusion, or a feeling of disassociation. Then, it is as though the truth itself acts like an energy torpedo: even when it is intentionally targeted, and the person aiming it understands that it is set for impact, there is no way to prepare fully for its aftermath. There may be debris and collateral damage.

However, truth-telling does not always have to be received this way. If there is openness and transparency, and there are enough available tools to hand, including language, context, and understanding when a piece of truth is shared, the energy of its landing can feel less like a torpedo and more like an energy pulse that is the catalyst for change and positive new beginnings.

Much depends on context. Whether an energetic disruption interrupts the status quo in a way that feels threatening rather than affirmative depends on how the information is delivered, as well as the audience's relative willingness to receive critique. At an individual level, a person's ability to process hearing the truth and challenging insights depends on a number of factors, such as their emotional state and levels of self-awareness, delusion, and acceptance or otherwise of the toxicity of the situation. It will be subject to how much of their ego is invested in the situation and whether the uncovering of truths, behaviours or insights feels like an attack on their own ego, sense of purpose, and personhood. The same can be said for the response to unearthing truths within a wider system, such as a company or organization, a family, a friendship group or, more generally, any group of people gathering for a set purpose. These factors are further affected by our own relationship to risk and how much we trust in the people around us (and vice versa). The system we live within and the nature of our relationships with others also contribute to the overall level of trust, creating a domino effect that determines how well a particular situation can weather an interruption.

I want to be clear in this distinction: a person who is overtly harming others by abusing their power is different to a person whom you feel is behaving in a way that is misaligned with their own integrity. These are forms of disruption on different scales with different implications and risk factors. The first is an example of an injustice that has an impact on others and the second is an example of an injustice that someone is performing toward themselves.

Because of all of this, the use of disruption requires judgement and discernment. Disrupting a system, institution, a direction of travel, or a way of thinking is very different to disrupting an individual's idea of themselves and crossing a boundary around their own life history, emotions, and lived experience. People are entitled to feel safe among others, to share or conceal private information when they so choose, and not be steamrolled into internalizing another person's perception of them. There is a subtle difference here in our exploration of the disruption of abuses of power, toxic systems, and situations of injustice. All of these spaces of disruption are spaces where harm is being caused and the act of disrupting them is an act of harm reduction. By way of contrast, commenting on someone else's life circumstances without their consent and giving unsolicited advice is not the type of disruption we will seek to explore in these pages. Rather, we will be working with this definition:

> Disruption is a tool to minimize harm with discernment;
> it interrupts an unjust status quo by initiating and
> catalysing change through an energetic pulse that
> highlights and transforms this injustice.

The difference between a mischiefmaker and someone who chooses to make good trouble lies in the difference between someone who is disrupting something for the sake of it – with no purpose, guiding principles, nor integrity – and someone who is acting from a place of integrity, with a love or care ethic, and disrupting the status quo because it embodies an abuse of power.

The idea that causing problems or difficulty is the same as inciting others to defy those in authority is a curious notion. Who says those in authority are not already causing trouble and in need of defiance, resistance, and a set of their own problems to tackle? The habits of troublemakers are something to be studied, understood, and cultivated. For those of us who are unable to tolerate injustice and feel compelled to address it, making good trouble is a behaviour to be commended. How to hone and better shape that compulsion into a choice that minimizes harm and maximizes impact is the key question we will explore together in this book.

The Energetics of Disruption

There is a subtlety to the energetics of disruption. We will be looking at these energetics in more detail in chapter 1, but for now it's important to understand that disruption is not a straightforward process of weighing up the obvious pros and cons of any given situation. That may be part of it, but it is not about pure logic, and it *is* about feeling.

Making good trouble is an intuitive process of weighing up the decision of whether to speak out or act about something. It comes down to the psychic and energetic weight of holding your words and carrying your beliefs with you. It is the intuitive, subtle, psychic, and energetic side of things that predisposes someone to pick up on the opportunity for disruption. This can be experienced as a sensation that lies below the emotional radar, and beneath the surface of our usual physical sensations and interactions with the world; it might also be experienced as a heightened sensitivity to imbalance, to the toxicity, dysfunction, manipulation, duplicity, and concealment that happen when an abuse of power takes place. That is certainly how I experience disruption when a situation goes against my values – it feels like a forcefield grating against my nerves. Our nervous system also has a great role to play in this process (but more on that later).

No matter the scale, spaces in need of disruption leave a subtle energy footprint and signature that can only be picked up by someone attuned to this leftover mark or debris. The signal is harm and when you make good trouble you act like a detector for this harm, sensing that an imbalance is afoot. You may not pick up on this consciously at first, but it is a warning sign that you can learn to detect. It often starts as a hunch, a feeling in the air, a vibe, an energy, an intuition. All of these forms of perception are types of information being fed through energetic signals that allow us to detect the truth of the matter – to pick up on its frequency and then investigate further.

This intuitiveness, and near-psychic perception, needs to be practised with consent, because it can cause harm. In the same way we aim to practise emotional hygiene by checking in with someone before we divulge something personal to them (for example, by asking them if they have capacity, energy, and if they are in the right headspace to receive it), we must do the same with our ability to speak "truths" when they relate to someone's personal life.

These qualities are part of the reason why the Tarot can act as an excellent guide to the energetics of disruption.

The Tarot as Our Guide

A number of women were involved in the creation of two of the most ubiquitous Tarot decks in the modern western world. The American-British occultist, artist, and illustrator Pamela Colman Smith was the illustrator of the Rider–Waite deck (a deck referenced frequently in this book), but she has only been recognized relatively recently for her contributions to the Tarot canon. Her ability to bring A E Waite's vision for the Tarot to life and imbue the cards with her own meanings is why I refer to this deck not as the Rider–Waite, but as the Rider–Waite–Smith deck. Similarly, Aleister Crowley's Thoth Tarot deck (the deck with which I started) was illustrated by Lady Freida Harris, another woman largely erased from the history of Tarot.[1] In describing the Tarot, the author Liz Greene wrote that "[t]hese images are archetypal, which means that they describe essential human situations and patterns, which all of us experience in life at one time or another".[2] The Tarot is also "allegorical – that is to say, it is symbolism . . ."[3] It is partly through this symbolism that we will be journeying through an understanding of disruption and our relationship to it in the chapters that follow.

The 78 cards of Major and Minor Arcana (or the Trump Major and Minor Arcana) have a disputed history. Some say the cards were imbued with their meanings by Egyptian mystics as a way to protect sacred knowledge that they knew would not otherwise be preserved via sacred texts or oral traditions.[4] Others say that the Greek mystics did this. More specific verified accounts of the origins of Tarot put their creation down to the Albigensians in 13th-century France, who permeated the cards with imagery of the Holy Grail, Christian iconography, and other occultist symbolism.[5] The cards have also been associated with the mystery traditions of Hermeticism.[6]

Whatever their true origins, there is no question that the cards are *old* and should be treated as such. Their symbolism, archetypal knowledge, and lessons may be as ancient as time. Whether used as divining objects or guides for self-reflection, they have a mystery unto themselves. They live on as a council of elders and require a relationship of trust and mutual respect in order to reveal their secrets over time. The Tarot is not just a deck of secrets and spells, but asks the reader to open their own heart and practise patience.

All the Tarot cards are assigned a position and number in the deck; however, it is important to note that both the Major and Minor Arcana tell a slightly different story and reveal slightly different archetypes for us to consider. Neither is more important nor powerful than the other, but the Major Arcana does not explicitly reveal a numerical symbolism, as is the case with the Minor Arcana. The Major Arcana, of which there are 22 cards, communicate their position in the deck via the symbol or concept depicted on each card, whereas the cards of the Minor Arcana, of which there are 56, have a specific suite and numerical value which is related to the themes of that suite. Moreover, the Major Arcana shares the story of the Fool – somewhat similar to the traditional structure of the hero's journey – which shapes and informs the backbone of this guide.

In this respect, *Make Good Trouble* takes a similar approach to Jessica Dore's book *Tarot for Change* by using the Tarot as tools for self-reflection. Dore is a social worker and writer who uses the Tarot as a means for transformation, often comparing aspects of the Tarot to psychological tools for self-healing. In her book, she explains the work of the American professor Joseph Campbell and his exploration of the commonalities among myths, stories, and legends the world over, which he described in his seminal work *The Hero with a Thousand Faces*. Akin to the key stages of the hero's journey, the thematic imagery of the Tarot deck traces the story of the Fool by mimicking their journey through life.[7]

The Fool is sometimes known as card zero in the Tarot deck. Traditionally interpreted as male, but representing the experiences of all of us, the Fool is the first card in the deck and takes us on a journey through the Major Arcana, during which the Fool encounters a number of figures, challenges and obstacles that finally lead to the World. The 21st and final card of the Major Arcana, the World brings the Fool's journey to completion, taking us and the Fool full circle to the end of the cycle of life.

However, my aim in these pages is not follow the conventional numerical sequence of the Major Arcana, nor to consider all of the cards in it. Instead, I will be focusing on specific cards as part of the journey to understanding the energetics of disruption. In chapter 1, I will therefore be inviting you to identify with the questing Fool, before encountering the outsider energies of the Magician and Hermit in chapter 2 and the Hierophant in chapter 3.

The Hermit is sometimes misunderstood to mean occult isolation, like that of a mystic who has retreated from society with his secrets,[8] or peace.[9] However, the Hermit actually signifies the truth that is secured by the Divine Mysteries for "their own protection from those who are unprepared".[10] In other words, the Hermit is a symbol of a seeker or a journeyer who has earned the secrets of truth-telling by protecting the truth itself, much like a disruptor who chooses to interrupt the status quo in favour of justice, thereby disrupting abuses of power, toxic cycles, belief systems, and harmful ways of being. This act of shifting the balance of power and energy toward truth and justice can, in my mind, be embodied by the symbolism of the Hermit's carrying a torch of light or, by way of A E Waite's description, carrying a star that lights the way forward to a new world – toward truth.[11]

Chapter 4 leads us on to Strength. One of the shared features between the hero's and the Fool's journey concerns reaching an "initiatory threshold". Dore describes this stage in her own explanation of the Strength card. According to some accounts, the Fool reaches this card and then begins their journey into the Middle Arcana, or middle mysteries. Dore mentions how these cards are thought to take the Fool beyond the binary symbolism of the early mysteries depicted by the Magician, the High Priestess, the Empress, the Emperor, the Hierophant, the Lovers, and the Chariot.[12] However, I do not believe any of the cards communicate their secrets only through binaries. When transposed onto our lives, their meanings are subject to interpretation (within reason) by the reader, guided by the reader's own knowledge and understanding of the symbolism of the cards. Rather than the cards signalling any one outcome, they may instead suggest a number of themes that might emerge around the question you have set them, or the area of your life you have inquired about.

The Major Arcana cards "contain the legend of the soul"[13] and, for our purposes in these pages, they also act as a legend to the key hurdles, challenges, and obstacles we may encounter on our journey toward a better understanding of the energetics of disruption – in which Strength plays a part. The Strength card means fortitude. To Waite, it signifies a "connection with the Divine Mystery of Union" in one of its most "exalted aspects",[14] while reversed or flipped upside-down, it denotes the "abuse of power".[15]

Another card we will explore as an archetypal lesson is Judgement, in chapter 5. This is traditionally the second to last card in the Major Arcana, which the Fool encounters before they reach the World. Judgement is a part of the Fool's journey whereby they choose to accept their calling.[16] Dore sees the Judgement card as signifying both "a call to adventure" and "resurrection"; she views it as an "invitation to change; that is, to leave behind an old way for a new one . . .".[17] According to A E Waite, "It is the card which registers the accomplishment of the great work of transformation in answer to the summons of the supernal – a summons that is heard and answered from within."[18] It also represents "change of position, renewal".[19] This card has been compared to the Temperance card because of its meaning as "a card of eternal life", or, as Waite puts it: "Herein is the intimation of a significance . . . [w]hat is that within us which does not sound a trumpet and all that is lower in our nature rises in response – almost in a moment, almost in the twinkling of an eye?"[20] What he is asking here is: what is within us, which summons us from within? That thing inside that rallies us to instigate change is driven by judgement, the judgement of what we know to be true within. This hints at the process of deciding to interrupt or disrupt a situation based on an inner knowing, an inner judgement that cannot be described or spoken of: it simply exists.

In chapter 6, we will encounter the Wheel of Fortune, and the need to embrace change as part of the natural order of things, before moving on to the Tower in chapter 7. When the Fool encounters the energy of the Tower, there is a moment of revelation that brings them back to an understanding of purpose in the world and away from the feeling of isolation and exile that they experienced when first setting out. This moment is another initiatory experience for the Fool, bringing them into contact with a set of celestial secrets – the cards of the Sun, Moon, and the Star.[21] As A E Waite states: "The disruption and upheaval described by the card of the Tower, for example, may indeed manifest through material circumstances. But its deeper meaning lies in its portrayal of the collapse of old and outworn structures, and such structures can exist within us in the form of stale and rigid mental and emotional attitudes and habit-patterns."[22] It signifies the "materialization of the spiritual word" and "the downfall of the mind".[23] The Tower has also been described as confusion;[24] it shocks the Fool into this understanding and brings them back to themselves, jolting them out of an examination of their inner life and into the context of the outer world.

The Temperance card, touched upon in chapter 8, symbolizes "the perpetual movement of life and combination of ideas",[25] but also the harmonization of our "psychic and material natures".[26] It helps us to understand "something of whence we came and whither we are going".[27] In other words, it gives us grounding and direction when we are navigating the ups and downs of life. In the context of the other cards and the journey on which they are taking us within this book, Temperance is a reminder to approach things with "temper" and balance; for, as per the

Oxford English Dictionary, to temper is the "act of a neutralizing or counterbalancing force to (something)".[28] As a principle of navigating the energetics of disruption, this card embodies a concept that is central to keeping one's sanity.

In chapter 9, we will consider the Lovers card as this pertains to choice, while chapter 10 explores Justice. According to Waite, the Justice card signifies "equity" and "rightness".[29] Beyond the notion of a moral order of things – a *rightness,* as suggested by Waite – this card is associated with "the spiritual justice which is involved in the idea of election".[30] This notion of election or choice comes back to the idea of agency. Justice is an act and a choice we make to secure equity, not just a moral compass or set of principles that lie static and which guide us but do not inspire us to take action. This card and its symbolism remind us of the action we must take to protect, reinforce, and maintain justice – itself not merely a moral principle we can observe and passively participate in.

All of which brings us back to the Fool in chapter 11 and how to embody the Fool's disruptive energy in everyday life, taking this out into the World in chapter 12.

Astrological Energies and Disruption

In addition to the archetypes of the Tarot, astrology is a useful resource to draw on when exploring the energetics of disruption. Astrology is a little like the weather forecast, except that it describes the weather of the entire cosmos, not just a particular place. Using it as a guide gives us insight into the emotional atmosphere, or just a general mood in the air. It can help put our emotions into context and allow us to understand those situations in our day-to-day lives that may feel like they came out of nowhere, especially when it comes to astrological retrogrades.

In astrology, the inner and outer planets (i.e. those closest to and further from the sun) go through a process of appearing to slow down and then move backward in relation to their normal cycle around the sun, orbiting away from the earth. Like its name suggests, a retrograde is an exploration of the "re-s": review, revisit, return, and revise. It is also a time of rest in some ways, because of the pace of the energy present. For example, the well-known phenomenon of Mercury retrograde is revered in popular culture as being a time in which technology and schedules go haywire, and miscommunication runs rife. This is because, from an astrological perspective, Mercury governs these aspects of our lives. Many see a retrograde period as a time of difficulty and challenge relating to the areas that the retrograde planet governs. However, although the difficulty and challenge they anticipate may actually signal which areas of their own lives they need to pay greater attention to, once addressed, this allows for smooth sailing rather than choppy waters for the duration of the retrograde period.

I mentioned earlier the Mars retrograde that occurred when I first started writing this book. In astrology, the planet Mars is associated with conflict, fighting, the need for courage, going into battle, speaking one's truth, and fighting for what one believes in. Given that this book is, among many other things, an exploration of the themes Mars represents, there is an alignment here with the purpose in these pages and the planets. Most notably, the potential turmoil, tumult and fracturing that Mars retrograde brings can create space for wonderful reflections, if we are open to them.

The notion that conflict is something to fear will be a central question that we will explore in this book. Why do we fear it? Is it because it creates the possibility of discomfort? Is it the risk of potential loss or rejection? Or is it because we prefer to remain in comfortable, calm, and orderly environments at all times? As we know, this would be an unrealistic expectation to have on the journey of life.

Mars rules Aries, a zodiac fire sign that is known to be spirited, reactive, and provocative. As a sign that initiates action and can easily be activated by situations of injustice, Mars has an energy that does not shy away from conflict. The ability to navigate and engage with conflict head-on comes down to the question: how are we engaging with our power, our life force, our energy and working with it?

The astrologer Chani Nicholas argues that, of itself, conflict does not ensure harm.[31] Instead, we need to understand better our relationship to the harm that has been done to us and the harm we have caused. When in situations of conflict, we need to own our power and understand our agency. By working with the characteristics of the planet Mars and the energies it embodies we can better explore and understand ourselves. It is Martian energy that fuels us to interrupt injustice and cause strife or commotion in order to help us understand what we are made of. When we are accountable for our power and our rage, we are more able to allow this to impart useful information to us; to discern where our boundaries have been crossed and, as a result, to take appropriate action – to behave in a warrior-like fashion and cause disruption.

Warrior energy has many faces and whether it is by way of the Tarot, astrology, or mythology, this energy is something we need to have more clarity about in our changing world. Over millennia, patriarchal societies have encouraged us to have certain notions of leadership – usually involving strength, steadfastness, and control – leading to warrior energy being moulded into something it is not. Let's move away from the principles of binary thinking and into the sphere of dialectic thinking, where opposites can exist all at once, in the same space.

Take Mars, for example. As I mentioned earlier, this is the planet associated with conflict, battle, and fighting in astrology and mythology. However, in the Tarot, Mars can be linked to the Chariot,[32] a card that, in the Rider–Waite–Smith deck, is symbolized by a warrior figure who has been through tests of initiation, and who ultimately aims to effect liberation.[33] As we have seen, being tested is part of the hero's journey that the Fool embarks on in the Major Arcana, and it is the Fool's blind faith in the journey ahead that enables the Fool to be open to the lessons they will receive. Their courage is what guides them. It is this courage and sense of purpose that guides a warrior.

Disruption as an Act of Love

Courage is an act of love, and a love ethic is what this book proposes and supports. According to bell hooks in her seminal work *All About Love*, we can only live in a society with a "love ethic" at its heart if we "let go of our obsession with power and domination";[34] moreover, to bring this ethic to "every dimension of our lives, our society would need to embrace change".[35] She goes on to explain that this radical change requires us to have the courage to live the truth of our values and that people may fear change because it can mean challenging the status quo.[36] "Fear is the primary force uploading structures of domination",[37] she notes, and argues that it is love that is the antidote to this fear of change. Love has an alchemical quality that can transform and transmute our fears. Within this framework we can see that, if disruption is about interrupting domination and shifting power, then it is an act of love. (We will explore later the ways in which we need to remain critical in the face of fear in order to have the courage we need to challenge it and transmute it.)

Interrupting abuses of power and the systems that maintain these abuses is how we can ensure and protect our collective well-being. This is what hooks calls a central part of "a love ethic", as well as what will be referred to henceforth as a "care ethic". Abuses of power are systems reinforced by a culture of domination that can be characterized by the archetype of Mars, a masculine warrior energy. But this is Mars when interpreted, applied, and discharged in an abusive way. It is not how masculine energy needs to be experienced and is thus an example of an abuse of power.

How we understand power, interact with it, wield it, and shape it or share it are central to our experience and quality of life on earth. Often people with power feel a need to exert control over situations and individuals, yet this compulsion is misguided. By using discernment and the tools we will explore in this book, we will discover there is no need to control the dynamics of power, only the situations in which to disrupt it. This act of disruption is an act of love that asks us to let go of our attachment to power and our fear of change. Once we can understand the importance of disruption to interrupt and end abuses of power, we can view disruption as an act of creating a better, safer world, and therefore as an act of love. It is in this way that "constructive confrontation aids our healing"[38] – a confrontation that has been chosen, discerned, and actioned with care.

Using Disruption to Live in Alignment with Your Values

There is so much empty talk these days about "finding your purpose" or being "values-led" that it's no wonder we end up searching for the deeper meaning behind it all. There are clear historical, technological, philosophical, economic, and political factors that have contributed to this perfect storm of our quest for purpose. Some may argue that it is simply another manifestation of our existential search – for meaning, for our perpetual need to question why we are here. Put simply: if we do not know what makes us happy, how can we pursue it? If we do not know what brings us ease, how can we encourage it? If we do not know what brings us peace, how can we create it? If we do not know what makes us burn with excitement, how can we feed it? And if we do not know what we do not know, then we cannot do what we do not know we want to do.

The situation is as simple as this: our values lead the way. Once we understand what is or is not in alignment with our interests, knowing our values allows us to live with more ease. "Alignment" is a word that has become consistently used along with "resonance" to describe things that line up with our desires – we speak of things that resonate with our way of being or our life philosophy. But what do these terms (and jargon) which have been dominating the wellness industry for the last decade actually mean?

"Resonance" or "alignment" could be described as inner feelings of knowing: of calm, of peace, of inspiration, or of any other inner spark felt in response to an experience, a concept, an idea, a person, a physical place, or situation. It is that (almost) indescribable embodied reaction to something that is pleasing or satisfying – an umami of the soul, or of our desires, you could say. It is that head-nodding, hair raised on the back of the neck (in a good way) sense of calm, security and safety that emerges as a reaction to an experience that washes us over with a sense of contentedness. This is the physical feeling of our values compass needle pointing north; it is all of those feelings that indicate we are experiencing the deep meaning of values. We are seeing it realized in the world and in a felt sense, right in front of us. It is the thought of: *this is the place; this is the person; this is the opportunity; and this is the feeling, here*. There are so many ways that we can experience resonance and alignment. What distinguishes it from simply knowing or receiving verification that our values are truly ours is that we feel it and experience it corporeally. It is not always something we can describe.

In our modern western society and culture, we have downplayed the importance of feelings. Instead, we have apotheosized the importance of rationality, logic, and thought. Our feelings and their relationship to our bodies have been dismissed as contrary to logic and rationality, which in turn are all wrapped up in our current disconnection from our bodies, our intuition, and ultimately the guiding principles that give us a greater sense and clarity of "purpose" in our lives. It is no wonder that we are living in a world where people are experiencing so much mental ill-health, to the extent this trend have been identified as a global public health emergency that needs to be solved. However, alongside the identification of this "problem", new research is uncovering some old truths: that ignoring our feelings and dismissing their presence in our bodies can cause us to become unwell and dysregulated to a point that we develop dis-ease. The reconnection between our feelings and our bodies is a journey of rediscovery many brave souls are pioneering in our wellness and healing communities.

The Embodiment of Our Values

The connection between our physical and emotional selves is why our values are not just something we can think and believe. Our values are something we must inherently *feel* and thereby know. This is where our feeling brain comes into the picture or, in other words, our intuition. The somewhat challenging and amorphous concept of "intuition" remains elusive to grasp and define for many. What is our intuition? Is it that nagging internal voice warning us not to take a risk? Is it a quieter, steadier voice that is always present? Is it driven by fear? Is that fearful voice inside of our heads actually our ego? What if we have no voice inside our heads at all – no internal monologue, which is how many people experience the world . . . then, what?

I believe our confusion around our intuition and our inability to identify it are the direct result of our disconnection from our feeling bodies and ultimately from an understanding of our values. Without a clear understanding of our values and what is important to us, and being able to put a name to this, how can we possibly define our reactions to the world, other people, and specific situations that cause us to deeply feel? When our spider-sense tingles that something is amiss, or we feel something has violated our moral code, but are not sure why, how could we ever act on those sensations? We cannot act without a clear sense of who we are and what we believe in.

Our intuition is not something we can think our way to. It is something we can only feel. We need to rebuild the muscle memory that allows us to feel into our intuition and our feeling brain, much like we need to rebuild a relationship with our divergent thinking skills. It is something we have fallen out of practice with and have been told fervently to ignore and deprioritize. This attitude keeps us cut off from a deep inner intelligence we all possess, which is like a first mate to the captain on the ship of our lives.

Using our intuition to connect with our values is not always easy. It is something that is conditioned out of us at a young age. Being in our integrity requires us to understand our values and the principles that guide our feelings, as well as how we choose to be in the world – to maintain peace, equity, and fairness. This is a large part of the process of understanding disruption for good and unearthing what being in our integrity means for us. It may take us to a space of self-reflection, deep reckoning, or thinking about what is truly important for us for the first time in our lives.

Like anything in life, we need to work at it. We need to build up our muscles to use our intuition like a toddler builds up muscles when learning to walk. This process is not something that comes quickly at first, but once the skill is developed and learned it cannot be forgotten, although we may sometimes let those muscles atrophy. Don't worry, this book aims to help you redevelop your relationship to your intuition with a number of exercises, tips, and tools that will help you practise using those muscles again or, indeed, use them consciously for the first time.

On Making Good Trouble

Disruption is chaotic. There is no way around this fact. Chaos for many is something to avoid, problem-solve, and prevent, rather than a state of being to encourage. However, for many artists and particle physicists, chaos is simply part of the stuff of life, and it is people's inability to tolerate chaos and their urge to avoid it that cause trouble. The fact is that chaos is the first step to rebuilding after destruction. It is the materials from which we create, ultimately, the stuff we need to grow. We can understand through the symbolism of the Tarot the need for moments of chaos and chaotic intervention as the catalyst for new beginnings.

I would like you to take this moment to prepare yourself for your first initiatory threshold, a liminal space that marks the end of what you knew before and the beginning of the journey we are about to embark on. This exploration is not for the faint of heart. It requires strength to embark on the journey of the Fool and warrior-like courage. In the chapters that follow, you will discover how, once you begin working with your intuition and reconnecting with your values, you will gain access to a form of inner guidance that can empower you again and again to make good trouble and, ultimately, change the world for better.

I
THE ENERGETICS OF DISRUPTION

The Fool is a misfit and rulebreaker who embarks on a journey of self-knowledge and understanding.[1] The Rider–Waite–Smith deck shows the Fool setting out – flower in hand, knapsack on shoulder and dog at heel – gazing at the horizon and treading close to a cliff edge. I want you, the reader, to see yourself as the Fool and to embody this archetype's wonder, openness, and a certain type of openminded foolishness regarding the journey you are about to embark on; to see yourself as the journeyer who is open to new knowledge, mysteries, and secrets that will ultimately bring you closer to yourself and provide you with a renewed sense of purpose, intention, and relationship to the world. One that brings you into alignment with your choices about what you will tolerate, support, and disrupt to create a more peaceful world for yourself, the people around you, and the people who come after you. A path to becoming a good ancestor and an even better neighbour . . .

Walking the path of the Fool to instigate change requires us to have courage and to progress with the uncertainty and the full spectrum of emotions that change brings, which is often uncomfortable. In this book, the Fool's journey relates first and foremost to understanding the energetics of disruption and embodying these in your life.

The very word "energetics" suggests the existence of a system that rules how energy works, much as the Law of Thermodynamics states energy can be neither created nor destroyed; it can only be transferred. This is a useful place to start. Energy can be used to heal, to hold, and to shift, and it can also be used to destroy, to manipulate, and to control. Yet energy is a form unto itself that has its own rules and ways of being outside of our human needs, our rules for engaging with it, and our understanding of it as a system, modality, medium, or form of matter. As fundamental as a gas, liquid, or solid, energy is its own thing – its own being.

In trying to define energy, there are many hurdles and difficulties. The challenge itself is like defining the very words with which I write this passage. Energy is entirely experiential, intuitive, and felt in the body like emotions, but cannot be defined by its mechanical parts, just as emotions themselves cannot be considered to be only a firing of the synapses, or a mere response to internal or external stimuli.

What is key in regard to energetics has less to do with the energy itself and more to do with who interacts with it. I almost wrote who "uses" it – but, in my opinion, energy has properties of its own. Even if we think we are "using" it, energy is ancient and omnipotent in ways that humans are not. It has been around since the beginning of time, the Big Bang that started existence as we know it. It defies any and all of our attempts to dominate it. We can, however, grow to understand it, honour it, and play with it. Energy is at the core of magic and magical practice. It is at the core of our life force. It is us and we are it. Energy is what exists at the centre of the universe and – provided we believe that we are made from the same stuff – energy is everything.

But what even *is* "energy" in the sense that I mean? Take your favourite city or your favourite spot in the place where you live. Would you say there is an energy to it? How does it make you feel? What are its properties, its unique features? How does this energy feel, look, sound, and taste?

This is not about how energy looks or feels physically, although that is most certainly an influence. It is an intuitive but very present quality to a place that sits just on the edge of our consciousness. It is something we can feel, but it is also something we can sense – a moving thing. We might experience it as one of our five senses. It might be a taste, smell, touch, feeling, or sound that only we can hear. Other people might pick up on it, but it will be unique to our experience of this place.

We are mammals, animals. We receive energy from being in nature and interacting with all of the elements: fire to cook our food, or as part of ritual ceremony; water to quench our thirst, or for its healing powers on our nervous system; air to fill our lungs, or to remind us that we are indeed alive and that the trees support us with oxygen; or earth, which helps us grow things and build our homes, but also grounds us when we are feeling chaotic, burned out, and outside of our bodies. The ecosystem of elements is a system that supports the movement of energy in our bodies as well as in the physical and spiritual realms.

With respect to the latter, we might sense energy with our clairsenses, because this too is how we interact with and make sense of the world. Our clairsenses are the five psychic senses that align with our five physical senses. We can have psychic sight or psychic smell, for example, which afford us a glimpse into a world of the past, present, or future, arising from an intuitive knowing that allows us to tap into the world of spirit, ancestor, and those that have passed on. It allows us to feel what things came before in time or space, or what might be yet to come.

Setting Out on the Journey

My journey toward understanding my own disruptive qualities and energy has been a long and hard-fought one. From learning how my ethical approach and voracious questions contribute to disruptive moments, to working to better understand how my neurodivergence contributes to my worldview, disruption has been a large part of my life.

However, it wasn't until 2018 that a narrative about my disruption clicked into place for me. I had recently walked away from a job at an arts organization after a situation of alleged abuse within the company was mishandled. The stress of the situation caused me to break out in my first bout of psoriasis; I had no family history of skin conditions, nor had I ever experienced this type of skin inflammation in my short life. In my spare time, I volunteered for a spiritual platform and podcast series dedicated to supporting people on their journey after experiencing a dark night of the soul.

Dark nights of the soul have been described by many spiritual seekers as moments of awakening. Whether these moments last for minutes or years, they reveal a spiritual need for change and enable a deep dive into the darkness of a transformative process. Some people experience this process as a literal fall or accident (much like the Fool risks, dancing along the cliff edge) which forces them to re-examine their relationship to themselves. A dark night of the soul can also be precipitated by a form of burnout, illness, or injury – signals from the body that your current way of living is not working for you anymore. In learning about the dark night of the soul, I had finally found some language for my experience of disruption.

For as long as I can remember, I have been someone who would ask a question or point out something that felt obvious to me, and which aligned with my understanding of justice and injustice, but which people would find incredibly upsetting or to which they would react in a way I could not understand.

I would always approach these matters politely, with diplomacy and kindness, but I would still raise the issue. At times, if a situation was not addressed, was ignored, or in some cases covered up, I would choose to remove myself from the situation. I would simply leave. Somehow, the act of leaving would be more disruptive than raising awareness about the problem itself. It was like leaving was an act of defiance that was too much for the organization, the friendship, the family dynamic, or the social setting to handle.

My choice to leave marked the disruption. I refused to ignore it, cover matters up, or compromise when a solution, a workaround, or a working through was not possible, desired, or addressed. *Why should I stay in a situation that goes against my values, continues to cause harm, is causing me physical stress, or is unfair to the people involved?* I would think to myself.

What I did not realize was that this way of being, working, and treating others is often so normalized that my inability to tolerate it or pretend that it was ok was seen as audacious. My desire to change things, question them, or leave was threatening and unusual. For a lot of people, it was easier to get on with things and not ask questions, but for me it had never been that way.

What happened over time was that my willingness or inability to ignore wrongdoing, harm, or injustice became a beacon for other people. It was subtle. It was energy. Sometimes, I would share my stories with others. I would blog or write about my experiences. These stories spread via word of mouth, or I would demonstrate my values by behaving in ways that stood in marked opposition to certain situations.

I have always been very observant and can pick up on details in my environment, which includes speaking to people who are more reserved. I have one of those faces that signals to people I'm a trustworthy person to confide in, so people have always shared with me their secrets, personal experiences, and unformed opinions on things within minutes of meeting me.

It turned out that in situations of wrongdoing, I seemed to be a person who other people would come to. Quite often in these situations nothing was being done; the embarrassment and shame were too stark. The friendships that protected abusers ran too deep, to the extent that people were worried that they would be implicated if accusations came out or were properly investigated. It was quite rare to have any kind of infrastructure in place (or even an HR department) through which to report and investigate abuse, protect those who came forward, and put in place robust policies to facilitate this – let alone one that didn't protect the company or organization at all costs. In work situations, the knee-jerk reaction was for people to ask why nothing had been done before and why things were only coming to the surface now, shifting blame to the past rather than taking responsibility for the present. On other occasions, I found that people were unable to understand what was wrong because it was simply customary to behave that way. They never questioned it, and they didn't understand why I had to.

Quite quickly the conversation shifts from "What is the problem here?" to "Why are you causing the problem?" It is easier to project the machinations of a harmful system onto a single individual, and to ignore the reality that the system – institution, company, family, workplace, friendship group, and society more widely – is designed poorly. It is easier to focus on one person than to zoom out and question an entire way of being. It is easier to call someone a troublemaker than to ask ourselves if one person can truly make trouble without questioning the system itself; by which I mean the conditions that lead to troublemaking – the people around us, their values, their behaviour, and the environment we find ourselves in.

While speaking out against the status quo may seem foolish to some, I have learned to be proud of my ability to disrupt – to make good trouble. It has connected me more strongly than ever to my inner values and taught me how, through acts of disruption, energy can be directed to heal and create, rather than destroy.

Different Energy Healing Modalities

In the healing world, there are many different modalities that work with energy. When I refer to the healing world, I am also referring to the health and wellness world, the medical world, the world of stories and tales that heal us, the world of plants and land, the worlds of elders and those who heal with smoke, the world of the clairvoyant, psychic, and intuitive, the world of those who communicate across veils, mediums, and channels. All these worlds are spaces, liminal spaces, in-between things, which communicate through and work with energy. We feel physical energy every day based on the amount of vitality we sense, which motivates us to move. We replenish our physical energy through rest, food, and being in the presence of (or *without* the presence of) others.

Energy healing modalities belong to many different schools of thought, practices, and ways of transferring energy for the purpose of healing. For example, yoga, though not often seen as an energy healing modality per se, is not just about physical movements; it is about ways of being and working the breath, or *prana* (life force energy), to control energy flow in the body.

Similarly, witches and healers interact with energy in various different ways. They may use spellwork, charms, altars, herbs, kitchen tools, incantations, and grimoires. They may work together or alone. They may follow the wheel of the year or practise beliefs and rituals that require certain initiations. Their craft might be deeply hidden or performed in plain sight. In all cases, they are manipulating, interacting with, and working with energy to change the world. It could be for their own personal ends, the ends of the group of humans they work with, or for more global or universal ends.

In my experience, trauma-informed psychology and psychiatry can also be forms of energy healing work. I have spent over ten years working with two therapists, one from the Freudian school of thought and another from the Jungian, to understand the energetic impact of years of childhood trauma and centuries of generational trauma. Whether this has manifested in my body as phobias, complex PTSD, ADHD, anxiety, depression, and other neuroses, my therapists' techniques, listening ears, and expertise have allowed me to transmute the energy of those experiences into something else entirely. They have been lifesaving and life-enhancing. I have grown leaps and bounds in understanding myself (and others), as well as having the energy to engage with a world that I find at times to be extremely noisy.

Bodyworkers, including massage therapists, craniosacral therapists, osteopaths, certain chiropractors, acupuncturists, Ayurvedic specialists, meridian bodyworkers, medical herbalists, homeopaths, aromatherapy specialists, some podiatrists, nutritional therapists, herbalists, physiotherapists, and other therapists use their understanding of the body, ancient techniques, ancient wisdom, natural remedies, and incredible expertise to move energy in the body to heal it.

For some healing modalities, while energy is key, the notion that our physical body is directly connected to our emotional body is not a belief they share. They may operate through the logic of meridian lines or energy centres linked to our body's eight chakra points, for example. (For more on the chakras, see chapter 10, page 185.) In contrast, the Human Design school of thought, which helps us discern our energy, combines the chakra system, the I-Ching and astrology into a massive system of energy flow through our bodies that helps us better understand our needs, values, and how we interact with others and the world with less resistance.

Other modalities also make an explicit connection between the body and mind, such as the method devised by Louise Hay. Hay initially became famous for her book *You Can Heal Your Life*, which outlines the underlying spiritual cause, meaning, influence, and emotional impact of our physical ailments. The same properties apply to energy healing modalities such as reiki and Theta Energy Healing®. Both reiki and Theta Energy Healing® work with the energy of brainwaves to heal physical ailments in the body.

Discovered by Vianna Stibal in the mid 1990s, Theta Energy Healing® channels theta brainwaves from Source energy (the universe, deities, or whatever higher power you believe in – if none, then yourself) to heal physical, psychological, and emotional ailments, while addressing patterns and core beliefs that cause discomfort, trauma, and ailments in the body. Theta Energy Healers® are able to bring context, connect to Source energy and make connections that tap into people's past histories, generational belief systems, and soul-level beliefs to shift energy away from trauma and toward healing. This is a modality that I, too, have trained in.

An Introduction to Theta DNA Energy Healing®

When a Theta Energy Healer® works with a client one to one, we are doing the work of unearthing what ails them. Otherwise known as "digging", this technique allows the practitioner to get to the root of the apparent problem – the belief that is causing discomfort, physically, emotionally, and spiritually. This belief can sit in a client's conscious awareness or just outside of it. Quite often, when you are working with someone and asking them a series of questions to better understand what ails them or what core beliefs they hold, they may stop speaking and shut down. Then, the client may say things like "I don't know", "there is nothing there", or "there is nothing else". A skilled Theta Energy Healer® will be able to identify this block as an important step before the emergence of the truth.

Knowing how long or how deep to dig is therefore a skill. The conversation must be conducted without asking leading questions, unless these are necessary. As Theta Energy Healers®, we are working very closely with energy, and, with a person's consent and permission, channelling healing to our client throughout a session. As we go, we may be asking Source to give that person a higher perspective on loyalty, for example. What we mean by this is that we can give them an energetic insight or "download" into what true loyalty feels like, not the manipulative or toxic kind. The aim is to heal any harmful beliefs and experiences by providing a new framework for loyalty, allowing them to work past trauma or negative experiences concerning broken loyalty, for example. It is an instantaneous healing and it is channelled by theta brainwaves.

Another important component to this process is the literal rewriting of experience on a cellular level. Vianna Stibal didn't call her method "Theta DNA Healing" for fun. When this energetic practice was channelled through her, she understood and experienced how this energetic healing was happening on a cellular level. Today, we know that our genetics impact so many different aspects of our lives from the moment they were encoded in us at our conception, from inherited conditions and diseases, to all of the physical, emotional, and psychological characteristics that make us who we are.

Our core beliefs do not exist only on one or two levels. They may have been passed down to us from our family through intergenerational trauma. Today, scientists, trauma specialists, and psychologists are well aware of the impact that these types of experience have when passed down through our bodies epigenetically. Through the work of psychiatrists, physicians, and psychotherapists such as Bessel van der Kolk, Gabor Maté, and Peter Levine, we know that the body keeps score in ways we cannot fathom for generations to come. Theta DNA Energy Healing® works to unwind and heal these connections at the DNA level and allows us to let go of beliefs, frameworks, mindsets, and ways of experiencing the world that have a detrimental impact on our health.

Receiving and Exchanging Energy: Downloads and Channelled Messages

For a Theta Energy Healer®, discerning between the energy of the person they are working with and the energetic "messages" that are meant for them is very important. What do I mean by energetic messages? Theta Healers® sometimes talk about instantaneous healing arriving in the form of energy downloads, which can manifest as a sudden sense of vitality, new knowledge or information, clarity around a topic, or channelled messages shared through a healer or person from the universe itself.

The ability to receive downloads is echoed by other energy workers, including astrologers and guides in the spiritual community. For them, downloads may take the form of solar energy flares, numerological energy portals, or auspicious interactions between planets in the astrological calendar. They may open themselves up to the significance of these by getting quiet on important solstice days, through meditation, by checking in with themselves, and through asking guidance from any guides, deities, or goddesses they connect with. Whatever their form, at the core of all these downloads is the receipt of wisdom, knowledge, and intuitive information through an exchange of energy that enables us to update our own operating systems – a bit like an update for our laptops, tablets, and phones. It gives us fresh divine insights about an idea, topic, and/or way of relating to ourselves or other people.

In Theta Healing®, clients can receive downloads based on the issue, body part, or human experience they are seeking to heal. When a Theta Energy Healer® clears stuck energy, a stagnant belief, or tricky core belief system based on bodily, generational, or soul-level trauma, they will ask the client if they would like a download of a new belief, energy, or belief system to replace the old one. As mentioned, it could be a download regarding a concept such as true loyalty, or it could be the reality of what true partnership feels like, what unconditional love is, or even just experiencing the fullness of being present in a body, for example. All of this comes down to the client's core beliefs and belief systems, which have been unearthed through the healing session. The "healing" is then a download of theta energy from the Source of life itself, which, in turn, enables the client and the healer to channel healing energy to and from one another. The focus of these healings and downloads is directed at the client, but the healer benefits from them too, by acting as the channel between Source and the person receiving the healing.

To receive a download when you are working with a Theta Energy Healer®, you simply consent to receiving the download, sit back, breathe, and accept the knowledge. It will not necessarily come to you in words, it may just be a feeling. You may get a sense of a weight being lifted and of lightness. You may immediately sense that you have gained a deeper understanding or a new perspective on something you didn't have before. Or you may not feel anything in particular at first and only later, when you revisit the belief system, realize that you feel differently about it, and that you react differently to a situation that relates to your healed belief, or simply no longer feel any sort of resistance around the idea anymore – for example, you may have changed your views about the idea that love has to be hard, or that you have to overwork in order to feel successful.

Those are just two small examples of the plethora of ways in which Theta Energy Healing® might impact your beliefs and belief system; however, it is not as straightforward as going into a session with a Theta Healer® and saying to them, "I believe love is hard and I would like help to stop feeling this way." Quite often, by the time you come to a Theta Energy Healer® with a physical ailment or mental ailment, you may feel stuck or tired. You may feel malaise. And it is only through the session and the process of talking over things that you begin to unearth what is at the heart of your "issue" and start to root out the beliefs that underpin them in order to heal.

There is much more that goes into the Theta Energy Healing® process and the training healers receive that I cannot reveal, nor would it feel right to do so. There is a great deal to learn about the nature of the universe, time, energy, and the way we interact with it that is fluid, adaptable, changeable, and infinite. We have so much more influence over our reality and our bodies than we may realize, but we have to learn how to use the tools to negotiate these different aspects of our realities. Without taking you down a rabbit hole of platitudes and vague references, I want you to think about how you understand your life at this moment. Do you believe you have power and influence over your decisions? Or do you feel that your decisions are not your own?

A Healer's Guide to Managing Your Energy

Healing might not just release energy inside the client, but inside the healer. We often interact in the world as mirrors of one another. We can mirror each other's beliefs, mindsets, and pain, for example. We can also mirror each other's joy, love, and bewilderment at the beauty of the universe. This is where like can attract like; another energetic principle shown in science through the rule of magnetism. It also references the theory of attraction and manifestation, but rather than dive into these different schools of thought, let us explore what the principle of being a mirror for another person, a place, or a situation might mean for us energetically and how we can then use discernment in these circumstances.

Theta Energy Healers® often believe that our clients or the people we work with are attracted to us for a reason. Maybe they are working through something we have worked through ourselves or maybe they are working through something we could be repressing, unaware of, or simply indifferent to. The beauty of this relationship is that we may discover things about our own beliefs and habits that would otherwise remain concealed from us. This is why it is important that we work on our own belief systems and energies regularly while we work with others.

Now, I have not practised regularly as a Theta Healer® since I trained back in 2019, so I need to take my own advice here. However, I do engage in energy healing work, and when I do, I always make sure to ask myself: is this energy I am picking up on (beliefs, ideas, feelings, pain, etc.) mine or does it belong to the person I'm working with? We are constantly picking up energetic debris from our environment, and depending on how sensitive we are to our environment and how often or well we remember to practise energy hygiene, we may be muddling up the energy of the person, situation, or dynamic in front of us with our own energy, feelings, ideas, beliefs, and physical sensations.

In Theta Healing®, practitioners learn to manage their own energy and clear it, which comes back to the fundamental principle of healing your own "stuff" before, alongside, and while you heal others. The notion that we will ever be finished healing reinforces the idea that we can reach perfection – but perfection does not exist. We can look at our healing journey and the people we work with as a process of learning lessons, being presented with mirrors, and discovering information to guide us on our way, including on our journey toward making good trouble and becoming disruptors.

Disrupting the Status Quo

In line with the principles of physics and the concept of inertia, we are designed to continue in the direction in which we are already travelling in order to conserve energy. It takes energy and effort to change direction, to interrupt the flow of energy and the flow of things – and, ultimately, to change the status quo.

Now, if we were to apply this principle to society more widely, what would we consider to be the status quo? What things are taken as given in your world, friendship group, family, or partnership? It is difficult these days to assume that anything is "universal" or experienced by everyone in the world (other than breathing) when we live lives that are so drastically different from each other. This includes our access to technology and information, and our customs, cultures, and beliefs.

I learned how to be a dissident from an early age because I often did not like what I was seeing around me. The things I noticed made me very suspicious of authority. It took me years to realize that this suspicion came from a sincere place of observation. I observed that people in power often behaved in ways that rarely demonstrated respect for others, yet which earned them respect in return. They often forced compliance and expected it without consent. Without doing the work to build trust, they would assume that, because they had been given the power they possessed and the position they held, this then gave them licence to expect subordination.

This is obviously not always the case for people in positions of power and those responsible for others. There are many examples of caring, community-based power-sharing structures, hierarchies that allow for coherence, not strict compliance, and a power dynamic that encourages collective agreement, not individual domination. However, if we look at world history as a whole, we can find a multitude of examples where domination, exploitation, abuse, and harm were the methods chosen by leaders. They created spaces, societies, and cultures built in the image of their desire to maintain ultimate control. This trend does not come from nowhere, but speaks to the dominating modus operandi of our time – capitalism.

Now, discourse around capitalism and exploitation has been dominated by socialism, communism, radical feminist theory, anti-racist theory, climate scientists, theologians, historians, sociologists, psychologists, anthropologists, and activists for generations. It is not as simple as "capitalism is bad", but it *is* as simple as "capitalism promotes efficiency and productivity in a world of scarce resources". This scarcity requires us to optimize those resources at any cost, which incurs a cost on our bodies, time, and the natural landscape. If we lived in a world of plenty and abundance, there would be no need to compete for resources, nor would there be a need to be guided by a market of supply and demand.

There is also no way to talk about the history of capitalism without talking about the history of slavery and colonialization. This is why people say that capitalism cannot exist without white supremacy and toxic patriarchy. The systems at play that benefit only a few exist and thrive due to histories of exploitation over centuries. Free labour is the foundation on which modern western society was built. The ability to see Black bodies as "less than" and the land loved by these bodies as "uncivilized terrain" to be taken – resources and all – is fundamental to our human history.

It may be that you read this and think, "What does any of this have to do with me and why is this topic constantly revisited?" It is revisited because it is important. Until we understand the scale on which human bodies were trafficked, exploited for free labour, and used as breeding machines, and of the unpaid labour extracted from women to maintain households over centuries, then we cannot understand why power used in this way has always been exploitative and violent. Harm comes from violence, and the way we have treated each other has been nothing but violent for centuries.

Rich spiritual traditions and an understanding of our relationship to our bodies, to our land, and to each other were also harmed in this process of systemic brutalization. The disconnection we experience from our bodies and our inner lives is directly related to the shame and guilt toward, as well as the erasure of, our past. The harm that was inflicted on Black people, people of colour, people with non-western traditions and ideologies, women, queer people, and other genders is deep. Our disconnection from our emotions is part of the coping process. For how else can a culture that exploited and harmed others so ruthlessly cope with generations of harm? This is supported by a belief in that culture's superiority – white supremacy and a belief in that culture's closeness to God – a divine right to rule, as in a Christian monarchy. Critiques of these belief systems sit at the very core of decolonial, anti-racist, intersectional feminist, womanist, and trauma-based philosophies. Audre Lorde, bell hooks, Angela Davis, Martin Luther King Jr., and Senator John Lewis are among the thinkers who have dedicated their lives to the unpacking of history and the unlearning of cultures of violence.

What does this mean for our own understanding of power and privilege? How can we understand our power in this world even if we feel we have none? How do the circumstances of our birth, our geography, our family history, our beliefs, our access to resources that fulfil our basic needs, our language, our sexuality, our gender, our neurotypicality, or our neurodivergence influence the role we play in the wider world? We can understand our energy and our impact. We can understand the systems, beliefs, and relationships we need to disrupt in order to minimize the impact of our history and build a better world – a world shaped in the image of care, love, community, and abundance. We can begin to see our way forward; for would it not be better to build trust collaboratively, based on an exchange of ideas, commitment, sharing knowledge, sharing skills, and a mutual understanding around who is best placed to be in positions of power? All it takes is a dream and the will to try.

Tackling Harm, Abuse, and Injustice

People often refuse to look abuse, harm, or injustice in the eye when they feel too close to these, because they realize that then they would have to admit their own role in wrongdoing. We have an uncanny inability to accept that we can cause harm, even if this is unintentional. The fact is that we all have the capacity to harm, and we have all caused harm. It is part of being human. Yet there is a moral framework in place that encourages us to ignore this simple truth. It dates back to Protestant values, if not further, and involves a delusional view of ourselves and the messy emotions that come with accepting these harder aspects of life. Negative emotions, self-reflection, and understanding our own power all factor into comprehending our capacity to harm. In the west, we live in a society that encourages us to hyperfocus on the good, the positive, and on the palatable aspects of being human, precisely because there is so much damage, danger, abuse, and difficulty in the world. Yet the good comes *with* the bad – although in many respects we are socialized to stay away from the bad in order to cope with the good.

However, there is more language available to us around abuse today, and a better understanding of why people do not speak out about it than ever before. We have more resources to work through the notions of shame, embarrassment, and the confusion that come with things not being as they seem. Realizing there has been harm right under our noses is not easy, but it is necessary in order to transmute that harm into healing.

While we have the tools to hold people or systems accountable by bringing them to justice, the same blind spots, flaws, and acceptance of the status quo also exist in our systems of justice, allowing abusers to be believed over survivors or accusers. How often do we give our power away in our everyday lives and let ourselves or other people excuse harmful behaviour? Do any of these phrases sound familiar . . .?

It is just the way they are.
Boys will be boys.
It's just a joke!
They didn't mean anything by it.
Are you sure that's what they meant?
They didn't realize they were doing it.
That's just the way it is.
We have always done it this way!
That's what happened to me, and I didn't complain.
They didn't mean to hurt you.
But they are your [insert family member here] and they love you!
I find that hard to believe!
Sticks and stones may break your bones, but words will never hurt you.
What doesn't kill you makes you stronger.
That may have been hard, but it made you who you are today – and look at where you are now.

All of these phrases are excuses used to justify harm and bad behaviour. These are tools to cover up, shame, ignore, dismiss, and, simply put, avoid facing the role we played in enabling the harm to take place in the first instance.

What we ignore in each and every one of these situations is the power at play; the ways in which this energy moves through, in, and around us in our lives. The way that power is an energy, and it is also a system. It has rules, ways of flowing, ways of working that we will all interact with on a daily basis, but because we are so used to it, we barely take notice of it. We barely stop to think about, unpack, or understand the forces at play in our lives because we were born into them and we assume that the way things are is the way they will always be.

This is where the disruptor comes in to disrupt these assumptions. A disruptor has a vision for the way things could be and ought to be, based on guiding values and principles. Each disruptor may not have the exact same vision, but they may and can have a common purpose. And that is what we are going to explore . . .

PRACTICE TO EXPLORE YOUR DISRUPTOR ENERGY

Are you a disruptor? Do you have the audacity to interrupt those who use their position, power, privilege, and relationships to others to manipulate, coerce, abuse, and push people to perform for their own ends? Are you ready to identify with this and admit that we live within wider systems that encourage this behaviour?

Being comfortable as a disruptor requires you to sit with discomfort. And discomfort is just that: it is uncomfortable. We are going to practise staying with the trouble and sitting with discomfort. This is a tool that will serve you well as you embark on your disruptor journey.

1. Take a moment to find a quiet space, or if that is not possible in this moment, close your eyes and begin to tune out the world.

2. Let's begin with a body scan. Start at the top of your head and imagine a gentle, pulsating white light enveloping your head. As you imagine this white light, allow it to travel from the top of your head across your

forehead, over your ears, nose, mouth, and the rest of your face.

3. Take a deep breath as you imagine the white light moving to different parts of your body. Allow it to move at whatever pace you like. Let the white light cover every part of your body until you reach your toes.

4. Now, bring this white light to rest gently in your mind, from where its glow surrounds you like a protective energy. You have just completed a body scan.

5. Next, think of a situation in the past or present that makes you feel uncomfortable. It could be a specific situation involving a family member, friend, or partner. It could be a situation you do not agree with at work or a decision made in a social setting. It could be an upcoming decision you need to make for yourself which might impact other people in ways that make them uncomfortable.

6. Imagine this situation or decision and allow yourself to feel into the discomfort of it. You might experience emotions such as anxiety, embarrassment, tension, or hopeful feelings such as excitement, pride, and ease. Allow yourself to feel into these emotions.

7. Now, focus on one of these feelings. While you focus on this feeling, take a deep breath and allow yourself to notice where the feeling comes up in your body. Try to pay close attention to where you feel a tensing up, a twitch, or a pressure on a certain part of your body. You may notice a shift in different parts of your body.

8. Next, imagine the white light moving to that part of your body. As it moves to that part of your body, take a deep breath and repeat the following mantra: "Breathing in, I focus my attention, and breathing out, I release any tension."

9. For each emotion that comes up in relation to the decision or situation, repeat this mantra every time you focus on the body part that connects to it.

10. When you feel ready to finish, allow yourself to take one last deep breath and scan your body gently again with the white light.

11. When you think about this situation or decision now, how do you feel? Do you feel any less tension and any more ease around it?

The purpose of this exercise is to help regulate your nervous system and bring some ease to your body. It will also help to ready your body for more discomfort and to have the capacity to process this when it arises in the future. Practise these steps as often as you like for the full effect. While you may not necessarily find clarity on what to do if you feel indecisive or if you believe you should have behaved differently in the past, you should feel less physically triggered by any emotions that a challenging situation or difficult decision brings up.

To be disruptors, we must be ready to do the work. We need to look harm in the eye and address it by confronting the perpetrators of harm. We need to address the wider systems of harm that encourage these behaviours and codify those ways of being into our culture. We need to do the collective work of changing policy and modes of operating. For example, we may have to do the work of changing cultures within our own families to enable family members to admit when they turned a blind eye to harm and, by default, played a role in protecting abusers. Or we may need to encourage space for friends who have felt overwhelmed, or believed that it was not their place to support another friend through the harm they experienced from their partner. We may have to give ourselves grace for what we allowed to happen before, and to have the courage to learn how to interrupt systems of harm *now*.

Are You Ready to Disrupt Your Life?

When was the first time you spoke out when you saw something wrong? Did the sheer force of energy around the knowledge that no one else was saying anything – that everyone was acting like it was normal – give you enough momentum to speak out? Did the pressure you felt to speak literally break the silence that stifled you?

Perhaps you have had the sensation that a piece of knowledge is building inside you, twisting at your insides, taking your breath away, the urgency of it keeping you up at night by interrupting your sleep in fits and starts so that you cannot keep it contained within you for much longer. I have had this experience more times than I can count and, trust me, it is not fun, but I have learned to embrace the feeling with the awareness that I need to choose between the internal chaos of keeping my newfound knowledge to myself or the chaos that ensues after I share it.

Now, I know that no one becomes a disruptor by accident, but I want you to hear me out. Disruptors can be disruptive without realizing it. They can be a disruptor by asking a simple question that reveals what should not be spoken in a situation. They can be disruptive by asking for more, or to be treated better, and by questioning why we do things the way that we do. They can be a disruptor by being willing to accept responsibility for both their actions and their inaction, and by being prepared to do something about this. We are a product of the world we live in, the values we cultivate from society more widely, and the choices we make. Do not blame the disruptor; the disruptor is simply the messenger and agent of change . . .

2

EMBODYING THE ENERGY OF LIVING ON THE EDGES

Those of us who work with energy and spend our days observing its subtle flows, changes, and nuances are highly attuned to the world around us. Many of us may identify as neurodivergent or simply sensitive. We are the artists, makers, and observers of our world. We often allow our empathy to guide us. We take note of signals that hint at the lessons and information we need to pay attention to. Historically, such figures were medicine people and keepers of the oracle. In order for these individuals to truly hone their craft and listen to all of the subtle signals in the world, whether to study herbs and botany, or to quiet their minds and receive divine messages, they would isolate themselves from society and live on the edges of it. They would become edge-dwellers.

In traditional lore and storytelling, these edge-dwellers were often known as wise people who would settle away from the village in order to gain enough perspective to guide the people in it. Similarly, seers and mages would need to be able to study the signs and practise their rituals and magic in peace. They would collect their materials from the natural world in solitude. In the Rider–Waite–Smith Tarot, the archetype of the Hermit is represented by a wise person with a grey beard who is dressed in a white travelling cape and who walks with a lantern and staff through hilly terrain on a journey illuminated by a guiding star. This image encapsulates aspects of a learned individual – in solitude, showing signs of age, and willing to walk among us, yet comfortable on the edges to pursue their quest for deeper knowledge.

The physical location of the edge of town or the edge of a village often has eerie, mystical, or scary connotations that suggest this is a place where little ones do not go. The edge of town is where the witch dwells or where those that do not want to be found make their home. Even today, we can drive people in society to the edge in the sense that they feel they need to isolate themselves in order to exist among everyone else.

Embodying the Energy and Magic of the Edge-Dweller

When I was about five years old, our science teacher in elementary school, Ms Jones, created a magical space in her classroom. She used this space to teach us the rules of the circle of life. As she worded it, the circle of life was the circle of life *and* death: all things that begin must come to an end – and that was something we needed to get comfortable with, because it was coming for all of us. However, her lesson was a subtle one, which she taught us with plenty of joy, love, and fun.

In her classroom, nearly 35 different types of animals lived in tanks and cages on shelves running the length of the room. There were tarantulas, garden snakes, chinchillas, rats, ferrets, hamsters, guinea pigs, mice, armadillos, iguanas, praying mantises, frogs, toads, turtles, gerbils, beetles, and pigeons. In the southeastern corner of the classroom sat a pen of her own construction built from pine and thick chicken wire. This space was called "the Peaceable Kingdom", where several species of animals that should not co-exist lived together – here, a pigeon-dove hybrid lived alongside baby turtles, and garden snakes zipped their way around rats.

Ms Jones was an early proponent of upcycling. She would come to the lunch canteen and collect leftover crusts, pieces of cheese and veggies. She had a little metal food trolley with wheels that clattered as she happily asked the little ones if they were done with their scraps. Eventually, there were dedicated trays where we could deposit our leftovers at the end of our meal, ready for collection by Ms Jones as soon as she arrived with her trolley. Ms Jones often hummed Stevie Wonder songs as she rolled the trolley through the halls back to her tropical animal oasis. Later, you could see bits of your salad being munched by the bunnies happily bouncing away in their cage in her classroom or pieces of pizza being devoured by the chinchillas when they rolled out of their self-created dust balls. (Pizza was always popular.)

I am not sure if school regulations were particularly relaxed in the late 1990s and early 2000s, or if Ms Jones got away with her unconventional classroom antics because she taught in a private school, but it was a wild time! Ours was an independent school for children from kindergarten through to 12th grade. However, the school suddenly went into administration, and I remember watching teachers sobbing after an emergency meeting. Most of them had just been dismissed and were tearful in the aftermath of losing their jobs. The arts teachers were the first to go, although our librarian volunteered to stay in her post until the school year came to an end.

It was, of course, Ms Jones, the stoic confidante, who I saw consoling other teachers after that fateful meeting. She was the one to offer them coffee, tea, and water, and provide them with a listening ear. I watched as fellow teachers sobbed on her shoulder, where the rat or two that she always had on her person would scurry away to avoid being crushed. She consoled others when her own fate was on similar tenterhooks. She always showed an incredible amount of compassion in the face of massive change. In the event, the actions of parents, teachers, students, and the wider school authority's efforts ensured that the school did not close, but Ms Jones gave us the equanimity to face whatever lay ahead.

It was Ms Jones who repeated in each science lesson: we must learn to let go. That life is too short to hold grudges and that forgiveness is key to living a long, healthy life. She talked about how holding on to resentments could build up and negatively impact the body. Little did she know, or maybe she was very aware, that she was talking about the energy that can build up from negative emotions and impact our bodies if not released. Her encouragement to accept endings came in very handy in the midst of our school crisis. She was also preparing me for an incredibly important lesson: that it would take an ending, no matter how difficult, sudden, violent, or unexpected, to birth new life or to bring about change. The beauty of a new beginning could not exist without the ending that would one day follow it.

By subtly understanding our energy and how it impacts or interacts with the energy outside of us, we can create an alchemical process and create magic. In this respect, Ms Jones was a magician because she transmuted an experience of loss and suffering into an experience we could absorb. In her classroom, we learned to face the fear of death together. Ms Jones could have avoided the pain of showing us this process. She could have shielded us from the realities of life, but she chose not to.

Ms Jones was very familiar with the suffering in the world, and even though we were little, she did not want her students to go out into the world without a nuanced understanding of it. So, she showed us suffering in an environment where we could process things together through discussion. Part of this involved watching the classroom boa constrictors feed. Yet the atmosphere that Ms Jones created was one of complete safety and control. Sure, something could go wrong. Occasionally, a snake might slither out of the Peaceable Kingdom or a baby rat escape, but other than those rare occurrences, things ran fairly smoothly. We were in the hands of an expert who understood and respected her animals and their needs, and who gently passed on lessons about the boundaries required in her space. These boundaries were clear rules that had a purpose. They were not passed on to use frivolously, like rules often are. Her leadership was demonstrated in how she maintained safety by negotiating the rules of engagement in the space through our collective agreement about the necessity to protect all the living creatures in her care. Some of those guidelines were: no running, no opening cages or homes without her there, and absolutely no entering the Peaceable Kingdom without her being present.

I often wondered what sorts of conversations Ms Jones had with the other teachers. She always waved to them, but seemed most comfortable when speaking to her daughter, who sometimes visited her, and to Olivia, the only blind student in the school, whom she helped acquire a guide dog. She often ate in her classroom because she was kept busy with the incredible list of tasks she had to complete in order to keep its residents alive, literally, but I also wonder if this was her choice – to be on her own, to live on the edge.

Living like the Magician and the Hermit

If we take Ms Jones as a living example of choosing a life on the edges, we can use her story to understand the energy of both the Hermit and the Magician Tarot cards. In fact, Ms Jones is a perfect manifestation of the Magician energy. In the Tarot, the Magician card depicts a magician using all four of the elements of the Tarot to influence the world, by employing subtle energies (i.e. magic) to affect what already exists in order to change it. What subtle forces might we use to influence a situation and become our own magicians?

In contrast, the Hermit card depicts a figure in a hooded garment carrying a lantern with a star inside and a staff to guide their way. Unlike the Magician, the Hermit is not retreating from society in search of truth to observe "occult isolation" but holds the star as a beacon in the lantern to suggest "where I am, you may also be".[1] This is the perspective of the seeker who is always able to share their knowledge with others while seeing others' experiences as spaces of possibility – of knowledge that they can cultivate through curiosity. Ms Jones helped my classmates and me to cultivate this curiosity by giving us the space to experiment and ask questions in her classroom. Cultivating the energy of the seeker seemed attainable and accessible to us because she modelled it for us.

Ms Jones lived on the edge in how she taught and how she lived. It was a way of life that was embodied in every pore of her being. She was committed to her life's work and to sharing it with others, so that they might have an ounce of the appreciation she had for sentient beings. If I remember correctly, she was a vegetarian before many of us had ever considered this as an option. I would follow in her footsteps only a few years later.

What she created in her classroom was an alchemy of sorts. She continued to embody the essence of the Magician. She turned snake urine into chalk in a way that was literally akin to the work of the alchemists who turned liquid into gold. The subtle alchemy of calcium interacting with urine to harden it and turn it into a white chalk writing medium can be seen as magic as much as science. It is an alchemical process. The Magician lives on the edges, so that they can experiment without interruption, while the Hermit chooses to live on the edge to better observe and guide society without the noise or interruption of other people's energies clouding the emergence of their inner wisdom.

Edge Theory and Edge-Dwellers

What brings us to the edge, the edge of things and the edges of our awareness? We have so many phrases for being pushed to our limits, such as being "pushed over the edge" and being "pushed too far". We also have many phrases for being pushed past our breaking point – but what happens between that point and the moments before it? Can we trace the steps or decisions that lead us past the point of no return? Where is the beginning of the edge?

In ecology and in the study of sustainable development, edge theory is an incredibly important concept. The edge is where different ecosystems of plant life and animal life meet. It is where many ecosystems thrive. Certain animals and plants only meet in the unique environment of the edge, a transition between worlds, such as the beginning of a beach and the end of a meadow, or even a hedgerow that separates two types of terrain. Birds fly through the bushes, mammals climb up the limbs of the hedge, and bugs scatter up the stems of the leaves, but these animals do not necessarily live here – they are travelling through, although sometimes they may make a home there.

When we think about the role of the mystic in mythology and old stories, they live on the edge of things. They are never at the centre of their community, much like the Hermit or the Magician in the Tarot whose experiments with the elements are tucked away from public view on a private altar. While these individuals may carry a community through times of struggle and strife, or even support and be celebrated by their community through periods of abundance, they also retreat to their own space to find solitude, gain wisdom, and to see things others cannot by distancing themselves from the influences of others. It is edge-dwellers whose wider perspective allows those living in the thick of things to gain some clarity and see the bigger picture, too. While you do not have to remove yourself from society or a situation in order to critique it, it is a useful skill to have – the willingness to remove yourself from the busyness and noise of others' opinions in order to find clarity and perspective.

I have always been an edge-dweller who has preferred living in solitude. Solitude gives me the space to process all of the stimulation, information, and feelings I absorb from the world. We empaths or highly sensitive people are attuned to other people's energy. First a therapist and then a shaman I worked helped me understand how much I absorbed or took on other people's energy as my own, which may be familiar to anyone who is neurodivergent or experiences life in this way. It was my therapist Gabriella who first taught me to ask myself, "Is this my energy or is this someone else's?" when I started to experience strong emotions or even states of consciousness that came on suddenly or that I felt stuck in. And it was Eileen, a shaman and artist I worked with for over five years, who first introduced me to Theta Energy Healing®. She also helped me learn some basic energetic hygiene I could practise at home. Though

Gabriella had encouraged me to envision a warm, white light that protected me, covering every inch of my body (similar to the sensation of a body scan), it was Eileen who reintroduced me to daily rituals including smudging and using essential oils as protective rituals.

When you think about solitude and living on the edges, is it an idea that holds any appeal for you? We all have very different relationships with solitude and how we recharge. The introverts and neurodiverse among us may need time for solitude away from the pressure of social cues that require us to be constantly engaged with our surroundings. Those of us who are neurodiverse can be sensitive to noise and incredibly overwhelmed by external stimuli. Our internal worlds are rich with colour, sound, and imagination – so the external world only adds to that activity.

Part of living on the edge is being willing to be by ourselves and being comfortable with solitude. It requires us to be comfortable standing alone or making connections where other people only see fractured pieces of experience. It is important to understand that we need to be willing to take a step back and be on the edges of things, so that we can see clearly – into systems, into relationships, and into communities. And from this perspective, we can discern where these systems need to be interrupted, altered, and shifted. We can decide how best to disrupt them. Being on the edge is also a form of protection, where we can step away to better understand who is supporting us. When we are caught up in the thick of things and constantly in contact with others, going with the flow of things and thereby passively supporting the status quo, it can be hard to know who is willing to sit on the edge with us to dream up a better future.

Tools for Protection – Oils and Crystals

It is very important for us to be aware of our energy in order to engage in the world in a way that reduces harm to all. To live in a way that allows us to experience more ease and live in alignment with our intentions, we need the tools to move through this energetic world with greater dexterity.

Take my own daily rituals, for example. In the morning, I brush my teeth and wash my face like most people do, but then I carry hand-blended oils with me, mixed by a friend and occultist that I trust. I use these regularly as a scent, but also as a grounding technique throughout the day. It is so subconscious that I do it automatically. If I am feeling the stress of a crowded commute; if I am picking up on the energy from a fight I have witnessed, or an aggressive shove when walking down the street; if I experience the microaggression of someone checking the whereabouts of their phone or almost unconsciously patting their pockets when I walk past or when I am standing near them, because I am Black and they are reacting to my presence – I take a moment to ground myself by rolling this scent onto my neck and the pressure points behind my ears and on the inside of each wrist. It is a protective ritual that pulls me back to myself through the sense of smell.

If you did not grow up asking yourself whether what you felt or experienced were your emotions or those of others, this may not be a fine-tuned sense for you, but it is like a muscle you can build by practising. Next time a strong emotion overcomes you, ask yourself: is this mine, or is this someone else's feeling, emotions and ultimately someone else's energy?

Eileen introduced me to two other important tools for an energetic disruptor's arsenal. These are not tools that everyone will respond well to or use, but they work for me: the protective energy of crystals and Theta Energy Healing®. I do not leave my room, let alone my flat, without crystals. They carry an energy that is foundational to moving around in the world as an energy body interacting with the 8.1 billion other energy bodies, objects, spaces, and fields as part of the collective energy interactions we experience every second of every day. I have found that I know a crystal has done its job once it has cracked, especially a protective crystal such as black tourmaline or obsidian.

Crystals do their work without you, although you can clear them and charge them. It is important to let go of them in the right way, which may be returning the crystal back to the earth once has completed its work with you. But otherwise, keeping crystals near you, in your clothing or in a bag, is a great way to work with them. Crystals have their own meanings and are associated with different archetypes, symbols, numbers, and energies that are helpful to explore before you work with them. Or you can be guided by your intuition and your clairsenses to pick a crystal that you are drawn to. You will be drawn to it for a reason and your intuition or clairsenses will make the crystal known to you if you trust these.

Developing Our Intuition and Sensitivity to Energy

Our relationship to our intuition is something we may have to develop. We live in a world that trains us to rely on logic, data, and tangible information to make informed decisions. In contrast, our intuition resides within us. By living in a world that values other forms of knowledge, we actually learn to distance ourselves from our intuition and our understanding of how it works may diminish over time. Our intuition can be steady and consistent, but it rarely sends us a signal more than once; many of us will know in retrospect that we had a feeling about something and wish we had listened to our gut. This learned distrust is down to which forms of knowledge we prioritize over others. We are traditionally taught to prioritize academic knowledge over lived experience, for example. This hierarchy speaks to a power dynamic at play that prioritizes rational knowledge acquired over centuries above what we immediately know to be true in our hearts and souls. Yet there is a time and a place for both. One form of knowledge is not more important than the other, nor should it be suppressed, discouraged, and erased in deference to the other. This is the same space that hierarchies of wisdom, experience, culture, and ideas around what is morally right or wrong come from. Rather, the underlying power dynamic at play privileges white, westernized knowledge systems and beliefs as being superior to all other forms of knowledge. This kind of thinking is at the core of racism, misogyny, and a number of other forms of oppression that drive our social belief systems in this world.

I have found that it is easier to work on strengthening my relation to my intuition by learning to trust it. However, it takes time and practice to build trust – to trust ourselves to listen to that inner voice. Sometimes, I work with my crystals to help me build this relationship with my inner voice. By sitting with my crystals and letting their cool surfaces melt into my skin, I give myself a moment to reflect and focus on my inner world. This also helps me cultivate the practice of checking in with myself and asking myself about my psychic state. If I am feeling tired or a mix of emotions, I can use these moments to ask myself whether the emotions I am feeling are mine due to a situation I am experiencing in my own life, or whether they are left over from a conversation I have had or an energy I have picked up from someone with whom I have interacted during my day.

Since we cannot always live in energetically quiet or calm spaces, we have to find ways to create moments of quiet and less distraction that enable us to focus in on ourselves. It is so important to be aware of the energy of our surroundings and to ask ourselves if the spaces we live in, eat in, socialize in, and look after our bodies in make us feel calm, energetic, activated, serene, at peace, frantic, on edge or at rest. Take a few moments now to ask yourself how your space feels. If that seems a little abstract, think about the space you are in at this moment, reading this passage.

Remember that we can influence the energy of the spaces we occupy. This is why it is important to extend our understanding of our influence beyond a physical space to our personal interactions. How we show up in a situation impacts the other people in it. This includes our mood, our energy levels, our level of engagement with the situation, how much we are listening or how distracted we appear, and how we respond to others. All of these aspects of our impact on an environment or situation are ways that we communicate our energy to other people. We are often not conscious of it or aware of it, but slowing down and being more intentional about our spaces allows us to make better choices about our energy and how we show up. Sometimes, we do not have the time, capacity, or space to think about this or take steps to change it, so simply starting to be aware of our energy by understanding our needs can be an important first step. Once we become more aware of our energy, and the energy of the space we are in, we can start the process of changing it.

Tuning in to Energy

Energy moves and changes, and certain energies have different weights – a literal heaviness that shows up as the feeling of a psychic load, which can be picked up through our clairsenses. I find I can pick up on the energy of a space fairly quickly. Though I may not always be able to pinpoint exactly what I am picking up on at first, I know I will soon be able to name or sense the energy. Sometimes I experience this as a deep knowing or a physical pressure like a headache. Since energy is power, I can also pick up on the power dynamics in a room, a situation, or an interaction through the same means. I ask myself certain questions when it comes to sensing a power dynamic. These questions are not always conscious, but they sound a little like this:

- Do I feel a sense of tension or restriction?
- Is everyone in that space able to speak freely and openly?
- Does someone appear withdrawn or shut down by something someone has said to them?
- What is everyone's body language in the space?

- Are they making eye contact?
- Are they looking down or looking away?
- Are they withdrawing into themselves and unconsciously holding themselves in self-protective ways by wrapping their arms around themselves or sitting with a sunken in posture?

Although you are likely to pick up on the answers subconsciously, these are questions you can also ask yourself to help you identify the dynamics in a space. As we live in a world that competes more and more for our attention, our ability to notice and then process the cues we pick up on is becoming compromised. This is why taking the time to pause and register our responses is crucial. You might walk into a new space and immediately feel a shift in temperature, or pick up on an almost imperceptible thickness in the air – but does this signify there is tension in the room or is there ease?

I think of energetics as being not only what you can pick up on and perceive about a situation, interaction, or space in the moment, but the energy of everything that influences how you perceive that situation. It is everything that is not said, yet which is psychically present in that space. Energetics are how all of the energy interacts with and responds to the wider environment. Like other healers, psychics, and mediums, I believe that everything leaves behind an energy signature or footprint (for lack of a better word) that we can read if we learn how to interpret the signals, and if we develop an openness to other ways of perceiving. It might be the signature in the form of energetic clues – feelings and nudges from the past, present, or even the future. (For me, the future is more like the potential that can be picked up on in a single moment, which lingers, or something that will emerge several moments later.)

When you begin to interact with this process, these indicators can seem subtle or barely there. Alternatively, depending on how you experience the world, you may perceive this energetic footprint or this piece of psychic information as unmissable, fully present, and loud. Like a slow reveal or a sudden realization, the energetics of a space or a situation will make themselves known to you if you know how to listen – which is what we are going to be focusing on now.

A PRACTICE TO IDENTIFY THE ENERGY IN A SPACE

This exercise will help you to tune in to your intuition and clairsenses so that you can begin to identify the energy of wherever you find yourself and, in this way, sharpen your clairsenses. What you are aiming to do here is to practise opening up your senses.

I. This practice can be performed outdoors; however, you may wish to work indoors initially as your confidence grows. Choosing a familiar room will make this exercise both more accessible and challenging in equal measure, because the room's familiarity may make it difficult to pick up on the energy in it. You can sit on the floor or a softer surface like your bed, a cushion, or the sofa.

2. Once you have chosen your room, it is good practice to clear your space before starting any ritual or activity. If you have not done so, please take the time now to clear your space; for example:
   – Sprinkle salt into the four corners of the room while setting the intention that the space is clear of any energies or entities that might inhabit it. Salt ought to be left in place for some time, often overnight, to soak up the energy in a space. Make sure to discard it afterwards. You can bury it in the earth or sprinkle it in a body of water. The most important thing is that

you do not leave it lingering for too long, otherwise it can trap old energy that can energetically pollute your space.

- If you choose to use a healing smoke to clear the space instead, use ethical cleansing smokes made from a herb that is local to you. This could be a bay leaf, rosemary, or locally grown sage, for example, which are commonly used for cleansing, but there may be other herbs you prefer working with. You can use either dried or fresh herbs. Before you work with a herb, it is important to familiarize yourself with its properties and meaning. Waft the smoke from the burning herb around both the space and your body, taking care not to set anything else alight.

- You can also burn a candle with the intention that the space be cleared, and motion for the energy to shift out of the room through an open window. Blow out your candle or keep it lit, depending on your preference.

3. If you wish, call in any guides, spirits, or angels you work with to hold you in a warm, safe, and sacred light and protect you. You can draw a circle or usher in the four corners of the universe if this is part of your practice. You are also welcome to work with crystals such as black tourmaline and obsidian for protection, or citrine for abundance, or whichever combination you prefer. If you are a visual person and would like to pull a Tarot or oracle card to watch over you, feel free to do this. If you like, you can pull the Hermit or the Magician cards to allow their energy to guide you. Oracles cards and Tarot cards can guide you with real strength, enhance psychic and intuitive abilities, or just give you the courage and confidence to try something new.

4. Once you have cleared your space, it is time to settle back into the space and start to open up your intuitive senses. Go inward and take a deep breath.

5. Now, set an intention that feels right for you in this space and moment. It could be for insight and clarity. It could be for ease or to easefully navigate a new practice. It could be an intention for fun and experimentation, or for focus. Words are spells and no words have a bigger impact on your practice than your own, which is why creating your own intentions is such an effective approach. Perhaps create a list of the types of intentions you want to set each time you practise this exercise. Give yourself a few seconds to reflect and then speak your intention out loud. If you prefer, write it down where you can see it easily during your practice, then begin.

6. Close your eyes if this helps you to focus on your clair senses. Take a deep breath. What do you feel around you? Are there things on the edge of your awareness that pull your attention toward them? Can you visualize the room you are in? Slowly scan the room in your mind, starting from where you are physically or, if you prefer, starting from a different part of the room. Visualize this starting point.

7. Give in to the sensations of scanning the room. Can you access a place or mindset you have when you meditate, engage with your intuition, or emerge from a deep sleep? If these sensations are unfamiliar, just allow whatever arises to emerge. Let yourself notice things that might feel insignificant and try to pull them into focus by breathing. You can also ask the room out

loud or silently to give you more clarity on what you are sensing. Asking for help in these situations is always useful. Or you can direct this request to yourself, your guides, or anything you normally work with. Ultimately, you are directing this to the energy in the room by asking it to become clearer.

8. What do you feel? Does that part of the room have any quality to it? This quality could be an emotion, colour, image, word, or something less easy to describe. That's ok. You might not grasp on to a sensation for very long. It may last for a split second, but that is enough. Just take a deep breath and try again. If you feel nothing, move on to a different part of the room with your mind's eye if you wish. Once you have taken 5 to 10 minutes or so to scan the room, come back to yourself.

9. If you were to describe the energy in the room, how would you describe it? You can focus on particular parts of the room or any sensations you felt. If you were to zoom out of these sensations and component parts, how would you describe the overall energy in the room? Remember: there is no right or wrong way to do this. Perhaps think about images, colours, feelings, smells, or anything else that strikes you and gives you a sense of what that room feels like energetically.

10. Maintaining your circle of protection by letting your guides know and keeping your space clear, you can walk out of the room now and re-enter it if you wish. However, if this is something you have not done before, I would suggest you stay in place. Depending on your practice and how you do ritual work, perhaps you never

break a circle in the middle of a ritual. If so, honour your practice and simply visualize leaving the room.

11. What does it feel like outside of the room? Ground yourself in that space by imagining your feet on the floor. Is there a noticeable difference now? Give yourself between 30 seconds and a minute to feel that space. Take more time if you need it. Then walk back into the room, or, if necessary, visualize yourself moving back into it and resettling in the spot you find your body. Do you notice anything different? How do you feel now? Can you describe the energetic properties of the room with more focus and clarity now that you have something to compare it to? Was there any difference?

12. Take some time to bring the exercise to a close by stating an intention to bring this energetic practice to its completion. Announce the end of this practice by concluding this ritual as you would normally – close your circle, blow out any candle(s), thank your guides, or simply acknowledge the time you've taken to do this practice. If you do not have a practice for closing a ritual you can say, "And so it is." Then thank yourself. You can express gratitude to yourself for this practice in any way you choose.

Over the next few days and weeks, repeat this exercise but without the visualization or quiet space. Choose busier locations in which to practise. You do not have to draw a full protective circle or close your eyes; you can simply notice the energy around you. Can you get quiet in the midst of busy spaces? Is it easier to pick up on energy in certain locations than in others?

This practice is a brilliant way to develop your relationship with energy as a whole by starting with the energy around you. You can continue with this practice as often as you like, but consider thinking about what it is like to be in different spaces. What is that new space, attitude, or dynamic's energetic footprint? As soon as you enter or engage with a new space, dynamic or situation, ask yourself, "What does this feel like energetically?" This could be an outdoor space, a shady spot under a street lamp, an archway, or a space that a lot of people pass through. It can be indoors or outdoors. It can be at home with your family, friends, partner, or flatmates.

Challenging yourself by tuning in to busy spaces with lots of distractions can really help you train your psychic intuitive muscles. Being able to get quiet and focus on the subtlety of energy in the busiest spaces is a skill anyone can hone and develop with practice. Use this exercise in the ways that make you feel strong and courageous – that help you develop your intuitive sense.

Remember, the feeling may not always last. It may be fleeting, a mere flash of a second, but it is still significant. You may also experience déjà vu – all of this is perfect. Energy is constantly in movement, in flux, and always evolving. Energy morphs. We all have different ways of reading, picking up on, and working with energy. If you find yourself questioning whether you felt, smelled, or heard something, chances are you did, but you can always check in with yourself to clarify by getting quiet and giving yourself the space to focus on what you picked up. Trust the space in between the known and unknown world.

As we move through this book, we will develop more tools to work with energy and cultivate a practice with it. It can be incredibly helpful to give yourself grace and understanding in the knowledge that this is a life-long process. Reading energy is a practice that healers spend their lifetimes cultivating. It comes to some of us more easily than others, but it is something each of us can develop or learn to identify. Energy is still a mysterious thing and the ways we each seek to understand it are unique to us.

There are traditions that study the relationship to energy as an alchemical process. These traditions are sacred spaces of knowledge, with their own customs and rituals which should be respected and revered. These are spaces we may be initiated into, inherit, or which are passed down to us by our ancestors. They should be protected. However, you can cultivate your own practice and your own rituals around energy as long as you respect the places from which you borrow these practices. Understanding where rituals come from, who developed them, and respecting the cultures they originate from without appropriating them is important. Take the time to explore what is indigenous to your own culture, to your family and to your local area, as part of interrupting the practice of extracting from others and instead building from a place of consideration and thoughtfulness.

The Edge-Dweller as the Critic

Now that we are aware that energy has different properties – and that there are different ways to identify those energetic properties, through language, images, or sensations that make sense to us – we know that how we interact with energies varies depending on who we are and how attuned we are to identifying them. The energy of a room, place, situation, or person can vary massively as these different energies interact with one another. This is where discernment becomes incredibly important.

We explored the role of the edge-dweller as the Magician and Hermit who can guide us through subtle knowledge and alchemize that knowledge into change. As edge-dwellers, we too become catalysts for this alchemy by continuing to practise discernment. This too is part of the work of mystics such as the Magician and Hermit. According to Jessica Dore, the "mystic can experience the totality of things".[2] That perspective upon and connection to the totality of things brings wisdom and a discernment that creates space for an inspired, empowered critical eye when working with energy emanating from a person, place, or situation.

In the same way that we can practise tuning in to the energy of a space, we can channel the habits of the Hermit into our rituals to learn to tune out the noise of our environment and better pick up on the energy running through it. The Hermit observes and holds the star of knowledge, the beacon of wisdom that acts as a guide forward, while the Magician makes use of all of the subtle energies available to them to create magic to transmute that which already exists. We can likewise transmute our relationship to the energy around us by using the magic of our attention and presence. It is by using this transformative magic that we can begin to disrupt and change the world around us, but first we need to hone the skills that both the Hermit and Magician teach us. How might you embody the energies of both the Hermit and the Magician in your practice of disruption to make good trouble?

3

GODDESS ARCHETYPES OF DISRUPTION

Disruption is a catalysing force. It is an energy that carries weight and power. However, it is important to practise discernment and put things into context. To that end, you could ask yourself: *Does the energy I am picking up on and the situation I find myself in align with my values? Does this fit in with my understanding of the world I want to live in?* Taking action to change the relationship, situation, or dynamic when you realize it is out of sync with your values and the values of the people around you is one way to apply discernment. And taking inspired action and being courageous enough to shift things into alignment with your vision for how the world should be is the sign of a good warrior. Inspired action – action that is inspired in response to a clear set of values – has been embodied by many warrior archetypes.

A warrior can embody Martian energy and be ready to take action no matter the cost. In the context of making good trouble, a warrior knows their principles and is willing to fight for them. They do not shy away from conflict or chaos. They hope to resolve conflict by moving through it, which can take many forms – defeating an enemy, engaging with a worthy opponent, or overcoming a seemingly insurmountable obstacle, for example. Warriors are comfortable and experienced with interrupting the world as it is to create the world as they think they should be. They know the right thing to do is not always comfortable, and they embrace the discomfort of change because they know that change is necessary.

Their very presence brings about change and their energy is a beautiful manifestation of disruptor energy. They understand that chaos may ensue, but they trust they will be guided through the chaos by their principles. Their need for justice and their willingness to embark on any journey to achieve it means they can navigate any perceived obstacle to defend, uphold, and protect the principle of fairness at any cost. Warriors are not afraid to interrupt things; and if anything, they relish being the source of the interruption. There are so many ways to be a warrior and so many different types of warrior energy – from taking a stand for our values in everyday life, to the examples set by the warrior goddesses, leaders, and truthsayers of ancient lore.

The Hierophant and Goddess Energy

In the Tarot, the Hierophant may not be the first card that you associate with Goddess energy. Historically, it has been linked with the Pope card – a card that denotes a teacher or an educational guide of some sort. In the Rider–Waite–Smith deck, the card features a figure who is wearing a crown and who is dressed in robes, and who sits on a throne with their arms raised, holding a staff in one hand. It is also a card that can signify discernment; of consciously deciding whether to support the status quo or to disrupt it. Given the attitudes that many of us today have toward organized religion and institutions, as well as the wider conversations we are having about the role of education, our collective relationships to institutional spaces of learning may be complicated. Our relationship to secularism and our belief in higher powers and to spaces where we can engage in conversation with higher powers may be becoming more fluid.

In many respects, it is this fluidity which suggests to me a link between the traditional interpretation of the Hierophant and Goddess energy. If the goddesses and their stories remind us of a connection to myths and lessons from other times, embodied by the wisdom of a figure known for certain traits, choices, and mystical powers; if we are able to continue to interpret and re-interpret what their experiences may teach us and how their wisdom may guide us on our path, why would they not relate to a learned figure that can symbolize our learning about ourselves and our choices (or the choices we are about to make)?

Jessica Dore suggests that the Hierophant can act as a reminder of our connection between what is above and what is below.[1] In a way, the Hierophant is a reminder of our relationship to our spiritual practice and perhaps even the container with which we do the work of connecting to whatever Source, spirit, or wisdom tradition we resonate with. As a means to surrender and engage with the mysteries of life, this connection to a guide or spirit allows us to open ourselves up to the possibilities that may come. Even in a secular world, we can make space for our spiritual practice and allow ourselves to be guided by another place, in this case the goddesses. Allowing ourselves to be open to their energy, their fire, and every aspect of what we know about how they might show up in a situation is a form of divine guidance.

As we will see, the warrior spirits of the three powerful figures in particular serve as powerful invitations to channel the archetypal energies they represent into our own lives.

Disruptors in Action: The Warrior Energy of Three Women Archetypes

In Wiccan cosmology and practice, there is the archetype of woman that moves through three stages: Maiden, Mother, Crone. This can be understood as a process for understanding the feminine energy that we all contain, regardless of our gender. Some of us may identify more with different aspects of the Maiden, the Mother, or the Crone. These three states of being all symbolize different parts of an individual's journey to maturation, wisdom, and back to the naïveté of new life again.

The archetype is also known as the Triple Goddess, sometimes associated with the goddess Hecate, and it can be understood as representing the different seasons of our lives. There is a period of exploration and newness that is often compared to the season of *spring*, when seeds are planted for fresh beginnings. These mature to bloom in *summer*; our motherhood can likewise be seen as the summer of our lives when fruit is fresh and ripe. Then there is the *fall*, a time of harvest, which we liken to that which takes us into the *winter* of our lives – or the crone period of wisdom, reflection, and preparation for our next transition away from life on earth. These cycles could be applied to any transitional period in our life with a beginning, a blooming, and an end, leading once more to a new beginning.

It is a trifecta comparable to trifectas in other wisdom traditions, such as the Holy Trinity of the Father, Son, and Holy Spirit in Christianity, or the Trimurti of Brahma, Shiva, and Vishnu in Hinduism. We can think of each of these groups in the trifecta, including the Triple Goddess archetype, as the embodiment of three aspects of an energy moving through different cycles. While these cycles are distinctive, with very different attributes, they are three parts of a whole. Let's take a look at three figures who embody the Triple Goddess archetype and thus the three seasons of disruptor energy.

Kalī or Durga – Spring

Kalī is a Hindu goddess who embodies the energy of the warrior. In the *Devi Mahatmya*, a religious text of *c.*600 CE, she is said to have emerged from the goddess Durga, fully formed, all black with four arms. Kalī is the goddess of death, and legend has it that when Durga summoned her to help her fight the demon Raktabija, each time a drop of the demon's blood hit the earth another adversary would spring up for Kalī to fight, resulting in thousands of demons. Kalī licked up the blood to prevent any more from emerging. She was whipped up into a blood-fuelled frenzy and devoured the demons. The god Shiva was horrified, so he threw himself under Kalī to calm her down. She is often portrayed as standing on Shiva with her tongue out, for this reason.

In other accounts of Kalī, she is the opposite of the goddess Parvati, Shiva's consort, an alter ego of sorts. Legend describes how Kalī was summoned by Parvati to fight Daruka, a demon who can only be fought by a woman. In this account, Kalī has a fanged mouth, appears with blue or black skin, and stands erect with a flicked tongue. In the 14th to 19th centuries, the Thuggee sect considered themselves to be children of Kalī and supposedly carried out ritualistic assassinations in her name. However, it is possible that English colonialists overstated the violence of the cult to justify their increased presence in their territory.

Kalī is often shown carrying important symbolic objects such as a severed human head, which is said to represent the ego, and the sword of Enlightenment. It is possible that she is liberating her children from earthly delusion. She is also referred to as "Divine Mother". She is known as a goddess of fertility, embodying the principle that to know life one must know death in the balance of the cosmic cycle. She still has over 750 million followers today, Hinduism being the third most popular religion in the world. She is worshipped in the goddess-centred denomination of Shaktism as one of the Mahavidya, the ten aspects of the goddess Parvati, Adi Parashakti. On a personal level, Kalī can help us conjure up righteous anger in order to vanquish our enemies. She represents time as well as the wheel of growth, creation, birth, and death.

Seen as the ultimate manifestation of *shakti* or the primordial cosmic energy, Kalī appears in the Atharva Veda – or the fourth Vedic scripture in Hinduism – in the *Kathaka Grihya Sutra*. She is often referred to as *Shakti*, Lord Shiva's counterpart. She also appears in the verse of the famous *Mahabharata*, one of the two major Hindu Sanskrit epics. She is depicted in many forms, including the MahaKali or "Great Kali" identified with the ultimate reality of Braham or God. Depending on different traditions, she has up to 21 forms.[2]

Kalī is time itself and the neverending cycle of rebirth. If we look at disruption as an act of destruction and rebirth, Kalī fully embodies this energy. Like the Maiden of the Triple Goddess archetype, Kalī is the beginning of a journey of transformation, but she is also the middle and the end. She embodies every stage of the process of change; and her ability to root out all evil – to act as a protective force for good, completely unafraid of change – is an energy we should channel at every stage of the process of the disruption. She is the Divine Mother and she is the seed energy in the cycle of destruction. Kalī's fierce energy transmutes situations through pure fire and alchemy; with her connection to spring, she can help you to prune fearlessly in preparation for the next season of life and growth.

Njinga, Warrior Princess – Summer

Njinga, Queen of Ndongo and Matamba, was a warrior queen who walked this earth in the country now known as Angola, my country of heritage on my father's side. In the 17th century, at a time when the Portuguese had occupied the Kingdom of Ndongo for 50 years, Queen Njinga singlehandedly fought their colonial empire. Her father was Ngola Kilombo Kia Kasenda and she was born into a royal family in which her brothers and half-brothers vied for power. Njinga had two sisters, Funji, the youngest, and her middle sister, Kambu. Her father trained her in strategic warfare, and she was a skilled diplomat.

In 1617, her half-brother Mbande took over the throne when their father was killed by an envoy disguised as a member of his royal court, in a rebellion stoked by the Portuguese. Mbande then disposed of his opponents in a murderous game of political chess, the casualties of which included Njinga's firstborn son and her brother Kiluanje, who had been next in line for the throne. Mbande viewed Kiluanje as being too diplomatic and militarily weak to fight with the Portuguese. Mbande had all his siblings' heirs killed and, according to some accounts, all of his sisters sterilized against their will, so that there would be no other claimants to the throne. He was willing to kill half of his family members to secure his rule.

Mbande fought for a few years unsuccessfully to maintain his hold over the kingdom. When the capital of the kingdom, Kabasa, fell to the Portuguese, he retreated to his defensive stronghold in the Kindonga Islands. Having fought with Imbangala mercenaries against the Portuguese Empire, disrupting their slave trade routes, Njinga reluctantly went to negotiate with the Portuguese on her half-brother's behalf, even though she didn't trust him after the murders of her son and brother.

This was to become the largest formal peace delegation to the Portuguese since their arrival in the country. Njinga's knowledge of Portuguese and her strategic prowess caught them offguard. She was determined to negotiate the release of Ndongo captives, protection from mutual enemies, and the removal of the Portuguese from the fort of Ambaca, close to Kabasa. However, the Portuguese attempted to humiliate her during the negotiations by refusing to offer her a chair. In response, a member of her delegation put themselves forward to act as a human chair during the discussions.

The Portuguese's insatiable appetite for slaves led them to ask Ndongo to pay tribute to them in the form of humans. The Portuguese practised chattel slavery, which meant they transported as many people as possible in horrific conditions to sugar plantations. The life expectancy of these people was only seven years. As the Portuguese nevertheless believed they were civilizing barbarians and spreading the word of God, Njinga decided to be baptized in the Catholic Church in order to encourage them to sign a peace treaty. While she didn't believe she could stop slavery, she did hope to keep it contained.

A few months after signing the peace treaty with the Portuguese, Njinga was forced to retreat to the stronghold on the Kindonga Islands herself, when the capital of Kabasa fell to the kingdom of Kasanje. This second loss of Kabasa reinforced the belief of Mbande's subjects that he was not fit to rule. Moreover, when the Portuguese sent a delegation to the islands in 1623, he agreed to be baptized. In Njinga's eyes, his consent to baptism severed their links to their ancestors and weakened the throne of Ngondo even further. The Portuguese then reneged on the agreements set out in the peace treaty. Mbande took this as further evidence of his failure as king and fell into a deep depression. He died; according to some accounts, this might have been due to poison at his own hand or arranged by Njinga herself. She was then to act as queen regent until Mbande's son came of age. However, she decided to wed Kasa, the Imbangala leader alongside whom she'd fought against the Portuguese. On the day of their marriage, she had Mbande's son assassinated and took her place on the throne as "Woman King" of the Ndongo.

Njinga ultimately appealed to the Pope himself to recognize her as a sovereign Catholic queen. She struggled to stop the slave trade around her, but dealt a number of blows to the Portuguese in the process of her reign. At one point in her reign, she was able to decrease the number of slaves captured by the Portuguese to zero, from an average of tens of thousands a month. In their 100 years of trading people in the Ndongo region, the Portuguese managed to traffic six million slaves from the region.[3]

Queen Njinga is the embodiment of the Mother archetype. As mother of her people, her kingdom, and the fierce protector of her subjects, she does whatever it takes to protect them – from fighting her adversaries directly, forming alliances, going against her half-brother the king, and finding her way to the throne after heartache and betrayal. In her rise to power and fight for liberation from the Portuguese, Njinga represents the archetype that embodies the energy of summer – the season of action, heat, and blooming. Her unrelenting energy to fight until the bitter end in order to protect her people from an unjust fate is the lesson we need to take from her; the energy of fierce protection and a determined fight for justice at all costs. Queen Njinga fought hard to maintain Ndongo's independence and to secure the future of her land and people. It was not until two more rulers had succeeded her that Ndongo finally fell completely to the Portuguese.

Cassandra – Fall/Winter

Cassandra is a name often given to those who tell the truth yet who are vilified for it. The daughter of Queen Hecuba and King Priam of Troy, Cassandra was known for her refusal to be silenced and her relentless determination in the face of adversity.

According to one myth, the god Apollo granted her supernatural powers known as "the sight" that enabled her to predict events before they happened. He was hoping that she would return this gift with sexual favours, which the young Cassandra refused. Enraged by this, Apollo punished her by inverting the abilities he had given her. He spat into her mouth and instantly turned her gift into prophecies that were doomed to be disbelieved.

Cassandra predicted the fall of Troy and though no one believed her, she continued to speak out bravely. She taught her brother Helenus the art of prediction and both of them prophesied that if Queen Helen graced Troy's walls, Troy would fall. Cassandra tried attacking Helen when her brother Paris brought her back to the city as his wife, but to no avail. Already viewed as a madwoman, she could not stop the siege of Troy.

Cassandra's most famous prophecy related to the Trojan horse. She warned the city of the danger, but they continued to disregard her. She took a blazing branch and a double-edged spear to try to attack the horse, but she was captured in the process by Ajax the Lesser in one of Athena's temples and then taken as a prize to Agamemnon. Cassandra was brutally assaulted by Ajax the Lesser upon her capture, yet she remained uninhibited in her predictions. She knew that her relationship with Agamemnon would be the end of both of them. Years later, Agamemnon's wife, Clytemnestra, murdered them, their children, and her own lover, Aegisthus.

The myth of Cassandra has been referenced throughout history by the likes of Shakespeare. The term "Cassandra complex" is used to describe a person who shares truthful warnings but is ignored. These sorts of situations will be familiar to many disruptors. It has certainly been my own experience.

Cassandra is an embodiment of Crone energy, the wise one who has lived many lives and observes what she sees with the insights afforded by age, time, and experience. It is an energy that does not need to be validated nor understood by others. However, the Crone is often disregarded and ignored in our modern world, which is obsessed with the cult of youth.

So what lesson can we take from Cassandra? To always speak the truth even if no one listens, because the truth will out . . . eventually. And what can we learn from her untimely death? There may always be someone who will try to silence you and at times they may succeed, but that does not change the nature of the truth itself.

Each of these embodiments of the Triple Goddess archetypes followed a set of guiding principles. Whether it was the belief that their purpose was to facilitate transformation in the universe, or simply to speak their truth, they always stuck to their purpose and never strayed. Being led by your values in a world that puts so much pressure on us to conform may feel like a tall order. But if you simply attempt to channel some of their energy in pivotal moments – when, for example, asking yourself whether to take a stand or stay silent – you can garner strength from their examples.

When you have the truth on your side and you are working to protect others like Cassandra protected the people of Troy, Queen Njinga protected the people of Ndongo, and Kalī protected the realms of the universe, you are taking on the work of a goddess. Having a purpose that is led by justice, by truth, and by vanquishing demons like these three figures did, does not always come with being liked or being believed. Yet trusting in the dignity of your values will nevertheless take you a long way. All of these three were seen as mad, terrifying, and at times untrustworthy. If you find yourself in a situation where you are being judged in this way too for doing what is right, take heart that you are being seen in the image of a goddess.

A PRACTICE TO CHANNEL GODDESS ENERGY

This exercise invites you to channel goddess energy into a situation to help change it for the better.

1. Find a space where you will not be interrupted. If you have a pen and paper or something to write with, these will come in handy too.

2. Now, select a goddess that you would like to work with in the steps that follow. This could be a goddess or figure mentioned earlier, or it could be another archetype or deity. If you have a description of this being, please keep it near you.

3. I want you to start by visualizing this deity or figure in front of you. Call them into your imagination and field of psychic vision. What are they like? If you were to describe them in five words, what would you say?

4. Next, think about which tools or instruments this figure has at their disposal. Are there certain skills, gifts, or traits they have? Take a moment to list five of the tools, skills, traits, or physical objects they use for their work.

5. What type of work do they do? Are they a truth-teller? Do they protect those around them? Are they called on for certain tasks, needs, jobs, or situations? Think about how they could imbue you with certain characteristics you might need in a particular situation if you were to call on them.

6. As you reflect on the various skills, tools, and gifts they have at their disposal, take a moment to think about

each one and how this is something you can conjure up in your life if you need it.

7. Are you aware of a particular situation in your life now relating to someone you care about, work, a friend, a family member, or the greater world? How can you call on the skills, gifts, tools, or traits of this archetype to support you through this situation?

8. Now, ask the deity, archetype, or figure you are working with to imbue you with whatever you might need in this situation. Literally feel the transfer of energy from them to you.

9. Thank them for giving you this power and take three deep breaths to close your ritual.

Afterwards, try to embody their essence and channel their energy into your daily life. If you need a reminder, refer back to all the aspects of the divine being that you've considered and listed in this exercise.

Disruption and Manifestations of Power

We cannot talk about Goddess energy without talking about power and the role the patriarchy has played in suppressing women's roles in leadership. Goddess worship is an exception to this rule in many cultures, but it has taken time for us to understand the histories and mythology of the many legends, archetypes, and deities that are represented by women. We are more aware now than ever that history has been written by men in power; the stories of women have not only been lost, but were hardly ever recorded in the first place – not to mention those of other genders, which have mostly been erased completely. Yet throughout history, women have often been disruptors of the status quo and that status quo was often a toxic patriarchy, a patriarchal system that promotes misogyny and gender-based violence.

The figures speak for themselves when it comes to the impact of the patriarchy on women's mortality rates in childbirth, particularly for Black women; and on the gender pay gap and how pay for women experiencing multiple forms of oppression as women who are also queer or disabled or of colour compounds the experiences of prejudice they face. Until relatively recently in the west, women were denied access to higher education, wrote under pen names, and fought for women's suffrage by occasionally using violent means. They have been continually misremembered in history.

Today, queer astrologers are reframing Greek mythology and other goddess figures with a feminist lens. They are starting to unpack the assumptions we have made about ancient myths. By reframing these myths from a woman's perspective, we can glean new meaning from old tales. Take the story of Medusa, for example, which the astrologer Chani Nicholas has referenced in a number of her podcasts over the years. Medusa was punished by Athena after Poseidon assaulted her in Athena's temple. Rather than show compassion and solidarity for Medusa's plight, Athena turned her hair into snakes and her gaze deadly. But how could Medusa have said no to a god? Other tales refer to women who chose to take an oath of chastity as part of their devotion to their temple, and which then cast their virginity as something helpless and naïve – some of the assumptions we still make today about virginity. In the same way that these interpretations of mythology are being reframed, our understanding of our own world is not fixed, but fluid. We must embrace the idea that nothing is binary or simple.

We cannot talk about power without exploring systems of power and how power shows up in our world. Power, in my opinion, is a form of energy that is very misunderstood. Often, power is described in terms of us cultivating it, hoarding it, stepping into it, and not wanting to let it go. Indeed, when we look at patriarchal descriptions and understandings of power, we can easily see why our understanding of power is about control, ownership, and scarcity. These are also the ideals our capitalist society is based on.

In a society like ours, the messages we receive about power can often convey subtle messages about the wider system in which we live, which is designed to ensure that those in power maintain their power. We have seen, for example, how politicians can become so worried about their next election cycle that they start making decisions that are out of sync with their own manifesto or campaign promises. They are so worried about potentially undermining or losing their power, that they do whatever is needed to maintain it. This is how many of our political systems are designed.

It stands to reason that if all "resources" are thought to be finite in a capitalist society, then power must also be. However, power is different. It is not just a resource. It is an energy and it is infinite. We are constantly renewing and regenerating it. It can be shared and redistributed.

A Quick Dive into Theories on Power

Alternative ways of thinking about power are presented by Professor John Gaventa, a social researcher and specialist in development studies, in his seminal work *Power and Powerlessness*, first published in 1980. In it, Gaventa gives us the language to think about how power is distributed, experienced, and moves in a social setting. The book was revised in 2003 to include the theory of the power cube.

Gaventa describes power as a three-dimensional force. There are various levels of society on which it exists; it has varying levels of visibility – invisible, visible, and hidden; and it occurs in different spaces – open, closed, or invited spaces. Thinking about these spaces of power or types of power invites us to consider where decisions are made. This can be in any setting – in a partnership (platonic or romantic), in a place of work, or in a family. When decisions are made, does this occur in open spaces, in which the decision-making process is open to contributions from anyone who will be impacted by the decision? Or are they made in closed spaces, where the people making the decision are the only ones involved in the process, and decisions are made on the behalf of others? Or are decisions made in spaces where others are invited to contribute to the decision-making? Who gets the invitation and when they receive the invitation is ultimately still decided by the people that hold power.

If we were to expand the idea of decision-making to exercising control over the decisions that impact your life, it becomes no longer just about a theoretical process but a question of autonomy – who truly governs your life and who makes decisions about it. What access do you have to the spaces in which these decisions are made and does some kind of hierarchy exist in your relationships, where power is imbalanced? Did you consent to that power imbalance or power dynamic? Has this ever been discussed or acknowledged openly, or agreed upon explicitly? Where is power hidden or visible in your relationship? Is there any invisible power that removes you, or someone else you are in relationship to, from understanding that their rights have been taken away – that somehow there is an unknown that keeps you from knowing what you do not know about your autonomy, rights, and needs?

This is an incredibly brief overview of Gaventa's theory, which applies to situations of civic engagement and democracy as well as many other contexts. I often use this framework of power when I do anti-racism training or when helping organizations to think about how they work: who holds power in their organizations and how can their leaders be held accountable?

A Simple Framework for Thinking about Power

In 2014, a consultant who worked for the Democracy Commission partnered with the National Union of Students in the UK to explore whether students in higher and further education engaged with their student unions.[4] Did they see their union, which they were automatically enrolled into (in most cases), as a force for collective bargaining and advocating for their rights, or did they simply equate their student union with the university bar? The report was called *Democracy is Dead! Long Live Democracies!* and explored whether or not student unions were truly democratic.[5] Its publication was followed by an intimate session on power for student union leaders, which was hosted by the lead researcher, James Robertson, in the fall of 2014 at that year's annual National Union of Students (NUS UK) Sabbatical Officers conference.[6]

At around this time, I was elected the first Black woman president of Edinburgh University Students' Association (EUSA). Coming from the States, where student unions did not have nearly as much power, influence, or resources, and where student unions did not have the same legacy of launching politicians' careers, I was fascinated by how students perceived their student unions. As a student who had transferred from an International Relations course to Edinburgh University's first MA in Sustainable Development, I was equally intrigued by power relations, dynamics, and power theory. Robertson's references to Foucauldian theory and Bourdieu's theories of networked power had me transfixed. His overarching discussion concerned other ways to think about how we can interact with power, including the way power moves, and included the following four categories:

- power over – control over people and resources
- power with – collective strength
- power to – individual agency
- power within – self-worth and efficacy

When I run anti-racism workshops today, or work with organizations like NGOs and charities to help them think about governance and who has decision-making power within their organizations, I still find this a useful framework to consider. When we start to think about how we have power over and with other people – and the power to make change, alongside the power within ourselves to be self-reflective or hold ourselves accountable – we have a better understanding of the relationship we have not only to power individually, but to the way power works as a type of energy. One of the most important tools in a disruptor's toolkit is understanding the power we have and how to use it.

Ways to Channel Power

It is incredibly important to understand how we approach power, and our relationship to it, when we work with energy. We need to think beyond power as being a resource that is there for us to use, because that encourages us to think about power in an extractive way. Our current way of working with power often presupposes that power is finite and needs to be maintained because it can disappear or be yielded to others. However, if power is energy and energy is fundamental to our understanding of ourselves because we are made up of it, then energy is as endless as our human potential; indeed, it exceeds it.

While the Triple Goddess archetypes offer examples of ways to express power, the Hierophant invites us to question our attitude to power and the status quo itself, so that we can make conscious choices about how and where we direct our energy for disruption. The Hierophant acts as a connector between our humanity and the cosmos, by linking what is above with what is below. As an energy channel and conductor, a disruptor is like the Hierophant. You are the power conduit. You can begin to think about how you experience power in your own life by asking yourself these sorts of questions:

- Where are the spaces of power you occupy and how do you experience them? Are they hidden, visible, or invisible?
- Are you practising power to, power from, power with, or power within?
- What is your take on your level of power in any given moment or situation?
- What are the ways in which you engage with and interact with your own power?
- Given your position of, proximity to, or lack of power – what potential is there for disruption?

It is often easy these days to feel powerless or to forget our power (although, of course, there may be those who feel they wield too much of it). A great deal of the health, wellness, and healing world speaks about how to step into our power, reclaim our power, and cut cords with negative energetic hooks or cords in us that other people have unconsciously planted. We are often asked to remember our power. Why? I believe it is because deep down we have forgotten we are all powerful, mystical, magical beings. Our circumstances, trauma, family history, personal history, and daily lives may have taught us that we have less power than we do or want.

Of course, this does not mean that people will not continue to try to have power over you. They will, and some people will exert more power over you than others. But how do you engage with your *power to* (your individual agency) and *power within* (your self-worth and efficacy) to use your power in spaces in which you have some control, which includes how you live your life, who you surround yourself with, where you work, what you eat, and how you choose to respond to the situations you find yourself in?

Will you have the power to disrupt things when necessary or to speak up when someone else cannot? Do you find the power within to withstand the scrutiny of bringing something not right to the surface or of being disliked? Can you start to think of this as being part of your life's work and your purpose here on this earth?

4

"RIGHT" LEADERSHIP IN THE FACE OF DISRUPTION

Leadership does not need to mimic the traditional models. Often, when we think of leaders, the first thing that springs to mind is the CEO of a company or a politician. However, leadership can come in the form of being a good friend, a good partner, or a good neighbour. It can be about being quiet and taking a step back. Leadership can also be about identifying that which guides us and the people we may look to, for hints on how to lead. This might entail looking to the goddesses or finding examples closer to our daily lives. Most significantly, it can be about leading yourself, which is one of the most important ways to demonstrate leadership – when you choose to live for yourself based on your own choices and not what works for other people.

Leadership in the face of disruption is all about how willing you are to disrupt yourself and your life for good reason, for what you believe in and in order to benefit others. In the Rider–Waite–Smith Tarot, the Strength card is represented by a woman greeting a lion. As Jessica Dore puts it, it is about the soft, gentle parts of ourselves meeting the "ferocious" part of ourselves.[1] According to Joseph Campbell's interpretations, this card also portrays the initiatory threshold.[2] The call to adventure that can signal disruption. Sometimes the hero answers the call, but sometimes the hero denies having received it. Oftentimes, it is their inner monologue that prevents them from responding to it. This card is about the Fool's call to adventure and the obstacles the Fool encounters on the way when they accept their call. The question is, will you be your own Fool and accept the call to adventure?

We can associate strength and leadership with things like brute force or a need to be steadfast. But what requires more strength is greeting our doubt, fear, uncertainty, and anxiety with a courageousness or an openness that allows us to respond to a call to action – to join the path of a leader taking charge of their own future or their own destiny.

What Are Your Circumstances Telling You?

When it comes to deciding the sort of leader you want to be, one of the best ways to work through what good leadership is involves exploring the opposite – what bad leadership is and what doesn't work. To that end, let's first explore what the word "leadership" currently conjures up for you. Do you imagine yourself completely in control of your life and following a set of principles that you dictate or decide on? Do you even know what principles are important to you? Or do you feel like you are spending your life just going through the motions and navigating the principles, social pressures, or rules laid down by the people around you, like your family, friends, or the people you work with? And what might this be telling you about yourself?

I believe we reflect what we project – and that like attracts like. These are all energetic principles in the rules of physics and light, which reflect the reality of our interactions with others. We are energetic, light-filled beings. We are 97 per cent water and the earth's surface is 71 per cent water, so we literally mirror our external world.

In much the same way, our choices, friendships, relation-ships, and connections not only reflect our outer worlds, but they reflect the people we want to be and choose to be, too. We can make the decision to change our outer world in a second, just as we can choose who we associate with. These choices about the energy we radiate are extremely important. As we have seen, paying attention to how we feel energetically when we are around other people, in new environments, or in any situation for that matter, is crucial. It means sensing whether these vibrate in harmony with us and our own values. (See the exercise in chapter 2, page 36, on sensing atmospheres.)

To demonstrate "right" leadership, with no ego driving us to seek power, requires us to be led by our values and principles. We cannot navigate the world with ease, certainty, courage, or confidence without a deep understanding of these. It also helps if we can find some clarity around the unique traits that make us who we are.

Understanding Yourself as a Leader

Developed in the late 1980s, Ra Uru Hu's Human Design system can be used to get a better understanding of our unique traits and gifts, and the qualities that we can each bring to leadership. The idea at the centre of the system is that each of us has a design, or what is called an "Individual Rave BodyGraph" or "Rave Mandala", which is formed by the combinations of the date, place, and time of our birth, the Hindu-Brahmin chakra system, the sephiroth of the Kabbala, the I-Ching, and the nature of our auras. Altogether, these describe how we individually function.

Human Design is centred around Rave Cosmology, which describes our nature as being that of "nine-centered beings" – arguing that homo sapiens are in a transitional stage, "with a binary consciousness", unlike our predecessors, and we are "moving through a duality of this and that".[3] One aspect of the system concerns the idea of "authorities", whereby our "inner authorities" are "our body's knowing or intelligence" and how we "know if a decision is the right one" for us. It explains how we can face less resistance in life by acting on the authority of our body's intelligence, rather than the conditioning of our mind and what we think we should do instead of what aligns with our inner nature. Our Human Design type – which includes our authorities, centres, and profile lines – thus determines our "strategy", which influences our ability to act in alignment with our inner authority and create less resistance and more flow in our lives.

Human Design is also known as the "Science of Differentiation", and I, for one, have found it a useful way to learn more about my own needs and what good leadership can look like for me.

The Making of "Good Leadership"

The author Simon Sinek talks about good leaders eating last and leading by example, by making sure others' needs were met before the leader's own.[4] Sinek coined the phrase "start with why", arguing that if a group of people are motivated by their "why" – their shared purpose – they will go much further together, aligned to a common goal and values. Ever since I learned this phrase in the early 2010s, "starting with why" has echoed in my head through every talk, workshop, project, campaign, and debate I've been involved in, but more importantly, it has motivated me in every situation where I have been responsible for leading a team.

Sinek is talking about a type of leadership that has long been understood in the healing community. Commonly referred to as "service leadership", this notion of leading by example and not from the front is a type of leadership that some groups have been proposing as the way forward for decades. You will often find service leadership in community-led, civic-minded spaces, within wisdom traditions, climate movements, and youth work, for example. In spaces like these, the notion that an individual has autonomy over their own experience and is therefore an expert in their experience gives them access to leadership. They can inspire others to live authentically in order to understand what motivates them – in other words, their "why".

As an example of this in action, in the sustainable development circles I have been a part of, we talk about leadership in local spaces, in which locals are viewed as the experts in their experience, as the antithesis to international development, philanthropy, and westernized models of white saviourism in the Global South. This alternative is authentic leadership. With respect to this, the question each prospective leader should ask themselves is this: "Am I centring myself?" This means: "Am I making myself the protagonist in a situation where my leadership or existence is not actually important beyond being a vehicle for other people to get the resources, time, energy, and support that they need? Or am I centring the true experts in this space – those that have the lived experience to understand how I can best be of service in this space?"

Similar to contests over who has a platform and who indeed has power in a situation, this narrative and line of questioning – critical inquiry – is something that many of us have been using for a long time to question the power we have over others as leaders. Leadership that dismantles power dynamics, rather than putting on shows of strength through appearing steadfast, staunch, stoic, and unwavering, is good leadership. Feminist thinkers, decolonizers, and community organizers have been using these techniques for centuries, but the real work comes on an individual level when a leader asks themselves if they are the problem, or if they are contributing to the problem.

How to Practise "Good Leadership"

I have worked with many leaders whose aim has been to make their visions a reality. From working with small community-led arts organizations to visionaries who build spaces to support other purpose-driven visionaries, my career to date has included working with thousands of social entrepreneurs, artists, creatives, freelancers, self-employed people, and start-up organizations. Whether legally incorporating these organizations, fund-raising, or helping small groups of people to realize a creative goal, I have encountered a number of different types of leaders. What I have noticed in this 15-year period is that there are some common characteristics or behaviours that indicate how *not* to behave in leadership positions. These behaviours will tell you when you might be venturing into a sticky, challenging, or deeply problematic situations. I learned the hard way. So that you do not have to live my mistakes or go through some of the deeply uncomfortable, soul-destroying, and patience-stretching situations I have experienced, I would like to share these with you now, reframing them as positive lessons:

1. A good leader does not feel the need to have all of the answers and always be right. More importantly, a good leader does not equate not-knowing with weakness. A good leader surrounds themselves with people who know more than they do about certain areas or things they want to accomplish – if only because they recognize that one person cannot know everything. When they bring in a co-director, consultant, or expert to support them in making their vision become a reality, they do not feel threatened by this person. A good leader does not conceal information that is crucial to the survival or existence of their vision coming to life. Good leaders do not view any team members who choose to step away from that work or project as an attack, assault, or personal affront.

2. A good leader creates some distance between their vision for the future and their sense of self. There is some separation between their self-image and their work. Entanglement between those two things leads to a number of complications and is a direct result of the messages we receive from society about our worth being tied to our productivity. We are inherently worthy of living and thriving simply because we are human. However, the energy it takes to bring something into the world – whether it is a creative endeavour, project, business, idea, or piece of writing – requires the person or group of people bringing it into the world to go through an energetic birthing process. This energetic birthing process can result in those bringing this project into the world as subconsciously relating to it as their "baby". Which means they are often very precious about who has any impact on their idea, project, creative process, business, or piece of work. Not only is there an unhealthy attachment to their idea, but they begin to treat others supporting them as if they are working directly with their own offspring, sometimes in a very protective, precious, and unhelpful way. There is nothing wrong with having an attachment to your work, and your creative process is your own. No one can or should take that away from you, but once you invite other people to join your process, it is important as a leader to change or renegotiate your relationship to whatever it is that you are bringing into the world before you negatively impact the people supporting you in realizing your vision. This can feel like a grieving process. Remember Kalī and embrace it as a natural part of the process of change.

3. A good leader encourages you to be open about your skills and interests, so as not to limit you, your potential, and the external influences that might contribute to the wider work you are doing. This also means that they are secure enough to let go of power and do not try to control the people they work with. Behaviour that suggests otherwise includes never asking other people about their hobbies or interests outside of their work. They may also draw attention away from or choose not to celebrate the other parts of you that you are proud of/love because these aspects of yourself do not seem relevant to work you are doing with them. This is largely about a leader's sense of self and security. If they are a secure leader, they will not feel threatened by anybody around them. They will encourage you and support you by being proud of the person you are and everything that might entail. A good leader encourages their team and colleagues or the people they are working with to be their full, authentic selves. They lead by example in this, and they do not inadvertently signal to others or explicitly ask them to leave certain aspects of themselves at home or cut off parts of themselves to participate in the work they are doing together.

4. A good leader does not overshare themselves. They do not expect their team to hold their emotions, needs, and desires – the rollercoaster ride of emotions that emerges when bringing something into being – without their team's consent. There needs to be a consensual exchange of personal information and energy in any group. An invitation to share and be open is not the same as sharing information, emotions, and fears or positive emotions with others without them consenting to receive that information. The invitation to share within reason is different to unloading emotions and thoughts onto the team in a way that they either cannot reciprocate or which means they feel responsible for the leader's emotions, feelings, fears, and expectations in a way that is disproportionate to the responsibility team members feel for the emotions of each other (or anyone else they are collaborating with).

5. A good leader practises energy hygiene regularly and is aware of the energetic frequency, build-up, exchange, toil, and nature of the work they are doing. A lot of this requires having the time and space to reflect on the energetics of a situation. We work in a world that encourages us to perform quickly and "efficiently" to optimize productivity, but we know that decisions made hastily can have a detrimental impact. Leaders who go at their own pace, who create an environment that allows everyone in their team to work at their own pace, who frequently revisit their values, who create space for everyone's well-being, and have time for self-reflection, are more able to tune in to and be attuned to the energy present within a process. As we saw in chapters 1 and 2, tapping into the energetics of a situation can be intuitive, but it can also be practised and learned. It is as simple as taking the time to meditate on a project, the people involved in it, and the next steps required for it. Good leadership includes practising good energetic hygiene, which means regularly clearing your work energetically, cutting energetic ties to decisions and people involved in that work, and having the clarity to look into the future of a project.

6. A good leader does not need to receive credit for their work (and takes responsibility when there is a crisis or things go wrong). Not everyone in leadership roles should have the same skill set, but when it comes to crisis management, a leader's skills can reveal their true colours. Think about how somebody reacts under pressure or in circumstances where they are surprised. This surprise may come with an element of challenge and a lack of control where the outcome they expected is no longer possible. A good leader is able to adapt to change and treat people with dignity when things do not go the way they planned. From an energetic standpoint, this may look like having the foresight, calm, patience, understanding, and an energetic reading of a situation that enables everyone to proceed in a manner that minimizes damage and supports the whole team.

7. A good leader is not an island. A good leader is as strong as the people they work with. Leadership can feel lonely, but a leader does not have to be alone – and this is often where some leaders can make mistakes. There are many different people who a leader can approach for advice, perspective, and to gain insights from their past experiences. A leader who thinks they can come up with a solution on their own – and that it is their responsibility to come to decisions by themselves, uninformed by the input of others – has got the wrong end of the stick. Good leaders ask for help, as often and as regularly as they need it. A strong group of advisors who do not necessarily hold the same views as you, but with whom you share collective values, are good critical friends for any leader to surround themselves with.

The Importance of Friction and Leadership in the Face of Disruption

There can be no change without some level of friction – whether it is the friction of the future coming into contact with the old world as we know it, or the friction of new ways clashing as they settle in. There is no change without navigating and negotiating discomfort. When you are attempting to make change, remember that friction is part of the process. If you are starting to notice it among your group of friends, family, or in a dynamic playing out in front of you, know that this is a good indicator that the process of change has started.

We must remember that tension and friction are energy generators. When we start a fire the traditional way by rubbing two pieces of wood together to get a spark, we can see the physical evidence to suggest that friction causes a spark, which can lead to fire. This fiery energy can be incredibly useful as a catalyst for change. However, if it is not managed or is left to its own devices – if there is not a good facilitator to support this spark in a manageable way – the spark can get out of hand and turn into a raging fire.

Part of showing good leadership is being able to facilitate and hold friction in order to bring about change. Managing friction and relationships full of friction is part and parcel of managing people. This can be true in a family dynamic or in a friendship dynamic too, when you find yourself mediating between friends, although hopefully that is not a regular occurrence. A good leader must be able to sit with discomfort and not take it personally; to bring together competing views and interests; to help facilitate a team in finding common ground among a plethora of ideas and viewpoints or differing ways of working. And a responsible leader must sit with the discomfort of discord and uncertainty entailed in guiding a team through to the other side – where beauty can come out of the friction. They must make sure that no one in the team is burned in the process by feeling unheard, dismissed, or pushed in one direction or another, but that the team reaches the decision via consensus, collective agreement, or rigorous discussion.

A leader who is aware of their own emotional landscape and their team's emotional landscape can hold together the vision for the big picture by understanding what everyone is trying to achieve. They are also able to take the temperature of their team, which includes understanding any points of friction caused by changes and in negotiating the different needs within the team. A leader who can do this has the best chance of leading well, whether they are responsible for just their partner, their family more widely, volunteers, or another group of people.

In contrast, trying to control a situation in an ego-centred and authoritarian way is never useful, because of the dismissive and overruling impact this can have on others, which may have a negative effect on their experience of the situation. This creates the kind of friction that is undesirable in any situation, which is not friction as a result of change, but as a result of needing to maintain power and control.

It is true that sometimes a leader needs to make difficult and swift decisions. Examples of this can include deciding to act when you witness someone in your group of friends being bullied or making a difficult decision about the family finances. Given how time-poor many of us are in a society where there are limited resources and constant pressures, it can feel like these sorts of hard decisions are impossible to make.

If you do need to make a decision without the support of anyone else, it is important to respect those people who will be impacted by your choices enough to explain your thinking and back up your decision as a result. If the answer is simply because a leader "felt like it", rather than a more comprehensive assessment of the situation, which takes into account the collective goals, the resources available, people's capacity, and the time in which the leader had to make the decision, then it will be difficult for others to believe in, trust, and follow the leader, who appears to be led only by their own needs or perspectives on the world. If your quick judgement of a situation allows you instead to consider all of these factors, you will be leading with integrity. And if you need more time to make a decision to consider all of these factors, take it.

How to Stand in Your Integrity as a Leader

I once worked for an arts organization that hired me as Creative Director five months before the launch of a major programme of events. The small fee I accepted for the role was much less than my usual day rate and a reasonable salary for this type of role, but I was willing to accept it because I believed in the work the organization was doing.

The organization was only a few years old. Between starting my role and getting to grips with the programme itself, I spent much of my time on incorporating the organization legally as a social enterprise, applying for funding (because the founder didn't have as much experience as I did with this), and supporting the team's delivery of the programme in the coming summer.

It was only after I'd joined the team that I realized quite how little funding we had. Rather than receiving an actual fee, which had been my understanding before I accepted the role, each team member was being paid a stipend as a gesture toward the amount of hours they would need to put in to make the programme happen. Because of the small fees, we were working with a limited capacity. At times, people were in roles they didn't have much experience in, which meant I was supporting team members even more than I would normally. Occasionally, I was even showing them how to do certain pieces of their work. We got to a point where we still did not have enough funding to run all of our events a week before we were set to announce our events programme.

Our planning reached a critical point. A week before we were set to launch our programme, I thought we should delay announcing it until we were sure we had the funding to proceed. The founder was not willing to do this and, after a short conversation, I decided I had to walk away from the project. There were a number of red flags that had come up in the process of our collaboration. While the pay situation was one, another was finding out the founder had some money in reserve which they were willing to contribute to the festival in an emergency, but which they had not made me aware of.

I had been working for months to secure enough funding for us and this information would have allowed me to plan the process much better. As it was, we were already coming across as disorganized to potential funders, whereas knowing about the money held in reserve could have made the process much easier. The founder's unwillingness to delay the programme announcement was the last straw. I resigned with my integrity intact. I did not agree with how things were being run. I tried to discuss it and the founder was too defensive and unreceptive to my perspective. I was trying to support them and prevent them from having to go through the sorts of experiences I had encountered with festivals in the past, but they took it as a personal attack.

How other people respond to you is not something you have control over, but it is incredibly important to know where your boundaries are around what you will tolerate and what will put you out of your integrity. Having the confidence to walk away and defend other people in the process – even if you are vilified for it or misunderstood – is good leadership. Standing in our integrity is not always easy but it is very important, because if we do not do so, that choice will eat away at us and our ability to stand in our integrity may be completely taken away from us over time.

Managing Crisis as a Leader in the Face of Disruption

I often run training sessions in which I prepare people to manage crises in leadership situations. According to the *Oxford English Dictionary*, crises are "times of intense danger or difficulty",[5] which is often how we experience them. But they are also times when "an important decision must be made". The urgency of the situation is part of what defines it as a crisis, but the fact that an important decision needs to be made suggests that there is an opportunity or opening for change, too. A crisis does not need to end in disaster, but it does suggest an imminent need for change. Crises are complex in nature and require action. Yet they can often involve a lack of direction, order, or clear way of "handling" the situation. Sometimes all of the factors that contribute to a crisis have not yet been revealed and aspects of the situation could rapidly evolve. Often when a crisis starts, we do not have all of the information we need about what has caused it.

This is where crisis management comes in. This term may sound incredibly corporate or bureaucratic, like advice from a human resources manual (and there is nothing wrong with that!), but believe me: understanding how to manage a crisis will come in handy for you on your journey through the energetics of disruption.

Learning and understanding how to manage crises, particularly when causing disruption, is critical. Over the years I have been in a number of crisis situations – from car accidents to social media disasters. At the moment, my role as an anti-racism and governance consultant means I strive to hold organizations and companies accountable to do the deep work of setting up ethical boards of directors, as well as embed anti-racist values and principles into their day-to-day business. I work with a lot of young women to prepare them to sit on the boards of organizations and think about feminist approaches to governance. What does truly ethical governance look like in these situations and, as voluntary board members of these organizations, what can they do to hold themselves more accountable both to the work they are doing and to each other?

A PRACTICE FOR CRISIS MANAGEMENT

When I teach workshops on crisis management, I often speak to young women who are looking to join boards for the first time and to people who have to manage crisis in their jobs in other ways. I ask these people to think about their own needs in a crisis: *How do you react when a crisis actually occurs? When have you been in crisis situations, and are there things you have done that have surprised you?*

The following step-by-step practice can be applied to any kind of crisis situation – whether an accident, a relationship, or a friendship crisis, for example. This also applies to an energetic crisis. The important thing is that it will give you some tools and steps to follow, which will enable you to assess the situation, understand what your capacity is (emotional, energetic, or otherwise), and take a step back in order to respond instead of reacting.

1. Establish a clear understanding of the crisis. This includes fact-finding and establishing who is involved in the crisis and what it entails. Use this moment to tap into the energy of the crisis. How does the energy feel?

2. Create a mental or physical timeline. Start to prioritize what is urgent and what is important. Does the energy of the situation shift at different points in the timeline? What can this tell you about the nature of the crisis? This step allows you to start making a mental map of what you need to act on immediately and what can wait. Prioritization is key to preventing you from getting overwhelmed.

3. Understand the resources you have at your disposal. What do you have available to you to help you address

this situation? What energetic guidance can you call in to support you through this situation and which of its characteristics will be useful to you here?

4. Delegate tasks to deal with the situation. What must you do and what can others help you with? Are you aware of the energy you need to complete a task and the energy that others can bring to it? Keep this in mind as the crisis unfolds.

5. Take action – respond, do not react. It is incredibly important that you respond rather than react to a crisis, as chaos begets chaos. If we remember that the characteristics of a crisis are complex, amorphous, unfolding, and uncertain, similar to how energy behaves, it is likely that our initial reaction to any situation with those characteristics will mirror it.

Leadership, the Stars, and World-building

For a leader working with and through the energetics of disruption, courage is necessary, but it is also important to have or develop a penchant for disruption. Uranus, the planet of change, disruption, and upheaval, is one of the key celestial bodies in astrology for helping us to better understand where disruptive leadership comes from. Named after one of the primordial sky gods in Greek mythology, the planet Uranus is connected with blue-sky thinking, innovation and change. In the Tarot, the Fool corresponds with Uranus – as if suggesting that these qualities are essentially part of who we are on our journey through life. Through encountering Strength, and the initiation that this symbolizes, the Fool is perhaps being called to take a step closer to their true self.

We can try to lead others without being a leader in our own lives, but that type of leadership is incomplete. If we make a choice to be a leader, we need to make sure we are leaders in our own inner worlds – starting with the flesh we inhabit. Leadership is both an inside and an outside job. This does not mean we need to be perfect or "strong" in a conventional sense, but it may mean we need to find more ways to support our nervous system when we are activated and stressed. It also means having a better understanding of how all of the systems of our body are connected and paying attention to how the outside world impacts us on the inside. It means resting more than we think we need to, and not shaming ourselves for needing rest in a world that thrives on our exhaustion – and doing what we can to support the people around us to do the same. It is about building better conditions for our bodies, minds, spirits, souls; and finding the care, self-reflection, and community to support ourselves.

Leadership can take many forms, and there are many philosophies about it. Ultimately, a leader is a visionary with a big imagination who is able to bring a new world into existence. Reflecting on the leadership roles I've held in the last 15 years, I know that my approach to leadership has always been grounded in my values, although this is not what all leaders are driven or led by. Without values, we do not understand what drives and motivates us, how we show up in the world and how we interact with it. It is like travelling to a new world without understanding if there is any oxygen to survive on. We are doomed to fail. We need to greet the lion with clarity and trust like the maiden on the Strength Tarot card: trust in what is guiding us and providing the world-building blocks to create a new future.

5

THE IMPORTANCE OF VALUES

We live in an era where people often tell us we need to live our truths and find our purpose. The question is: how can we find our purpose when we do not know what is important to us? Many of us have been living in the shadow of economic recession after economic recession, as well as within the growing chaos of the climate crisis. Faced with daily crippling anxiety about our future, our livelihoods, and survival, most of us don't know how to even start thinking about what our purpose might be.

In the Tarot, the Judgement card is often seen as a card that – like Strength – represents a call to adventure, as well as resurrection. The card shows an angel sounding a trumpet in the sky while people rise from their tombs with their arms reaching out toward it. The call requires us to leave behind all of our preconceived notions of ourselves and only take with us what we need for the adventure ahead. We may not always be willing to answer the call to adventure, because sometimes we do not feel ready. Other times, we feel the task ahead of us is too immense or we may be scared of what the call to adventure might ultimately ask of us. It could ask us to make sacrifices that we are unwilling to make. It might require us to put ourselves in uncomfortable situations. It might embolden us to follow our instincts. And even scarier, it might ask us to leave behind the life we knew before for something entirely unknown.

A call to adventure requires us to keep an open mind about what we might encounter. And it will very likely involve getting clear on our values – on what is important to us in the everyday details of our lives and what we want to take with us on the next steps of our journey.

When it comes to values, people often think of morals and ethics. However, this book is not intended to be read as an ethical treatise, although I do believe we live in a world in which our moral and ethical framework is compromised – for example, large companies get away with polluting our air and making profits while millions of people live in poverty, and the pollution is causing the world's largest ecological crisis to date. Young people in poverty may be forced into trading whatever they can get their hands on, which in many communities is drugs, so they end up in jail and caught in a cycle of incarceration that profits from the number of people in jails, while in comparison a blind eye may be turned to those committing corporate fraud and embezzling money. We are raising our young people to value digital connection, augmented and virtual realities instead of valuing spending time outside with their neighbours. Words are being removed from the dictionary at exponential rates – words to describe nature are being replaced with words about our digital and virtual lives.

In all of this noise, all of this messaging about the ways in which we are supposed to be and to live our lives, how do we know what is important to us, and more importantly, what is important at all?

The word "values" may feel substantial and suggest a system of beliefs that are immutable and unchangeable. However, for the purpose of this book and the work we are embarking on together, I would like us to think about our values differently. Our values may shift and change. It might be odd to think that our guiding principles can change at all, that something so fundamental to us could or should shift, but it is important for us to approach our values with a more fluid mindset. This allows us to embrace any changes to our values in the future by affording us some room in which to evolve and to grow.

Understanding Your Values with the Values Compass

When I was growing up, I had the luxury of enough time to be bored. I had to entertain myself by inventing things; like the terrible homemade newspaper I put out for a week when I was about nine or ten years old, which had so many typos in it I don't believe any local newspaper, let alone a major newspaper, would ever take me on. I once had a lemonade stand, where only one customer ever bought a glass for 50 cents. I tried so many things that did not stick, but in the midst of it all I learned so much about myself and other people.

I learned about my creative drive, and about what I thought was fair and what was not fair. (I see you, M, who stole about 45 of my Pokémon cards out of my binder in the fourth grade. I also see you, Headmistress, who told me this was not possible – because we attended a Christian school.) I also learned very fast, due to the fast-paced and status-obsessed environment I lived in as a teenager, where unless you had something to give or offer by way of personal connections, even in an informal setting, other people would quickly lose interest in you. The corridors of power and how power operates in an environment obsessed with scarcity require you to be strategic, swift, and opportunistic in ways that still make me feel unwell writing this.

When you think about the environment you grew up in and what unspoken rules there were, what do you remember? Were you always praised for your appearance, and did you experience a lot of pressure to be successful in whichever way success was defined? Or were you not expected to do much of anything and were you considered a waste of space? Or was it more subtle than that, so subtle that you need to do some serious exploration to discover what those unwritten expectations, ways of being, and ways of interacting with others were? When you think about the things that bring you joy, that conjure up indifference, or that make your face burn with embarrassment, rage, or vengefulness . . . what are those things? What moves you?

Discovering Your Values System

The values compass is a system that can help you find clarity around the areas of life that are important to you.[1] However, it is more than a "check in" and unearthing of your current values or what is important to you. It can act like the big reveal of your inner guidance system.

Quite often, when I deliver the values compass to groups, I explain how our values are changeable and the compass is mutable. What is important to us on a daily basis will shift, based on what is happening in our life, such as whether we are going through a major life transition or if we have experienced an illness. We might think that something like our values are core to who we are and that they will never change, but this would suggest that we never change as human beings – and, of course, we do.

I speak of the importance of doing the values compass exercise regularly, perhaps every six months or once a year. It could be any time you are making a big decision that has found you stuck or in a place of unknowing. However, as any coaching practice reminds us: we always know. Our job is to reveal and uncover our inner knowing – in some ways to reveal our inner truth to ourselves. The values compass is a simple tool that allows us to switch off our conscious mind in order to support the subconscious (or pull the subconscious into focus). And it's an exercise we must regularly engage in, in order to build a muscle memory that enables us to direct our focus in this way more easily in the future.

Unless you grew up in an environment that encouraged you to discover, explore, and develop a language around your values, they may feel incredibly difficult to access. Your values may also be wrapped up in and conflated with values passed down to and projected onto you from authority figures such as family members and friends, or from religious belief systems, society and unspoken social rules; but, in actuality, values are something you probably need to spend time excavating rather than searching for. Like a sculptor working with marble who reveals the sculpture within, your values are there, albeit hidden underneath layers of conditioning, social pressure, and belief systems around what it means to be in the world, or, in other words, what it means to be human – although our humanity is inherently ours, something that we cannot get wrong. It is part of the animal of who we are and therefore embedded into our instinct for life as fundamentally as our reaction to oxygen hitting our lungs is to breathe.

Our values are the guiding principles for how we live life. They are the things that bring us joy and help us relate to or connect with others. They are the ideas that give our lives shape and the boundaries that we believe a life should be shaped by. They inform our passions and create the parameters of our windows of tolerance for how we believe the world should operate. They are influenced by our "lived experience" of our families, friends, and anyone else we have come into contact with who has had a significant impact on us. While you may not always know precisely which people, situations, and experiences have shaped your values, you can begin to understand how your values have been shaped by them.

Understanding our values can feel daunting, like a task that asks us to examine ourselves with a magnifying glass. We may feel threatened to the point of existential crisis, but it does not have to be this way. For some of us, our values are things that come easily to us when asked or reveal themselves quite quickly in the right situation. Approaching our values with lightness and humour, and through the people around us, will allow us to uncover our values through our environment, which – as we have seen – acts like a mirror for us. It goes back to the adage that is often repeated in spiritual circles: that our judgements of others are what we judge in ourselves, and that the people closest to us mirror our own beliefs, needs, and desires back to us.

A PRACTICE TO LEARN ABOUT YOURSELF WITH THE VALUES COMPASS

The values compass will allow you to understand your values through the world around you and the things that are close to you, without forcing you to confront yourself in an incredibly vulnerable way. How you experience or interpret the questions and what you think of first is what you should write down. You do not have to share your answers with anyone.

Before you start, take a moment to get a piece of paper or a device that you can write on, and find a timer. You will have a short period of time to respond to each question, statement, or prompt. This means you won't be tempted to spend too much time reading into each question or trying to come up with the perfect answer. Let yourself move on within the time allocated, which will be 30 seconds or a minute at most.

Let us begin:

1. Name one of your traits that, if you could, you would like to pass on to someone you care about.
   (30 seconds)
2. List two of the most important people in your life.
   (30 seconds)
3. List one word for each of the people you have chosen that describes them. (30 seconds)
4. You have discovered a new place or established your own space. Imagine this space is exclusively yours, and with this space comes its own currency. On this currency it says: "In —— we trust." In what do you trust? (30 seconds)
5. Finish this statement: "Give me —— or give me death." What would you die for? (30 seconds)

6. What two qualities do you look for in someone you spend a lot of time with? (*30 seconds*)

7. Describe yourself in one word. (*30 seconds*)

8. Finish this statement: "… life, liberty, and the pursuit of ——." (*30 seconds*)

9. If there were just two rules you felt everyone should follow in life, what would they be? (*1 minute*)

10. Think of the person you most admire, and explain in one word why. (*30 seconds*)

11. After you have written down your answers, take a few minutes to consider your responses and circle the eight responses to the questions that resonate with you the most.

12. Then, after you have circled or selected the eight words that resonated the most, draw a circle on the page in front of you.

13. Next, separate the circle into eight sections. Each word gets its own section. (If you have enough time, allow a couple of minutes per word to jot down what that word means to you.)

14. Now, look again at the eight words in front of you. You can approach this diagram like a compass. If you were to find yourself stuck on a decision or an idea, for example, you can decide that you would only make that decision or move forward with that idea if it allowed you to live more in alignment with your values, as written down in front of you. For example, you could frame a question to yourself along these lines: "Does this [insert idea/situation/or decision here] allow me to live with more [insert value here]?"

15. In this way, you can employ the rule of five or six by deciding that in order to move forward with your decision, it would have to enable you to live more fully in alignment with five or six of your values. Those values can be anything you have come up with – from trust to justice and creativity and joy. And now, you have a working values compass. Use it to guide you whenever you see fit!

The Values Compass – A Window to Your Creativity

The timing factor of the exercise is key when it comes to the values compass questions, because of the constraints this presents. The process is one of allowing lots of ideas to come to mind and then narrowing those ideas down – creating space for everything, before getting specific. As we saw in the values compass exercise, constraints from the beginning limit your ability to overthink or feel pressured to choose the "right" answer. Rather than constraining you, it opens you up to more possibilities, since you do not have enough time to judge your thoughts in the first place. It removes the instinct to self-censor and encourages divergent thinking.

The fact is that one cannot create with no constraints in a finite world. There must be some material constraints or, indeed, a framework to create something, whether those constraints are as simple as the materials at hand to use (wood, metal, gas, liquids) or that one's story has to fit into an 80,000-word limit in order for the book to go to print . . . The values compass and other design thinking exercises and activities like it can help unleash our imagination while at the same time encouraging us to work within agreed-upon or externally imposed constraints. That process of reacting to boundaries, finite resources, or time limits is central to a creative process that has some end. Otherwise, we would simply be creating, reshaping, building models, and testing them ad infinitum, which is a very common approach but is not the goal of the values compass tool.

The values compass itself acts as a starting point for a process of discernment. It is a point that we can use to anchor ourselves and gain some insight into what is most important to us in this moment, which is a wider indicator of which principles are guiding our lives. As our values are fluid entities, rather than fixed, I would encourage you to revisit the values compass exercise in three months' time. Compare the two sets of results and see what has changed. Have your fundamental guiding principles shifted? Have the values you've unearthed changed?

This process reminds me of the poet Rainer Maria Rilke's advice to young poet Franz Xavier Kappus in *Letters to a Young Poet*: "[a]nd the point is, to live everything. Live the questions now. Perhaps then, someday far in the future, you will gradually, without even noticing it, live your way into the answer."[2] That is what is most important . . . living into your questions and being guided by your values with the help of your values compass to live into the answers too.

In 2018, I was part of a collective called Povo. Co-founded by me and two others, Povo was a thought-experiment and practical "conductancy" that explored what a 21st-century consultancy could look like. The notion that ideas are conducted, rather than using our creative minds to consult for the people we worked with, was central to the project. Drawing on our youth and practices that were the opposite of a lot of existing ways of working, Povo sought to explore what helping our "un-clients" facilitate their own creative process might look like.

The idea was that we did not have all the answers. In fact, we didn't have any of the answers. However, what we did have were tools and techniques to enable whoever we were working with to unlock their creativity, divergent thinking, and imagination to help them through a process that might have an endpoint or maybe a starting point for them. Our aim was not to be opaque about the creative process nor obtuse about our methods, but simply to invite in the notion that being creative with no goal was ok. It was more than ok. It was essential to the process.

Katherine Snow, one of our co-founders, was a product designer and is a now a design researcher who wrote her dissertation on the importance of play in the creative process. She was working with Linda Peilin Ma at the Edinburgh College of Art School of Design Informatics as researchers in residence to explore what play in the creative process could look like in practice. I was their chief collaborator, and together we explored what Povo could be or might look like. While our freelance, self-employed lifestyle was not for everyone, within a short few months we were working with the Church of England, Cambridge Regional College's Hub-of-All-Things (HAT),[3] and our relationship with the School (now Centre) for Design Informatics led to me co-producing an executive education programme called Project Mercury for Tesco Bank with the Chair of the centre. If I said any more . . . well, it was all top secret.

Anyway, this whole notion of creating space to "conduct" ideas was key. Rather than "consulting" with others and offering our expertise on ideas that were theirs to develop, we would create the optimal conditions for them to "conduct" their own ideas like electricity and play with the current. We simply equipped them with the mindset, head space, time, and tools to start conducting electricity – we created the conditions for divergent thinking to prevail. We were all big fans of the late Sir Ken Robinson at the time (and we continue to be).

Sir Ken beautifully illustrated the conditions needed for divergent thinking in his seminal RSAnimate, "Changing Education Paradigms",[4] in which his illustrated manifesto perfectly summarized how schools were encouraging convergent thinking, monotony, and conformity. Divergent thinking is often literally discouraged and something we unlearn in the modern education system. The solution lies in not restricting everyone to thinking the same way and giving people the freedom to use their divergent thinking skills.

These skills are perhaps best illustrated by a classic design thinking exercise involving a paperclip, in which participants are asked to think of about eight different uses for a paperclip. Someone who is self-censoring or still in "convergent thinking" mode may well think of the paperclip as being small, made of metal, and somewhat malleable. However, the exercise has never specified the size, shape, and composition of the paperclip, because in a creative world or space, the paperclip could be any size, shape, or composition. The exercise thus involves exploding any physical constraints to encourage out-of-the-box, divergent, or non-conformist thinking, which is essential to any creative process.

I have to wholeheartedly attribute to Katherine Snow and Linda Peilin Ma the notion of our approach at Povo being all about creating "a starting point". The fact is that often we need a starting point, any starting point, to have the confidence to embark on a creative process or journey. A starting point acts as a point of entry or inquiry that allows us to begin to ask the questions we need to truly explore an idea.

Often in the creative process, it is the beginning that is the hardest. We may be plagued with the thought of "well, I don't know where to start", when the task ahead of us feels overwhelming or insurmountable. While the blank page is often the most creative space for an artist, brimming with endless possibilities, at the same time that blank page can feel like a trap full of potential failure and failings. We all know that there is no failure when it comes to a creative process. There is no failing, really, when it comes to making something for the sake of making it.

For many artists, creatives, and people drawn by their creative needs, there is no question of what their purpose is. They simply cannot wake in the morning without thinking about the things that make them come alive; they process the world through various creative mediums. And it is not just artists who feel this way, but anyone who has a passion for their purpose, which does not necessarily come down to one thing. Like our values, it can change over time.

The Importance of Grey Areas

Grey areas are crucial when it comes to understanding our values, because our values may apply differently in different situations, or we may prioritize certain values over others in certain contexts. For example, flexibility may be one of your most important values, but where justice and flexibility overlap, you may choose to prioritize justice over flexibility. Also, the way that flexibility might be applied in a particular situation could suggest deception, the bending of rules, the bending of truth, or outright falsehoods. In contrast, imagine a scenario in which you need to make a choice that is not as simple choosing as one thing or the other – where flexibility may be your priority *alongside* justice, in that you believe that everyone should have access to flexible working conditions, for example. In this instance, there needn't be such either/or black/white thinking.

Binaries – in particular, binary black and white thinking, which does not allow for any grey areas – is one of the attitudes left to us by the Age of Enlightenment's philosophy of logic, reason, and rationality. It is part of a larger problematic legacy we need to critique, where a creative approach to grey areas can be helpful.

Today, artists and creative people often give us the space to consider nuance and complexity in a world of rules and tight definitions. It is frequently an artist's world-building abilities that allow us to suspend disbelief and hold two opposing ideas in our minds at once through storytelling or other clever creations, for example. These imaginary worlds, which may sit within the confines of a medium such as a film, a stage, a story, or a piece of art, allow us to embark on thought experiments that enable us to change our minds, perceptions, and understanding of certain topics. Their mere existence allows us to embark on a thought experiment without any immediate repercussions; however, the very act of being willing to be taken on the journey in the first place can have a very real impact on the world, often enabling us to shift into different futures. It is the very stuff that creates change.

A PRACTICE FOR USING THE VALUES COMPASS ON GREY AREAS

So where do grey areas fit into your own values? The following exercise will allow you to explore in more depth what your values actually mean to you, and the grey areas around them – which is where the free-writing component of the values compass exercise comes into play. This is where you will have the opportunity to explore not only the true meaning of the value to you, but how or why it might apply in different scenarios and contexts.

1. After you have identified and written down your eight values in the exercise on pages 86–88, spend 2 to 3 minutes allowing words, associations, images, feelings, textures, memories, or shapes to arise from them in whichever form these take. For example, if one of your values is "creativity", take some time to expand on what that word means.

2. You can use a free-writing technique, where you allow yourself to write down whatever words come up, even if they do not make immediate sense to you or seem unrelated to the word you have selected. If you choose not to write, you can doodle, walk, think, or move. Whatever feels best . . .

3. What is each value's shape and how does it relate to your daily life? This will allow the value to become known to you in a sense that is more personal and less abstract, in a way that has more meaning and where there is less projection onto it of what you perhaps believe the value should mean, rather than what it actually does mean to you.

4. If "justice" is one of your values, for example, what might that look like in the workplace, versus among a group of friends? How can this value change shape and fit into the grey areas of life?

5. How can you practically apply each of your values to your life by better understanding its meaning in order to facilitate your interactions with the world in a way that promotes peace?

Welcome to the grey areas of the values compass.

On a Philosophy of Values

Given that they may change and take us into grey areas, why then are values so important? And what has caused the subject of values in our culture to be so important today? Values are not new, and in many ways our public discourse around them has been consistent for centuries, but what we have seen recently, in the last 25 years or so, is the use of the words "purpose" and "purpose-driven" interchangeably with the words "values" or "values-driven", which suggests that somewhere along the way these are ideas we are collectively rediscovering. It is also clear that this values deficit – or search for purpose – does not impact all of us sharing this earth equally. These questions seem to emerge in capitalist, western, and increasingly secular societies where a moral compass, wisdom traditions, or indeed, even belief systems are no longer shared or readily accessible. The rise in secularism and move away from organized religion is contributing to these societies' search for purpose.[5] With respect to this search for purpose, values are important because more than ever we need disruptors. And to be disruptors, we need values as our guiding light.

The rise of the multi-trillion-dollar health and wellness industry in the midst of a mental ill-health crisis in the western world is no coincidence. The adaptation and indeed appropriation of indigenous wisdom traditions or philosophies is also indicative of this search for meaning – for purpose. More importantly, the emergence of purpose-driven businesses and the need for transparency around their social impact is a direct response to decades of what has been arguably quite the opposite. The production of goods and services for no other purpose than to generate wealth or the accumulation of resources is finally under question. This emptiness or bereftness we are reckoning with has come about as a direct result of our actions. We can also see the impact of this behaviour, philosophy, and activity on our environment, given the climate emergency.

An Introduction to Resistance

In 2016, I spent six months working for an organization that created retreats for high-growth social entrepreneurs. Each of the social entrepreneurs had been selected by their contemporaries to take part in our retreats through a referral system. We took them out of the office to destinations ranging from the Scottish Borders to the Grecian coast to give them an opportunity to connect with like-minded, purpose-driven business owners whose collective goal was to have a positive impact on society. They were working to support a number of causes – from eradicating homelessness to creating crucial medical technologies.

The idea of the retreats was to create a space for these entrepreneurs to bring their full selves to work. To that end, we used a wide range of techniques and practices to create bonds of trust, mutuality, and confidence, which allowed the social entrepreneurs to share their challenges, hopes, dreams, and aspirations with each other. The retreats in part channelled the Theory U principles devised by the academic Otto Scharmer, which are facilitation practices based in research and nonviolent communication techniques, and while deeply spiritual are unrelated to any particular wisdom tradition, meaning that anybody from any background would be instantly at home in a retreat workshop.

One of our team members always hosted a session on resistance. In this, participants were asked to develop a relationship to resistance by understanding its purpose or its usefulness as an aid or clue for us to better navigate our world. Interestingly, a key concept that emerges during the values compass exercise is resistance, too. This resistance may come in the form of past memories, reactions, or ideas that emerge after the self-reflection free-writing exercise, on page 93 above.

Resistance can also creep in when you have identified your values, done your self-reflection, and then realized that you are not "living any of your values", or you cannot see any "alignment" with your values in any aspect of your life. This can be a jarring realization, but it can also mark the beginning of a deeply beautiful and transformational process when properly investigated.

A PRACTICE TO REFLECT ON RESISTANCE

I often say that identifying where we are not living in alignment with our values is the first step to making some changes, as this creates a space that helps us to adjust our perspective. However, for those of us who have never thought about this before, it may be quite challenging to reflect on it. It is up to you to be willing to wade into that space and if you prefer not to, there are other ideas to play with. Maybe you can return to this practice another time, if you are willing to.

1. Now that you have your list of values, grey areas, and associations, take 2 to 3 minutes to reflect on any resistance that arises from what you have written down. This resistance may come in the form of past memories, reactions, or (unwanted) ideas.

2. Next, I would like you to think about where you feel you are out of alignment with your values and to sit with how that feels. What is this discomfort telling you? It takes a level of open-mindedness, curiosity, and playfulness to sit with the discomfort long enough to work through it. (Oftentimes we say the only way out is through our emotions, but if you do not want to sit with the feeling of discomfort or explore your resistance, that is ok too.)

3. What would living in more alignment with your values look like practically, in one aspect of your life?

4. What is one thing you can choose to do to facilitate living more in alignment with your values from this moment forward?

5. Are you living in alignment with your values in any aspect of your life? There are certain aspects of your life that you may not be able to choose or control, but there are many you can, like who your friends are and what you do with your free time.

Because of how we are socialized, we tend to start by thinking about how our values align in relation to what we do. Our productivity-trained and capitalist mindset can kick in, where we attribute our value and worth to what we produce rather than who we are as a person. Some of us may feel these things are inextricably linked, but let me explain. Who we are as a person is also who we are as a friend or lover. It can be who we are when we are doing something we love for fun, not for anyone else's benefit. So, I would like to ask you to reframe where a values alignment might apply by thinking about yourself outside of a work or public roles context. Think of who you are when no one is really looking. Does that person even exist? Remember the Judgement card: could this realization mark a moment of both initiation and resurrection in relation to who you are, your values, and how you can channel these to make good trouble?

6

MAKING THE CHOICE TO CHANNEL DISRUPTION

People will often suffer quietly for years in unhappy situations, because they refuse the discomfort or uncertainty of change. We see this time and time again when people finally end a relationship or leave a job they hate. We even hear this when people talk about making positive changes, like trying something new, such as a different form of exercise or putting themselves out there to meet someone. It takes gumption to forge a new path. So, what enables someone to make the decision to change their lives? It means having the vision to help realize a future world different to the one they are living in.

It takes a true visionary and initiator to make change happen. It also takes someone who is very clear on their values and who can discern when something is not in alignment with these. When you are aware of your own values, it will be much easier to tell when you are out of alignment with them. Your energy will be off when you are out of alignment, which can manifest as a physical discomfort.

I know that in the many situations that I have ended up disrupting – whether a relationship, a system, an organization, a practice, or a way of doing things – I have felt the itch and even pain that grows when I do nothing. The lack of action is like the sound of nails dragging down a chalkboard and my choice to disrupt calms the noise.

I have often been asked by people who do not feel this itch, why I would ever whistle-blow, disrupt, or change things, knowing that there will be an inevitable (in their view) negative impact on me. The answer is always the same. There is no way I could tolerate harm. Leaving things as they are, especially when there is a blatant injustice taking place, leaves me feeling so unwell that it grates against my very soul. For many different reasons, I believe people who ask me this may have a different values system to mine. They are less inclined to disrupt the status quo because of the risk and impact this may have. They want to preserve and protect themselves. They may benefit from the status quo, or lack motivation to change a system they do not believe needs to change. That is their choice and they are entitled to it, in the same way you are entitled to yours. The choice to disrupt, once you have made it, is what we will explore here together.

Understanding Change through the Tarot

Change comes up constantly in Tarot readings – how to navigate it and what it might be, and sometimes as a warning about what might be coming in the future. I use readings myself as marker points for how much I have changed over a period of time. For example, before I returned to Edinburgh in the summer of 2022, I had spent two years in Glasgow. I needed some space from a city where I felt I had developed a reputation as a disruptor, and I wanted the room to be anything else – to simply be. Years of reflecting on my relationship to my work as a disruptor prompted me to think about how I might channel the role of disruptor into something I not only accepted, but understood as part of who I am. No matter where I went, this way of being would be there because it was part of me, something which was confirmed for me in a reading with a trusted Tarot reader.

In the Tarot, the Wheel of Fortune has traditionally signalled change, and I have always felt this, too. Perhaps I can blame it on years of watching the American TV show *Wheel of Fortune*, where contestants spin a wheel for different cash prizes. Where the wheel lands is partially due to chance (the result of velocity, speed, and a number of other factors), because once the wheel is out of your hands, so is the outcome. The card's image of the wheel suspended in air, surrounded by mythical figures and symbols, is curiously similar to the gameshow prop. I cannot help but think of this reference point whenever I come across the Wheel of Fortune card.

As Jessica Dore suggests, within the inevitability of change, we can find grace – the grace to allow ourselves to accept that change will happen, and it is out of our hands. We cannot predict when we may choose to disrupt because there are so many factors at play, but when change does inevitably happen, how can we give ourselves a little grace to be open to the inevitable? How might we prepare for the inevitability of disruption and identify what might happen – because one way or the other, change will occur anyway.

The Lead Up to Disruption

Experiencing toxicity in any environment is a major energy drainer. Where harm has been caused there will be toxicity, especially if the harm has not been addressed, has been covered up, or has gone unnoticed. Acts of harm and abuses of power leave an energy footprint. The energy required to maintain power in these dynamics, to conceal information or, indeed, ignore it, is massive. For those of us who are sensitive to them, such dynamics can start to impact our experience of a space, whether it consists of a work environment, personal relationship, or family situation. We can feel tired, lethargic, or get sick easily when we are in these environments. Our bodies can start to feel heavy yet we can find ourselves on high alert.

It is easy for us to try to dismiss what we see, ignore it, grin and bear it, or simply wish it to go away. This build-up of tension in our body can manifest in a number of ways. Sometimes it looks like:

- tension headaches or migraines
- burnout, with symptoms ranging from irritability, racing thoughts, to malaise and confusion

- insomnia – not just having trouble falling asleep, but problems staying asleep, interrupted sleep, nightmares, restless leg syndrome, and other things like night terrors, which can be caused by stress
- unexplained body aches and pains
- anxiety, specifically a feeling of paranoia and general distrust of the world – a sense of an "us and them" mentality or a defensiveness that comes from feeling like people are out to get you, talking about you negatively, or trying to create a false narrative about you given the context of the situation/ risks you are taking to whistle-blow or call out harm

There can be so much tension that mounts in the days, weeks, and months as we come to trust our instincts. It is important that when we start to feel this way we channel these feelings and natural body responses into the point of release: revealing the situation for what it is. Once we do this, we can begin to take steps to address it, whether it concerns our family, our work lives, or our relationships. Often a point of release turns into multiple moments of release, depending on how long it takes the truth to come to light. Those responsible may never accept their role in causing harm, but taking the first step where possible can begin to relieve your own tension. (We will explore ways to cope with what comes next later on.)

Disruption at Home

I am not sure what type of home you grew up in, and I will likely never know. However, avoiding assumptions about whether you had siblings, your relationship to them, what your parents or caretakers were like when you were growing up, and how comfortable you were at home, allows us to be open to thinking about what your experience was truly like. Is this something you speak to your friends about often, journal about, talk to a therapist about, or is this a topic you have ever considered?

I hope for your sake you do not spend as much time thinking about your family, your upbringing, and your current relationship with your biological humans as much as I do. Understanding trauma is something I have been a student of for my entire adult existence. And you may ask yourself why this has been a fixation for such a large part of my life; well . . . it has been my partially effective attempt at understanding why I am the way I am. Why I love the way I love and why I value the things I value. It also helps me to process things that happened when I was growing up that had a massive impact on me as an adult and how I see the world. Some of it may be to do with unpicking my ever-fluctuating mental state and also asking myself what impact I might be having on the people around me.

Psychologists have debated the idea of nature versus nature for very many years, and different schools of thought have leaned in a number of directions when exploring mental health conditions, neurodivergence, or simply to better understand the human condition. I lean more toward the nurture side, though I know nature is important. I think I do this because the people who raised me often dismissed the importance of nurture, as they associated anything I might say about it with their own sense of guilt, failure, and self-judgement – things I do not necessarily agree with or believe. As I mentioned before, it can be incredibly challenging to be self-reflective and self-critical, because we might not like what we see or what we discover. It is often advisable to do this sort of work with the support of a professional or someone you trust – whether that is a therapist, a doctor, a teacher, a coach, a partner (within reason), a mentor, an elder, a family member you trust (again within reason), or a reliable group of friends.

The millennial generation that I, and perhaps you, belong to have been known for doing quite a bit of so-called navel-gazing around issues like this. I, for one, believe our generation is focused on better understanding ourselves than some generations before us, because we see the mess people can make when they make decisions for others without having a deep understanding of themselves, their own blind spots, neuroses, and drama, and what is actually driving their decisions. Just look at the state of things and you can understand why we are searching anywhere and everywhere for answers!

When it comes to the family front, it is important to ask yourself some questions to begin exploring your family values. You can start with questions such as whether your family valued school and academic subjects – or was more emphasis put on the practical side of things? When you were growing up, were you constantly worried about having enough money for food and choosing between the heating and electricity, or is food, heating, and electricity something that never crossed your mind? Did you grow up in a big community or family that was around you constantly, or did you grow up in a smaller family unit? Was there someone or multiple people to care for at home, like a sibling with support needs or an ageing grandparent? Did other family members or friends live with you, and did you live in an intergenerational household where people of all ages lived together?

Did one parent look after you, which may have meant you had to take on a parent-like role too at a young age? Did you have to contribute to looking after the household? Did you live in a neighbourhood that felt safe, which meant you could stay out late at night or leave your door unlocked? Or were you constantly negotiating the streets outside of your house and having to manoeuvre through them as safely as you could at night? Did you not go out afterhours at all? Did you have access to fresh air and nature, or did you live in a more urban environment with less access to green space? Are these things you think about now and have they impacted your choices about where you currently live? Have you had much of a choice in where you stay? Can you trace the ways your upbringing and what you learned to adapt to while you were growing up may have impacted any decisions you have made or are making now in your life?

Unpacking Our Home Life to Better Understand Our Choices

We learn so much before we are verbal that trying to pin down which factors contributed to our tastes, preferences, and needs is almost impossible. What we can begin to think about, though, is how we interacted with our family when we were growing up.

I, for one, grew up with two parents in a cis, straight, and very international environment. Unlike households with traditional patriarchal gender dynamics, my mother travelled for work and sometimes had to work in the evenings, while my father worked from home. This schedule meant that my father was mostly the one who took me to school in the morning and picked me up from school in the afternoon. He was a great cook, he knew my friends' names by heart, and he was responsible for taking me to playdates. What was also unique about our relationship was that he listened to me and had conversations with me that signalled to me he truly valued my opinion. I was a precocious child, so we would listen to the news, read stories together, talk about travel and geography, and always, we would talk about food.

Even with how my family functioned while I was growing up, there were a lot of things over time that persuaded me to make different decisions to those my family members made. From choices about work to where I live, stories of trauma and harm in my family gave me cause for pause. As you may well know, taking the decision to disrupt ways of doing things and questioning patterns in your own family can be incredibly tough. Disrupting the way things are and the ways things have always been in a family system can have serious consequences. Quite often, if there is guilt within that family, or a sense that accepting claims of harm would require certain family members to do some self-reflection and think about whether they contributed to, caused, or allowed that harm to take place, this will likely result in denial. If only the one person is speaking out within an entire family system, which could include extended family, family friends, and grandparents, or members of the family that have long since passed, it is often easier to apportion blame to that person. It can feel easier to subject this person to a smear campaign, as everyone else in the dynamic seeks to maintain the status quo.

It can be more comfortable for them to believe that they have done nothing wrong, rather than address the harm. Depending on their worldview and self-image, they may not see your disruption as a path forward to help build a healthier future. If they are defensive, they will see it as an attack. If they are insecure, they may see it as a comment on their parenting or that their relationship with you has failed somehow. If they do not interact with the world in terms of its complexity and grey areas, they may interpret this bid to change things as your calling the entire family system bad or wrong. Or, indeed, you could experience all of the above.

So, what do you do in these situations? In these situations, you always, always return to your own values. The injury you cause yourself when you know something fundamentally contradicts your values is a soul-deep harm that is hard to redress. However, I am not promoting going cold turkey and cutting all contact with your family. Nor am I suggesting that having a conversation with family members who have been abusive is always safe. I am asking you to practise discernment and consider what might be possible for you in this situation. Do you rely on your family for support, either emotionally or financially? Are you close to members of your family? Are there certain members of your family who might have had a shared experience? Do you feel your family has the emotional maturity, language, and capacity to do this healing work? Depending on your answers to some of these questions, you might take several courses of action.

With respect to a family member who has already cut ties with the family, this person is often regarded as the "black sheep" of the family. If we stop to think about what this might mean, we can recognize that they may be a black sheep because their values or decisions do not gel with the wider family unit – but do they align with your values? Consider if there is hidden knowledge, unspoken truth, or odd dynamics in your family that you have never questioned before. It goes almost without saying that mental health histories may be a contributing factor here.

Disruption at Work

For many of us, there is no place we spend more time in our adult lives than at work. When it comes to the hours we spend in a day, the relationships we have at work, how we view ourselves in relation to our work, and the environment we are in at work, it is clear that our working lives have a massive impact on our mental health. I suspect that this is why we have been having national conversations about our relationship to work in recent years. More employers are bringing the four-day work week into place. Since the pandemic there have been several articles about "quiet quitting"[1] and the "Great Shift",[2] because some of us finally had a moment to consider if we wanted to be spending so much of our time at work or in the office. Over the last 20 years, as the spheres of social entrepreneurship have grown, the notion of finding our purpose and doing meaningful work has become central to our journeys of self-discovery.

While I was at university, I was part of a collective of people supporting other students in finding their purpose. We were part of a movement of young people at the University of Edinburgh who were asking questions about what university was for and who supported the growing movement of social entrepreneurship in Scotland. All of this was taking place in the wake of the disastrous 2010 election cycle, which saw the promise of the Liberal Democrats – that tuition fees would not rise – being completely ignored, which decimated the party in many of its strongholds, come the local elections. In the opinion of many of us, the fee regime change signalled a turning point in the privatization of higher education in the UK. Students from outside Scotland would have to pay tuition fees to attend university for the first time – and to say people weren't happy about it is an understatement. In response, there were student protests across the country, organized by the national student movement, the NUS, as people chose to take a stand and make good trouble.

Alongside this movement were further conversations among millennials about doing our own thing. We had come of age after one of the largest recessions in modern history, the 2008 financial crisis, and our prospects were looking grim, on top of the fact that it was becoming more expensive to get a degree. (In my opinion, this hustle culture is just another iteration of late-stage capitalism finding a way to turn something we love and enjoy into a productivity-measured commodity, but that is a conversation for another book.) Jobs were scarce and people began to make a living any way they could. However, we were determined to stand up for our values and, where possible, to find our own way through the trouble.

It is often at work that we will find ourselves in the most compromising position in terms of our values. While we cannot choose our family, we can choose how we interact with them. And we most certainly can choose our friends and who we are romantically involved with. However, when it comes to work, it may be hard for us to predict the values of a potential workplace and the environment we might find ourselves in until we start working there. The interview process and the process of searching for work, even if we are self-employed or run our own companies, is deceiving. We do not know who we are really working with until some time has passed, and we face some challenges together.

I think there is a special place in the universe for micro-managers and toxic managers, but then I've had a lot of experience with these people. Once, a manager told me they were disappointed when I left their organization because they had invested too much in me in the last year for me to just go. This same manager told me they thought my next role would be a "stretch" even though I'd had a similar role before. At another organization, my manager demanded to proofread my emails to our clients three times before I sent them out. This was the same organization where I was forced to share a bed with my colleague because we were "saving money" (although thankfully this colleague was a distant friend of mine from university, so it felt more like a sleepover than anything else). I had another boss who hired their friends for freelance work, and when they did not complete the work anywhere near the deadline or to brief, I was blamed. The common thread that draws together these and other such examples is that when people are desperate, they love to blame others. In each of these instances, the managers were feeling financial stress, fear of losing a staff member, or fear of missing a deadline that would impact an entire project. The fact is that a bad manager rarely takes responsibility for their own part in the situation.

By being honest and taking responsibility for ourselves and our own mistakes, we can be incredibly disruptive to a culture that values skating over problems, not being honest about finances, or a culture that only sees shame, and not an opportunity for learning, in "failure". I put failure in quotation marks here because rarely do I see failure as an endpoint, but mostly as providing useful information about something that did not quite work in order to change it later.

Disruption in Friendship

The American entrepreneur Jim Rohn once said we are the average of the five people we spend the most time with. Not that I agree entirely with this saying, but the notion that we are influenced by the people around us and the choices we make about our experiences of them makes some sense. Our ideas, worldview, mood, ways of talking, dressing, eating, and even how we walk are influenced by the people we surround ourselves with. We all know quotes and platitudes about friendship being for a season or a reason. However, our friendships may often last longer than our romantic or even our family relationships. Our friends know us and see us in times that our other loves or partners will not. There is a mutual love, appreciation, reverence for, and joy that comes from a fulfilling friendship.

At different stages of our lives, we may be more intentional about who our friends are, because we have more choice in the company we keep. When we are at home with family or carers (or people who did the opposite of raising us); when we are at school in a classroom of people we did not choose; or when we are in the workplace in which we cannot screen our colleagues before we get the job – in all of these common situations we have much less choice. However, there are critical points in our lives when we can make choices about who we spend our time with. We make choices about our partners and significant others. We make choices about our best friends. If we go to college or university, we can usually make choices about which institution we attend or which classes we take. When it comes to our hobbies, exercise, and leisure time, we can make decisions about where we go to drink, eat, and play. But how often do we pay attention to the energy of these activities or, indeed, to the people and places around them? Have you ever stopped to think about how the people closest to you make you feel?

When it comes to my own closest people and best friends, I have always adopted the mindset of them being my chosen family. Not only because my nearest and dearest friends feel like family I can rely on in times when my birth family has not been emotionally available to me for various reasons, but because I can select who those people are in my life. They are *chosen*.

It has taken me a lifetime to discern who is safe, trustworthy, loving, honest, direct, loyal, and wise enough to be called part of my intimate circle. There have been many trials and errors. There have been explosive ends to friendships that were toxic, codependent or abusive, when I had to learn how to have a voice, to stand up for myself, stop people-pleasing, and stop being friends with someone based on the expectations of our parents, social group, social status, proximity to each other, or shared interests. But it takes so much more than that. It also takes a capacity to repair a friendship when there is rupture, which the Gottman Institute – a leading body on relationships – also speaks about in the context of long-term romantic relationships.[3]

To the dismay of some members of my biological family, who liked to remind me that "blood is thicker than water" when they felt belittled or affronted at my description of friends as chosen family, I came across the origins of the full quote a few years ago, in the middle of the first 2020 lockdown, when I lost my father: "The blood of the covenant is thicker than the water of the womb."[4] To believe that there is only water and not life-giving amniotic fluid in the womb is nothing short of blasphemy, but the notion that biology is thicker than a covenant of friends or an agreement (which here I believe references a brotherhood of knights sworn to protect their king or whatever they have pledged their allegiance to) increases the significance of this statement. Chosen family means we choose them again and again. That they indeed choose us, and that consensual bond may break – is allowed to break – but we find our union even stronger because we do not take it for granted, nor do we treat our chosen family with any disrespect or presumption, because this is a love we intend to work on to maintain.

What becomes tricky is when rupture occurs among our chosen family. Disruption in a friendship can happen without us wanting it to. It could result from the revelation of abuse or the abuse of power, or from choosing sides within a group of friends. Whatever the cause, disruptions to these covenants can be earth-shattering, but I believe there are ways to navigate these ground-shifting situations with grace, integrity, and pureness of intention by exemplifying "right leadership", by staying true to your values, and staying true to the friendship.

Disruption in Romance

How often have you swallowed your feelings, your intuition, or not addressed issues that come up in your relationship dynamics because you did not want to rock the boat? If the answer is many times, this might have to do with your insecurities, attachment styles, relationship histories, and trauma. All of this requires us to disrupt our instinct to let things slide and to decide instead to take an active role in building a mutually supportive, consensual, and kind dynamic that we actually want. We must stop subscribing to odd messaging from films, friends, family, and society that do not align with our values.

How we feel in our relationships reflects how honest we are in them. If you are not in a relationship, you can apply this to dating and the stories you may be telling yourself when you are looking for a relationship, whether serious or casual. Are you being honest about your needs and desires, or are you riding a wave of peer pressure about what you think you should want in your romantic life just because of the age you are or the stage you are at in your life?

I can relate this to my own romantic journey. I have known for a very long time that I am at heart a monogamous person who simply wanted to find a life partner and get on with the other things I'm interested in. The constant thought of "is this my life partner or my person?" plagued me, no matter who I met and felt a tiny spark for. I was always open to whatever happened when I met someone, but I spent so much of my teens and early 20s convincing myself that I needed to be less serious about my search, and to experiment, have lots of experiences, and put aside the idea of finding a life partner – which is actually what I really always wanted.

It goes without saying that dating is very different depending on your sexuality, upbringing, values, and needs. Where we live geographically can have an impact on our romantic lives, too, even though phones and apps have enabled us to meet people from different cultures more easily.

I believe there are many different types of love and that we may not have one person we love in our lives for the duration of it. I also do not consider a relationship ending as a failure. However, I must say that traditional, heteronormative gender roles make me more than a little queasy; unless a couple has decided that it works for them, this model can often funnel people into incredibly limiting, pressurized, and sometimes demoralizing categories with respect to how they feel they ought to act in a relationship dynamic, rather than how they want to act and what is right for them in a partnership.

Now that all of those views are out there, there is something I want to ask you . . . How often have you stayed with someone because the thought of disrupting what you already have to risk finding something else is too overwhelming? And how often have you spent time with someone who raises a number of red(ish) flags, but because of social norms you've stuck with this person anyway? In this case, I mean the kind of toxic social norms that do not help us navigate how to have healthy and pleasurable relationships – because quite often these social norms mean that we are not given the tools we need in order to understand what healthy looks like for us. I am keeping this broad because the nature of their relationships will vary for different people. However, the fundamental element that does not change is a consensual and kind relationship (or situation-ship) dynamic. That is a must.

Disrupting our romantic relationships entails having the courage to be honest with ourselves and use our discernment when something does not quite align in them. Bringing this to the surface allows us to address it, work on it, work through it, gain clarity and understanding of our needs, do the exploration needed to understand if things could properly align, and to go from there. This will often enable us to change things for the better in our romantic set-ups or to find the courage to look elsewhere.

Mantras for the Energetics of Disruption

Once we have identified areas in our lives that feel out of alignment, we can begin the process of creating change in them. Centuries of activists have provided us with examples of how to make good trouble, including those set by the likes of the civil rights activist and United States congressman John Lewis, who coined the term. We also have many examples of disruptors thanks to wisdom traditions that have passed down stories of goddesses, gods, and courageous figures who were never afraid to do the important work of standing up for what is right. Various music movements have also embodied this energy, from the DIY punk scene that kicked off in a massive way in the 1980s in my hometown of Washington, DC, to modern DIY music movements. We can all draw upon the examples of wisdom, ferocity, and pure inspired action to fuck up the status quo when this is called for.

Often, political parties or groups of people coming together for a common cause will write a manifesto that acts as a loose contract between the members of the group, which outlines why they are coming together or what they are working toward. Manifestos are also extremely practical because they can contain pledges that need to be fulfilled. They can be time-bound or broader. They can consist of small commitments or they can speak to a bigger picture of how we want to live our lives.

As a self-taught disruptor, I have made a promise in a manifesto of my own to disrupt systems of abuse and the abuse of power. I understand that by living in a world which promotes productivity and profit over health and wellness I may need to speak out against abuses of power more often than not. While I know I will not do this in a way that compromises my own health and well-being if I can help it, I also know that I will not stay silent in the face of injustice. I understand that my values are important to me and that I will work my hardest to always live in alignment with my values so that I do not compromise myself. I will always commit to building a more just world and will support anyone who needs my help in the fight for equity, fairness, and a sustainable, beautiful future. I commit to shaking shit up for the better and in order to hold those that need it accountable for their harm or wrongdoing.

A good manifesto starts with an introduction to who is writing it and a statement of intent. Here is mine, which you can use as inspiration for your own, if you wish:

1. I will always investigate when a feeling, situation, or energetic inkling comes into my awareness.
2. I will follow my gut instinct, especially after I have honed my intuition, to believe myself when a power dynamic seems off, a situation feels unjust, or when I feel like I do not have all of the information I need.
3. I will always have the courage to speak my mind and bring attention to an injustice or wrongdoing because I know if I do not, it will eventually make me unwell.
4. I will enlist the help of people I trust to further explore, investigate, or do the research I need to understand the situation to the best of my ability.
5. I will practise energy hygiene and make sure that I am aware of what my and others' energy is at any given point.
6. I will speak the truth with kindness, compassion, and with the intent to improve a situation for the better by sharing my knowledge, insights, and perspectives on a situation.
7. I will challenge authority and power structures where they are unjust, unfairly balanced and/or causing harm, and there is no accountability for the harm being caused. I will assess when it is necessary for me to intervene and when I need to self-protect.
8. I will seek to restore balance in any given situation. I support relationships that honour fairness, respect, and honesty in ways that allow me to practise discernment, live in alignment with my values, and not betray myself by accepting anything less.

9. I will always make a choice to protect my energy in these situations, by passing on anything I cannot shoulder myself to those that might help me, to systems I can report them to, or I can choose to take a situation as far as I can manage in any given moment.

10. I will always have the choice to walk away and change my mind, no matter how involved I am in a matter, dispute, situation, or disruptive dynamic.

Take a moment now to look at this manifesto. Note the tone, the "I will" statements that start each manifesto point, and the content of each action point. What shape might a manifesto of your own take?

A PRACTICE FOR WRITING YOUR OWN MANIFESTO

This is an opportunity for you to write your own manifesto. There are many philosophies on manifesto writing, but the main thing to focus on is putting your values at the centre, writing down statements that you feel are realistic, and focusing on the act of disruption; for example, when will you need to speak up and when will you stay quiet? What do you need to make an informed choice in each situation and how can you use this manifesto as a reminder of the principles that guide you?

1. Take 5 to 10 minutes to write a list of points that make up your own manifesto. It is important to write these down to get a sense of what is guiding you. If you like, you can use the first three points in my manifesto, above, as a starting point. However, if you want to make a manifesto that is entirely your own, please feel free to disregard these.

2. Each point you write down should conclude with a real action you plan to take to be more disruptive in your life.

3. You can revisit your values through the values compass exercise on page 86 in chapter 5 and, if you like, write your manifesto framed around your values, dedicating one manifesto point to each value.

4. It is important to keep in mind what you feel is a realistic commitment for you to make. Manifestos are about our philosophies and values, but they are also practical statements that we can revisit in times of need. Remember to put your values at the centre and think of these as your own guiding principles to disruption. You can adapt them to different areas of your life, including your work and home.

When working with the energies of change symbolized by the Wheel of Fortune in the Tarot, remember that you are disrupting the now to right the wrongs of the past, and reflecting on the present in order to build a better future. Your disruption is an act of love, sacrifice, and service. It is an act of care in a world that does not always demonstrate care. In this respect, making good trouble is not an act of destruction, so much as one of creation.

7

THE IMPACT OF CHANNELLING DISRUPTION

The moment you decide to disrupt, something happens. It is as if the choice itself causes a sea change and a down drift – a wind that ripples across the cosmos. Your part of the universe, your mini universe, has been altered forever. There is a turning point that cannot be mistaken, a point of no return, which signals the unveiling of a truth, a reality, and a hidden state of being.

This turning point will cause a number of chain reactions. A bit like the grief cycle (which we will be exploring on page 124), the revelation of truth affects people differently depending on how honest they are being with themselves, their feelings about control, and their vested interests in the status quo being maintained. If disruption impacts the power dynamic, or people's access or relationship to power, they may perceive you as a threat. It may feel to them that you have a power you did not have before.

This moment of disruption is like an energetic lightning strike. Once the energy has been released, the environment it has been unleashed into will never be the same. It is an energizer and a call to action. Lightning can obviously be risky, but where it strikes it can also be the source of the creation of a beautiful new material like glass.

The Tower and Disruption

In the Tarot, the moment of the lightning strike is symbolized in representations of the Tower card. The card depicts an image of two people being catapulted from a tall tower struck by lightning bolts and surrounded by flames. The Tower is a high impact card that often send shudders down people's spines when they receive it in a reading. As infamous as the card of Death (a state that does not exist literally in the Rider–Waite–Smith Tarot deck), the Tower card is kryptonite for some and an absolute boon for those addicted to change or tantalized by the idea of it.

I received the Tower card in my very first Tarot reading. I was 11 years old and my cards were being read by a trusted librarian, who was providing me with guidance on the next stage of my education. I was leaving the safe haven of my elementary school and embarking on the confusing path to a new middle school. What I did not realize was that my choices that year would have a massive impact on how I would be received in this new learning institution.

At my elementary school I had formed a band with my two best friends. The other girls in our year quickly became jealous, either because they were not getting the time and space to practise music in the music room we used for band practice or they didn't play cool instruments awfully, like we did. Either way, they were not performing in front of an audience of eager elementary school kids and their parents.

One of the girls in my year ended up at the same middle school as me the next year. That year the tables turned and she started to make my life a living nightmare. I was no longer one of the most popular kids in our peer group. It was subtle, but now she got to make the rules. Thankfully, I did not care much for hierarchies, rules, or social orders.

When I arrived at my new middle school with my frenemy, who we will call Mary, people could not quite work me out. In large part this was because I signed up for the boys' tackle football team the first opportunity I got, as I loved the game. If it were not for an incredibly supportive and queer head of the athletic department, Ms Hall, I would have stood no chance of playing. She asked me if I was really serious and when I revealed to her I how much loved football, so much so that I played every day at recess, she told me I could go for it. I should say as an aside that this didn't mean I was any good at it; although I could run fairly quickly, my understanding of the rules was a bit hazy. Still, she did everything in her power to protect my right to play.

Not only was I the second girl in the school's history to play middle school boys' tackle football, but I was also placed in gender-segregated math and science classes, acting as a guinea pig in this kind of class set-up. Imagine me in a classroom full of 12-year-old boys who couldn't believe there was a girl in their midst! I loved science but struggled with math and my confidence in the subject was on the floor by the end of the academic year. I also chose, unintentionally, to stick out from the crowd. I just wanted to play football, but given my band membership, I was also a card-carrying emo goth kid who sported fishnets, combat boots, *Emily the Strange* shirts, fingerless gloves with netting, spiky necklaces and bracelets, as well as thick black eyeliner. Add to this the unsettling year I'd had of living through my parents' separation and you can understand why my experience of starting at this school was miserable.

Without knowing it, the way I dressed and the sport I chose to play challenged every unspoken rule of how a 12-year-old girl was supposed to behave. It was something I had never considered before, because thankfully I had always been encouraged to pursue whatever I was interested in. But what had been cool and accepted at my last school was not only not accepted, it was judged as odd, weird, and divergent. I was disrupting the way things were done simply by being myself.

We have to remember that mainstream trends and counter-cultures serve a purpose by existing in tension with one another. Trends can speak to both counterculture and popular cultures. Yet there is a fine line between pushing the boundaries of mainstream culture and running past them too swiftly to be acceptable. My school was not ready for me and neither was the culture in the rest of the country.

Nevertheless, one of the girls who was close to Mary did consider playing football with me – until her parents told her it was too dangerous. This girl had similar taste in music to me and didn't dress in traditional ways either. She bucked the norm of gendered clothing and also what sort of sport or hobby she was supposed to be interested in, but her parents held her back when they thought, I assume, she was pushing it too far.

I experienced my first bout of cyberbullying soon after. The evidence suggested that Mary and her friends may have been involved in this. But why would this friend of hers participate too, when she wanted to do the same thing I was doing? The inverse of the saying goes that if you can't join them, beat them. Often when others see aspects of themselves in you that they wish they could have the courage to embody, but they feel unable to, their reaction is to make you feel bad about it. They are projecting their repressed needs and desires onto an unsuspecting, but in my case, conspicuous target. Or perhaps I was just being punished for sticking out.

It was not until the end of that tumultuous year that I thought back to the fateful Tarot reading on my last day of elementary school. Its predictions had been exactly right. My library teacher had predicted that my first year at this new school was set to be a Tower year and it was, in more ways than one. I would be chucked out into the world in a way that was incredibly disruptive, but if I was to follow my own desires there could be no avoiding it. I was seen as a disruptive presence at school because I was unsettling social codes that I was not even aware existed. Thankfully many teachers supported me and my parents clearly believed, although not without protest, I should do the things I loved as long as I was staying safe.

By the end of the year, I had made a dear friend in the year above me who loved Tarot and music like the Strokes, and who would accompany me on walks home after school. Her friends and the kids that hung out in the photography lab, art studios, and computer labs were people I would come to admire. I also found refuge in weekly band practices with my best friends a short metro ride to a neighbouring city. These spaces for creativity and like-mindedness brought me so much joy.

A Tarot sceptic might read this and think: well, it was that Tarot reading which planted the seed for disruption through the power of suggestion. Through the power of suggestion, my actions contributed to a self-fulfilling prophecy. A year of bullying and outsider status at school is what happens in the 2000s when you're a girl in a rock band who plays on the boys' American football team. Someone else might read this and think, what about self-determination? Do we not have control over our lives and was the Tarot reading just a coincidence?

In this respect, it's important to highlight that when it comes to the Tarot, a spread of cards is a reflection of the most likely future in that moment, based on the decisions you have made in your life up until that point. It also takes into account your beliefs, choices, and circumstances, which could completely change by your next Tarot reading. A number of things may impact your future and your circumstances, which could affect your reading from one moment to the next. The Tarot gives you options and respects any changes in your psyche – it is nuanced in its approach.

The same nuance applies to the meanings of the cards themselves. The Tower card is also a depiction of the human journey on various levels through life; as A E Waite puts it: "The disruption and upheaval described by the card of the Tower, for example, may indeed manifest through material circumstances. But its deeper meaning lies in its portrayal of the collapse of old and outworn structures, and such structures can exist within us in the form of stale and rigid mental and emotional attitudes and habit-patterns."[1]

Ultimately, the Tower card allows us to understand that the nature of disruption can be the result of our choices or it can be imposed on us. Often, the message of the Tower is that if you do not make the changes you need to – that you desire on a deep level – the changes will be made for you. You'll be chucked out of the window of the tower of certainty you have built around you. Just when you think it is safe, circumstances can change – in the way that a move to a different school changed my relationship to my classmates completely and how, no matter what I did, I would have been received in the way I was, because I would have stuck to the things I loved to do.

Change will come whether we like it or not. However, the inevitability of change and the suddenness of it may bring some comfort. Our lives will be disrupted, so why not disrupt our lives in the ways and in the directions we desire? We may have no control over change, but we have control over how we respond to it.

The Cycle of Grief and Disruption

How we respond to change can entail grief; changes bring with them the loss of what has gone before and the grieving process can be part of this. Elisabeth Kübler-Ross described five stages of grief in her seminal 1969 book *On Death and Dying* after researching the impact of grief on people experiencing terminal illness. While these stages have been disputed and adapted over the years, the basic principles remain well supported: denial, anger, bargaining, depression, and acceptance. (Shock is a sixth stage I have added to describe the period before denial.)

But why am I talking about grief when it comes to making good trouble? I believe this cycle can help us understand how someone might feel in response to our disruption, especially if it is a disruption of their own abusive or harmful behaviour. Moreover, if you can identify these stages in the person you are disrupting, and understand them, you can take a radically empathetic approach to guiding that person through it. But only if you wish to support them and they have consented to your help. This is not always advisable in situations where someone has deliberately intended to cause you harm, although it can be very useful in other situations.

The Grief Cycle and Other People's Reactions to Disruption

If we can identify the stages of grief in another person's reaction to disruption (or even in our reaction to ourselves, which we will be exploring in more detail in a moment), we can support ourselves and each other through it. Understanding grief is a form of radical empathy, especially as it is a process that we sometimes avoid talking about. Think about these stages of grief as stages that may impact anyone involved in disruption:

Shock is to be expected in moments of disruption, because the act of revealing something that has been concealed will prompt shock in those who previously disbelieved something, or were unaware, or who chose to conceal the truth themselves because they have been engaging in coercive, manipulative, or abusive behaviour. They might simply be in shock because they are processing new information. They might not have had any malicious intent. Alternatively, part of their shock may be because someone has had the audacity to call their bluff, reveal their cards, and expose them and their behaviour for what it is. Or it could be because a situation is not what it seems and your experience of it differs greatly from theirs.

Denial is the next stage. Others may act slowly, or simply not respond to, or acknowledge your revelation. Denial is particularly prevalent if the person has acted wrongly, or if they benefitted from your silence. They may experience the other emotions that are part of the stages of grief, but they may choose to live in their denial while they cycle through these. Denial means that they never have to acknowledge their behaviour, take responsibility for it, or experience any accountability for it. Denial means that they can shift the blame and make you the problem for being the messenger. Denial is where the desire to scapegoat is born.

Anger is a difficult emotion, but it is valid and incredibly important. Anger reveals where our boundaries have been crossed. Anger also allows us to understand what we value and to know when what we value is at risk. Anger reveals where harm has been done or where there has been an injustice. Anger can also be used as a tool to harm others. Repressed anger can be dangerous. It can take the form of deep sadness or grief that goes unaddressed, unnoticed, and unacknowledged. It can then build over time in a way that ultimately results in an explosion of feeling that can lead to incredibly dangerous behaviour. But most importantly, anger is a powerful tool. When it is directed at a situation or people to hold them accountable for wrongdoing, it is one of the most important emotions we experience.

Bargaining is a process that can be incredibly challenging in this situation or dynamic. This is when the reporting process starts or the revelation has hit the press. In more intimate situations like a relationship, friendship, or family dynamic, this is when a process of negotiating begins. Depending on how self-aware, willing to change, and able to acknowledge harm the other person or people are in the dynamic, they may begin to gaslight you or offer a trade-off so that they do not have to do the work of acknowledging their wrongdoing.

From the perspective of an organization, company, or team dynamic, this is where those responsible might begin to explore what happened. An investigation of sorts may be on the cards, but when it comes with the threat that mistakes may be found out, those responsible may begin to bargain to prevent this process from beginning. This is where they may start to doubt the whistle-blower or disruptor. They might try to find fault with their argument, with the facts of the situation, even with their personal character. We see this in criminal cases all the time. This is the stage of the legal process when a defence lawyer tells someone to avoid pleading guilty at all costs, even if they committed the crime. The headache and heartache this creates for the victims or survivors of crime is immeasurable.

When it comes to your own disruption of the status quo, expect it to be challenged and look out for signs of bargaining. People may try to discredit you or strike a deal with you. This is when they are bargaining to maintain their power at all costs, because the risk to their power, their reputation, and/or the status quo is too great. They are still trying to maintain all of those things at your expense. In some ways, they may see you as a small problem to get rid of – something that is disposable and easy to remove. If they can stop a formal process from beginning – such as an investigation, a grievance process, or the involvement of any external parties or factors like a counsellor in a relationship or a person in a position of authority, like their boss – they will do so at all costs. This bargaining process is, in other words, an attempt for them to contain the situation and maintain control.

Depression can quickly emerge next. If the person being held accountable realizes that the jig is up, they may start to feel the walls closing in on them. They begin to realize that they will soon be found out and they begin to feel desperate. The ensuing depression can result in a number of behaviours, such as lashing out and fighting to the death. They do whatever it takes to minimize the damage, regardless of the truth or the impact on the people they've harmed. They are thinking in a very short-term manner and often their actions, words, and behaviours do not take into account the long-term impact of the issue being revealed. They might not accept that their behaviour has irrevocably eroded the trust they built with the people around them. They might not realize that their fighting has the opposite effect. It may act to reveal their guilt and make it obvious to everyone involved that they have been abusing their power. They might have some support from other people who are invested in maintaining the status quo, but ultimately they will give themselves away.

Depression can appear in the guise of someone who appears incredibly dejected, detached, disassociated, removed, and going through the motions. They might not want to reveal this to others, but there will be noticeable impact on their mood, actions, personality, and behaviour. Any other people involved might put this down to the stress of the situation and the unpleasantness of a process that has started to reveal the truth of the matter, but it is likely to be the second to last stage in the Kübler-Ross cycle.

Acceptance does not always look like acceptance. It sometimes looks like the end of an incredibly gruelling process, which might have an unsatisfactory outcome. This is something you must be prepared for. Those exposed might not be willing to accept the situation; their acceptance of the situation may only come in the form of winning, which could look like continuing to obstruct justice or conceal the truth of the matter. Even those who abuse power can be disgusted by their own actions. They might not initially see their actions as abuse, so being faced with the reality of their behaviour and the impact it has on others is not something they will easily or willingly accept. Rarely in this world, with its bias in favour of those in power, do we see true justice, accountability, or somebody's acceptance of their own wrongdoing. Therefore, prepare yourself for the opposite of acceptance taking place and brace yourself for your response to this.

It could be that, as a result of your disruption, the wider world gains a greater insight into the wrongdoing or harm that has taken place, even if no substantial change occurs within the situation or organization itself. There may no longer be an external acceptance of that behaviour, and people may be more wary of engaging with the person, situation, or dynamic involved in it. However, acceptance is a tricky thing, even in the cycle of grief. It can be hard for people to accept that their world has been categorically altered in a way that means it will never return to how it was before.

The Grief Cycle and Your Own Reactions to Disruption

Now let us reverse engineer the grief cycle from your perspective – the perspective of the disruptor. If we were to rewind time to start this process again from your perspective, it might look something like this . . .

Acceptance can be a fickle friend, depending on the outcome of the situation. You have brought something challenging to someone's attention and, depending on how much of a risk that posed to you, it may leave you in a tricky situation.

Depression is almost inevitable. The act of revealing harm or abuse unleashes that harm or abuse. Trauma therapists talk about this in detail; it is something that survivors of PTSD or Complex PTSD such as myself live with on a regular basis. Retelling a traumatic incident or experience(s) from your past activates the same part of the brain, the amygdala, which has stored the bodily feeling of that incident. That is why the flashbacks that PTSD survivors experience tend to come with bodily connections like sweating, deep breathing, or hyperventilation. That is also why being "triggered" – a much overused term at the moment – is not simply a feeling, but a physical reaction. Depression in this situation is normal and to be expected. Hopefully, you can avoid it with the right support, but if not, it might help to think of the depression that can occur as part of this process as a simple release and activation of the original harm. Even if it was a harm that you did not experience first-hand, but a harm someone else experienced, it will still have an energetic impact on you. If we did not experience a natural emotion like depression in response to harm or an abuse, this might indicate an even more worrying situation that could suggest avoidance, disassociation, and repression, which will come out in other ways later.

Bargaining can look like bargaining with yourself around whether or not you've made the right decision. Was it worth it? People you thought you trusted or who you thought would support you might begin to turn their backs on you. They might find it all too messy. Perhaps they "do not want to get involved", or they are "not sure", or find what you are telling them "hard to believe". It may feel like the earth is shifting under you. What you thought was firm ground might turn out to be quicksand or a sinking muddy bog. It's ok. This is the moment you look to your foundations – the people you love who are not involved in this situation, or literature, films, music, or a connection to nature that you can rely on. This is where your hobbies or tools for healthy forms of distraction come in handy.

You do not need to bargain with yourself and take yourself on a winding loop of unhelpful thoughts, which may include overthinking, catastrophizing, and imagining the worst. You have done the right thing. It was not easy and it took courage. Do not let the chaos of the moment shift your belief and your convictions. Take the time to find ways to energetically ground yourself. (There are tools for this which we will explore in more detail in chapter 10.)

Anger is necessary and important in this process. Anger might be a big motivation for why you decided to disrupt things. If an injustice has occurred and harm has been experienced, there is a need for anger. Anger, as a reminder, indicates where a boundary has been crossed and a harm has been done. Without anger, we do not have the adrenaline and motivation we need to react, respond, and protect ourselves. It is just as important that we do not live here. As with the denial stage, whistle-blowers and disruptors risk finding themselves stuck in a loop of anger for the rest of an eternity if they are not careful. You may experience a range of passing emotions, while at the same time being perpetually parked in anger mode. It is understandable that you may want to stay here. Anger is powerful. There are many things in our world to be angry about, but if we are not careful it can become our single motivating factor. Remember that anger is not the only reason why we call out injustice. We call out injustice as an act of love, care, and empathy.

Denial/Shock are listed beside each other here, because it is possible you will experience one, the other, or neither of these states as the result of being a disruptor. It is possible that shock might come right in response to other people's reactions to your revelation. It might be that denial emerges in some stage of the process, because a part of you wishes the disruption had not happened or you are in denial about how people react to you unearthing this truth. They may react in vicious, vindictive, and nasty ways, or even with ambivalence, which may feel even worse. The pure act of ambivalence is that of dismissal or skating over the severity of a situation – going back to ignoring it in order to maintain the status quo. You may find out people's true modus operandi. When they are presented with a sticky, complex, messy, and tricky situation, do they take action or do they remain paralysed in the face of the task at hand, finding it too overwhelming? Regardless of what you might face or experience, give yourself the time to feel the shock and recognize the denial for what it is – a potential pathway into even stronger emotions and simply part of the grieving process.

A Protective Measure for Disruptors

An incredibly useful tool throughout this process is a cord-cutting exercise, which I find very helpful in any situation where an energetic link or tie has been made. In Theta Healing®, we call these energetic ties hooks or cords. It might be that an energetic tie has been hooked into your energy field without you realizing. You may not have invited it, but the desire to connect or link with you came from elsewhere.

Cord cutting is practised in a number of magical and energetic traditions. It is something you could practise every day if you like. Quick versions of this include using salt, smoke, or other elements to cleanse your energy body and space. You can also use water, which is an element deeply linked to the emotions. For example, I try to practise a cleansing ritual every time I shower. I stand under the water and imagine the energetic debris falling off me. I imagine it sinking into the drain in the shower and my body being released from any energetic lint I've picked up throughout the day. This is a ritual many healers, psychics, mediums, and light workers use when they are doing energy work and it is a ritual they will often suggest to people they are working with to maintain their own basic energy hygiene. If you do not have access to a shower and badly need a cleanse, visualize a white light engulfing you that washes away any stuck energy. Repeat this as often as you need to. (We will practise this together in more detail below.)

Oils, talismans, and crystals are incredibly helpful to use during this time as well. During particularly turbulent times, I carry black obsidian or black tourmaline with me as an energetic barrier. As I mentioned at the start of this book, I always have a small crystal in my bag or pocket, but for a feeling of even greater protection you could wear one where it actually touches your skin. This could be in the form of a necklace, a ring, or a bracelet, or you could slip it into a piece of clothing that touches your skin if it will be secure and you won't have to worry about it slipping out.

A PRACTICE FOR RELEASING CHAOTIC ENERGY

The beauty of being an energetic disruptor is your sensitivity. You can pick up on the subtleties of energy, interactions, and dynamics that allow you to cut through deception, ego, and complex systems designed to confuse, confound, and befuddle. However, this clarity of thought and of intuition may also leave you vulnerable to the energies around you and the impact they may have on you. The following ritual can be practised regularly, as often as you like, in order to protect your energy, cleanse it, and cut ties or cords to any energy hangovers, people, and hooks that attach or cling on to your energy body.

1. Sit down in a quiet space and imagine there is a ring of white light around you that is protecting your energy body. You can visualize this ring of light as pulsating, as a solid wall of light, or as moving in a way that it has an amorphous quality to it. This protective shield of energy is yours and it can have any qualities you would like it to have.

2. If you cast circles, please take this moment to cast a circle.

3. Now you can set an intention for the ritual. Your intention is to release any energy that is not yours and any energetic ties you have to others, including other situations and dynamics that you no longer want to be linked to.

4. I want you to take a moment to do a body scan by pulling your awareness to each inch of your body, starting at the tip of your toes.

5. Using your energy and psychic awareness, feel into where there might be what we call a "hook" or "cord" attached to your energy field. It is not important to know where or who it has come from, but to sense it is there and to release it. When you feel these hooks or

cords you might experience them as a density around a certain part of your body, like a thickness or change in energy around that space. It may also feel like there is a certain colour or temperature around that body part. All of these sorts of subtle changes that you sense while you are doing this body scan will be an indicator of a hook or cord that shouldn't be there.

6. Once you sense a cord or hook, you can sever this by saying aloud or silently, "I release this hook or cord and return this energy to where it came." Finish this statement with, "And so it is and so it shall be."

7. Continue to scan your body and repeat the cord- or hook-cutting portion of this exercise until you reach the crown of your head. Then, to close the practice, thank yourself for being present and thank any powers that you believe in – you can thank the universe or your gods or simply leave it at thanking yourself. Close your circle if necessary and thank the light that protected you throughout the process.

Disruptions as Destabilizing Events

Whatever scale they occur on, disruptions are destabilizing events. Quite often we think of these as occurring on a massive scale, such as plagues and natural disasters, or the death of individuals whose passing impacts people enormously because of their notoriety and connections. Take, for example, the death of a tyrant. Their death, a destabilizing event, can usher in major changes, signifying a new era. It could signal the end of a period of abuse, subjugation, and oppression. These sorts of situations can result in economic collapse and mass illness, or a new way of living that is entirely better than what existed before. Now, if we were to apply the principles of these mass destabilizing events to a narrower network of interactions and a smaller radius of people or situations, they would obviously have a smaller range of impact. But are they any less significant? They might not usher in a new era of global leadership that impacts our entire planet, but the impact – energetically – of these smaller scale events is still significant. The same principles apply.

A destabilizing event of any size triggers an interruption and disruption of the status quo – whether intentional or not. The revelation of a secret or the act of holding someone accountable to wrongdoing are all examples of these interferences. Something shifts in reality's energetic field. The ways we were once living, operating, and interacting with the world around us shift. Our understanding of a person, interaction, event, and the system we are part of – whether it is a family system, a romantic relationship, a friendship, a school system, a wider community, or a workplace – is forever changed.

Chaos as Energy – Embracing the Universe's Randomness

In the Tarot, the Tower card symbolizes destruction. As the Tower represents things getting shaken up and the collapse that must occur before a period of growth, rebuilding, and remodelling, for those of us who like a little mischief, the Tower card can be a friend and guide. The Tower is the companion to the universe's chaotic energy. Destruction and demolition are required before anything new can be built.

Everyone has a different relationship to chaos. For some, chaos is an energy that is the source of all creation – a necessary starting point and the origins of all that is. In scientific studies and mathematics, chaos theory is the interdisciplinary study of systems and their random, unpredictable behaviour – a paradox of behaviours in systems of deterministic laws.[2] Another illustration of the beauty of paradox. Chaos magic in the 1970s stripped back the notions of religious affiliations and symbolism to create basic rules concerning the properties of magic. As studies of the transmission, dilution, and shift of energy, both of these traditions can inspire us to think of chaos as simply energy. What this energy inspires in us can vary, and is based on how we embrace it, and how much control we believe we have over a situation. In other words, what power we think we have in the presence of chaos is up to us.

We may think we spend our days making a plethora of choices that can dramatically change our future. The truth is that while we have the power and potential to create change, the majority of our choices tend to be about maintaining things as they are. When we maintain the status quo, rather than make choices that dramatically alter our lives and futures, things will get shaken up anyway.

It takes inspired action, discipline, a will, choice, and perseverance for us to genuinely choose chaos, discomfort, and uncertainty for a different future. That is why it can be so difficult to disrupt our lives, our beliefs, and the people we care about or are surrounded with at any given time. But while it can be painful and involve feelings of loss and grief, it is part of the work of making good trouble.

8

IMPLEMENTING DISRUPTION IN OUR LIVES

Disruption may be something that is easy to talk about, in the way we talk about innovation as something exciting, yet it can be hard to implement. Talk is a useful means for understanding ourselves, but it takes true commitment to turn words into action. We could spend a lifetime getting to grips with understanding how to live our lives closer to our values, using discernment and making difficult choices when we need to. But a difficult choice requires us to follow up that decision with challenging changes if we truly wish to improve a situation, dynamic, or relationship.

There can be a gap between what we say and how we behave that speaks volumes about our character. This is where the people emerge who walk the walk and who don't just talk the talk. This is where we learn who truly shares our values. More importantly, in a world where we have a multi-billion-pound health and wellness industry that produces more healing modalities, self-help books, and roadmaps to healing than ever before, we have to remember that even though we have a plethora of maps to guide us, they mean nothing unless we are willing to use them.

Each time I have made the decision to point out wrongdoing, or to report something that was not right, or to stand up for myself or someone else, there has never been a question of whether or not I would do it. It is part of who I am – and I do not believe in regret. I know this might sound like a lofty approach. I remember once telling a friend that I didn't believe in regret and he guffawed so loudly, I was sure the noise echoed across the entire neighbourhood. "What do you mean . . . you have no regrets?" he said. "How is that possible! Surely there is something you regret in your life?" I am sure that there are many things I wish either had not happened or had happened differently, but those situations do not translate to regrets – I have none. Everything that has happened in my life has led me to this point, for better or for worse. I have always made sure to take risks, so I am not left asking myself "what if" or wondering, for example, if the person I was meant to be with was on the other end of a number left on the back of a receipt or a napkin. I have always asked the question and made the call.

I have no qualms about taking a risk and failing, either. This doesn't mean that I do not feel rejection or seek to minimize rejection in my life, but if I am honest, rejection is not something I seek to avoid. This is despite the fact that I am a hard worker and have at times run myself into the ground to make sure I have put my all into something (though this is not an approach I'd recommend). The prospect of taking a risk and it not working out doesn't fill me with dread. It simply is and simply will be. I have come to approach disruption with the sort of equanimity portrayed by the figure of Temperance in the Rider–Waite–Smith Tarot. My advice to you is to practise temperance too when thinking about the choices you make around making good trouble.

The Practice of Temperance

In the Rider–Waite–Smith Tarot, Temperance is portrayed as an angel pouring liquid from one goblet into another at a gravity-defying angle. One of the angel's feet rests on dry land, while the other is dipped into water. It is a card in the Major Arcana that speaks of the virtues of balance, patience, and moderation. Rather than focusing on extremes of whether we have succeeded or failed, feel satisfied or have regret, it is important for us to remember that life is never about experiencing one extreme over another. All of these experiences are true to our experience of life.

In Jessica Dore's reading of Temperance, she discusses the card in relation to binaries and all-or-nothing thinking.[1] Seeing things in black or white, as one or the other, is a way of thinking often associated with anxiety and depression. This is why various forms of therapy encourage us to think about the grey areas of situations rather than in terms of extreme opposites. Even though our brains have evolved over time to need to label things in order to be able to discern if something is safe, our predisposition to pair things into categories of opposites can become amplified when we experience trauma. By learning to hold more than one truth in a situation and to allow ourselves to step back from our assumptions about how well we are handling a situation, or what true failure looks like, we can make the space to contain various different parts of our experience without condemning any of them. We will be able to seek more balance in our lives and patience for our life journey.

Italian physician and educator Maria Montessori once said, "Progress isn't linear"; in other words, our journey to self-actualization will always be winding. As I'm a recovering perfectionist and overachiever, this quote resonates with me deeply and it is unsurprising that its originator is the woman behind the philosophy that inspired the first school I ever attended. The Montessori philosophy allows students to find their own way and be led by their own curiosity. With certain core values embedded within the Montessori principles of education, pupils are left to their own devices in the early years of school. This gave me a lot of time to develop my understanding of the world, take risks, learn to fail, and also learn to approach everything with curiosity. I believe that because I was left to my own devices, I was encouraged to make my own connections and develop a unique understanding of the world. I could call this my personal style – and the building blocks for being disruptive. No question was ever discouraged; in fact, Montessori education taught me to question everything. It also taught me to live my values out loud.

Acting with Discernment and Consent

There have been many situations over the years where I have tried to avoid being disruptive. However, when I have tried to address them through the appropriate channels, I have found that the people who should have accepted responsibility in those situations often chose not to. It could be that they felt it was not in their interest to take action or not important enough to act on – perhaps they simply did not care.

I think this can happen for a number of reasons. The people who are less likely to be disruptive because it is not in their best interest, for example, are also less likely to be attuned to the subtitles of energies required to understand the need for the disruption in the first place. What motivates people to speak truth to power and challenge injustice? It often comes down to a person's lived experiences and the amount of oppression they face in society. Some choices for them are not choices at all, but actually necessities for survival.

One of my dear friends from university is an incredibly passionate, justice-driven, emotions-led, and sensitive soul who simply cannot stay silent on matters of injustice. She often speaks out on behalf of people who cannot, and as a privileged white woman, she chooses to use her privilege, unlike many others, to put herself on the front line of social justice. She is loud, mouthy, and direct. Three of my favourite qualities in the fight for justice. I would consider her my soul sister for these reasons alone, but something that bonds us even more is her sensitivity to the world and her enormous capacity for empathy. She is able to pick up on subtleties, facial expressions, tones, and unspoken thoughts. Though you may think these abilities contradict the confident and bolshie aspects of her personality, in my eyes they only affirm them. Her sensitivity makes her fearlessness and aplomb all the more impressive.

The act of simply sharing knowledge is not only disruptive, but – as we saw in chapter 7, when we looked at the stages of grief – it can be traumatizing and hurtful to a person who is not ready or willing to receive it. This can have a particular impact on our intimate relationships. When the feedback we are providing does not involve the other person's consent, we can accidentally push someone to a point of shutdown or serious discomfort. There is a tangible risk and potential for harm if we are not careful. Our observations, which may seem obvious to us, may not be obvious to the person with whom we are sharing them. What might appear to them to be a provocation may not seem like a provocation to us at all; however, the statement of our observations may have an impact which we simply do not appreciate until it is spoken. Our words have power and the practice of articulating something that has previously remained unsaid is even more powerful.

Not a Calm Matter, but a Matter of Consent

Now, I will not for one minute claim that disruptions are calm affairs that are going to be tolerated by everyone, let alone welcomed. We all make mistakes and we can all push things too far. This is something we are all capable of. We are all on a journey of understanding each other's boundaries and limits. Many of us are still developing our understanding of our own limits, let alone communicating them to other people. We need to learn in the meantime to sense other people's boundaries when they are struggling to communicate them with words. They might be communicating their boundaries in other, more subtle, ways.

This is where our intuitive and psychic tools need to be practised – with consent, because without it, we can cause harm. The responsible thing to do is ask and respect someone's reply, especially when it is "I do not know". In the same way we aim to practise emotional hygiene, by checking in with someone before we divulge something emotionally loaded to them, we must remember to ask the other person if we can check in with them before we speak a truth to them.

You can ask them if they have the capacity, energy, and if they are in the right headspace to receive what you have to say. You should do this when the truth you wish to share has anything to do with someone else and you intend to disrupt their reality or experience of a situation. I want to be very clear about this. Disrupting someone who is harming others by abusing their power is different to disrupting someone whom you feel is behaving out of their integrity because you know them well enough to notice. There is a gentle way to ask for consent in the latter situation, which enables you to share your observations or thought processes by asking that person if they would like feedback or your honest opinion, rather than providing it to them in a cavalier way.

As Jessica Lanyadoo, a brilliant queer Tarot reader, once said, "Acceptance is not consent. It is awareness."[2] This is a useful guiding principle for our conversation about consent. In more recent years, consent has come into conversations about healthy relationships and how to prevent gender-based violence. The work I do with Rape Crisis Scotland and that I have done over the years with the Young Women's Movement in Scotland is part of a sea change on how we talk about consent in school, at home, and in society more widely. The prevention-based education that exists now for young people is information I only wish I'd had growing up, as a young person navigating a culture of rape and toxic patriarchy.

There is understandably a lot of shame and stigma around causing harm. Until we acknowledge that we are all capable of causing harm to ourselves and others, both intentionally and unintentionally, we will be living in a constant state of denial, pain and shame. It is very important that we reach an understanding of our own capacity to harm, because in that process we come to understand that harm is something we can reduce. We live within the bounds of a world that systematically causes us and others harm, so – as participants in that system – we are not exempt from the capacity to cause harm ourselves. Understanding our capacity to cause harm and choosing to disrupt it is a powerful choice we can make to transmute harm into healing.

Balancing Your Values and Your Close Ties

Navigating your changing values and discovering your personal boundaries can be particularly jarring when it comes to the family you were born into or the people who raised you. As you get older and become more familiar with what is important to you, you may discover that this deviates from what you were raised to value or believe. Your changing values may entail a sudden departure from those of your origins, or a gradual, steady move in a different direction.

You may find that you no longer have much in common with your family. You may choose to visit them less frequently, or stop seeing some family members altogether. Perhaps you will experience those dreaded extended family occasions, such as when that problematic uncle makes comments that not are not only galling, but reveal a values system and a worldview that is completely contrary to your own. You may avoid discussing certain topics with family or indeed you may choose to work through these "differences in opinion". However, the likelihood is that not only are there differences, there are also fundamental discrepancies and a fundamental misalignment between your values and those of the people you were once close to.

On the other hand, it may be that you find through this sometimes tricky, often humbling process of discovery that you are much closer to certain family members now. You might come to find that family members who are distanced from the main family unit share similar values to you, or have made certain choices because the family ways of operating no longer align with them. This is the beauty of understanding ourselves and going through the natural process of separation from our caregivers. This process of discovery is not necessarily about severing all bonds, nor is it about closing yourself off. It is about disrupting the notion that you have to stay anywhere with anyone whose values not only do not align with your own, but who chooses not to respect your boundaries in the process.

No one decides to go no contact with family members or friends on a whim. The painful decision to cut ties with someone to whom we were once close often comes after years of negotiating painful situations. These painful situations are about boundaries being crossed or simply ignored after they have been lovingly set, described, and discussed.

The process of setting boundaries for the person on the receiving end of them can feel difficult, hard, and challenging – again, like a grieving process. It can disrupt their understanding of how you once interacted and it can seem like a personal attack on the ways things used to be. It can feel like how they usually behave toward you is being rejected, or as if you somehow disagree with them – how they are – fundamentally. It can also feel like you are now "offended" or "bothered" by things you once were not, which can seem trivial to the person receiving your new boundaries.

The truth is that others might struggle with the fact that you have changed and you are confident in expressing the changes that have taken place. However, it is less a comment on them and more a comment on how you want to interact with them. Having the autonomy to curate or choose how you wish to interact with someone when that person has never had to consider their behaviour toward you before, in a self-aware and proactive way, can make them feel self-conscious and judged. They may respond to this negatively.

It's ok for someone to need time to adjust to your boundaries and you theirs. And it's ok to feel a sense of loss when your interaction with someone changes in an explicit way or in an implicit way; but it is not ok to shame someone, demand things go back to how they were, or to completely dismiss someone's needs when they are asking you respectfully and honestly for a change in the way you interact with them. This can often happen after discussions of views and perspectives that are not only different, but harmful. The notion of a "difference in opinion" only holds when that difference in opinion does not deny another person's existence, rights, and autonomy to make choices in their lives that do not harm others.

When someone's belief system prevents other people from making choices in their lives that do no harm to anybody else, and stops them from accessing things such as healthcare or citizenship, or loving who they want to love, or simply existing, then that itself is a form of harm. If they claim it is their spiritual tradition, family values, or beliefs that cause them to feel and act this way, thereby causing suffering by preventing others from making their own choices for their own bodies and/or reinforcing harmful beliefs about marginalized people and people who are different from them – then these are not simply "differences in opinion", as if this concerned something as innocuous as a food choice at a restaurant.

Maybe this sounds familiar? Maybe you have experienced family members telling you that your "expectations are too high" or you are "too sensitive", rather than lovingly and respectfully engaging with what you have to say, with the intention of trying to understand your perspective or needs? Maybe their lack of understanding is driven by fear, stubbornness, or the belief that if they accept what you are saying they will lose some of their own power, privilege, rights, autonomy, and choices. This is often a false dichotomy and a false belief.

What we need to be willing to examine and disrupt is the belief that we have to tolerate being disrespected, harmed, and dismissed by people simply because we are related to them by birth. This can be hard to understand or accept, but those who have experienced grave harm from their relations in the form of physical, psychological, mental abuse, or sexual harm – or the rejection of their spouses, their sexuality, and their life choices – are often forced to find their own chosen family. The truth is that abuse thrives in silences and festers within belief systems that put pressure on us not to hold other people to account simply because we are related to them. The ways in which family loyalty can be used to cover up harm, abuse, and mistreatment have allowed people to get away with these crimes since the beginning of human history. We need to disrupt the notion of whom we call family and why we call them family.

Learning to be more discerning, willing to know your boundaries, discussing your needs, and knowing when to walk away is important when it comes to any relationship – whether familial, platonic, romantic, sexual, or professional. Our sphere of influence in these different relationships depends on our level of safety, our proximity to our relations, their ability to exert control over us, our ability to make choices about our relationships with them (which, ultimately, we always have), and our willingness to tolerate discomfort.

I've touched on earlier how the phrase "blood is thicker than water" was regularly used to shame me when I caused discord in my family by exploring and challenging belief systems in our family unit that other family members did not want to examine. This unwillingness to have the conversation, and the way in which family members would make assumptions about our collective viewpoints that were often inaccurate, made me realize that even my approach to setting boundaries was completely different from theirs. In their view, I was not allowed to have boundaries. I needed to fall in line with how things were done or I would be branded as an outsider with words like "weird", "odd", "sensitive", "strange", "different", and at times "difficult".

I learned over the years to find community, love, understanding, and safety in select family members and my chosen family of friends. My ability to use discernment with my friendships over the years has allowed me to develop an even deeper understanding of love, love that is unconditional by choice and not by association. I have learned that conditional love and manipulation due to my family relationships and my origins do not equate to how I want to love. Yet I have also always understood that this way of approaching love was not their fault. This came from the lessons passed down from generations who lived through incredibly traumatic times and who were making do with what was available to them – including the examples they had of how to love.

Learning to Disrupt When It's the Last Thing You Want to Do

Sometimes family values can be masked in things such as frequent criticism and high standards, which may translate into feeling like you are never good enough or that you constantly have to perform for the people around you in order to fit in. If this is something you have never experienced in your family, perhaps you have experienced it with a particular group of friends or at work? When this is a way you are used to being treated, it can feel even more challenging to interrupt or disrupt it.

In part, I put my own reluctance at times to challenge others down to my double Libra rising and moon signs. I constantly look for balance in any situation. It actually also goes against my nature to interrupt the flow of things, make people uncomfortable, hold them accountable, draw too much attention to myself, and state things plainly. Libras are the ultimate diplomats, but when people are invested in your relationship staying the way it is, they can easily "mishear" you or ignore your needs. At times, being plain and being direct are required. And it is also important to follow through and for there to be consequences when somebody promises to change or says they hear you, but their behaviour stays the same.

Libras like me can sometimes appear indecisive or wishy-washy, because we don't like disruption. It fundamentally does not agree with us; but given my entire life has been about learning to navigate disruption, I promise you that if this is not your natural approach to the world, it is something you can most certainly learn.

It is also an approach that you can adapt to your own style and way of doing things. Disruption does not need to be loud. It does not need to be intense. It does not need to be dramatic – but it does need to *be*. It usually starts with something as simple as disrupting your usual way of thinking about things. It means being open to exploring alternatives, especially when the current state of things is causing you harm and deep down you know (through your intuition and practice of discernment) that things are not working as they should. We can say these things are not serving us, if we want to use the popular language around this, but it is not as simple as this. When you are not being completely honest with yourself and others – when you are concealing hurt and playing along to keep the peace – that situation is not serving anyone. Ultimately, things will out somewhere down the line; the situation will disintegrate or even implode from the build-up of stress and the pressure of keeping things in. And no one wants that.

A great way to better understand your own style and your approach to maintaining your relationships is through astrology. When you can understand from an astrological perspective how you like to communicate, what you need to feel emotionally stable (and rich), as well as which areas of life cause you disharmony if they feature certain types of situations, personalities, and pressures, you can live more harmoniously, which is ultimately the goal of making good trouble. It may feel counterintuitive and to run counter to everything this book espouses, but we are looking to disrupt in order to bring balance to our lives and the lives of the people around us.

If we define disruption as any situation where injustice is present, a healthy boundary has been crossed (not a boundary that is in place due to unresolved trauma and pain – more on which later), or when a manipulation (i.e. a massive abuse of power) is taking place, then we can define disruption as a necessary action to address a system or situation causing harm.

A Path to Harm Reduction

What do I mean by a system that causes harm – and do I think we live in a world where people are constantly trying to manipulate us? No, it is not so simple. While I don't believe the world is full of people looking to take advantage of us, I do believe we live in a system that incentivizes people to do what they can to get ahead of others. Without getting into capitalist theory and how game theory comes into play, we need to acknowledge that we live in a society that reinforces the assumption that we live in scarcity. After all, why would we need to compete with each other for work, for attention, for partners, for "likes", for housing, for clothing, and for basic resources such as clean air or water if we had enough of these things to go around? Moreover, the way our days are often structured (and I appreciate this varies due to our personal circumstances, geographical location, family needs, and financial situation), we are all wrestling with the constant pressure of having limited time. This does not impact each of us equally. There are those of us that work two jobs a day and return home to people we are caring for – from children to ageing parents – and there are those of us who spend our days in leisure, but collectively, the notion that we are ageing and we are running out of time for leisure is reinforced by a society that believes in a market system. If there is a supply and there is a demand for products, services, and our bodies, then we are constantly being measured by our productivity levels, accolades, and status in that society.

This is a very basic explanation of concepts that sociologists, anthropologists, gender studies researchers, decolonialization experts, climate scientists, economists, queer theorists, and anti-capitalists have explored, expanded on, and described much better than I can here; however, hopefully you get the gist of this argument. Disrupting a system that exploits us for our time, labour, and happiness by constantly selling us the next best product to buy us more time, less labour, and more happiness is a bit of a losing game.

Even if we are aware of the big hamster wheel many of us are running in, we are not separate from the systems in which we live. Even though we may try our hardest to move against these systems where we can, by making different choices, by choosing to slow down, or deciding to come together to live differently, there are wider forces at play and there is a larger power structure to shift (or, indeed, fundamentally disrupt and restructure). If we are going to disrupt the systems that reinforce patriarchy, racism, homophobia, xenophobia, classism, climate crisis, ageism, ableism, and a number of other forms of oppression, we need to pace ourselves and find ways to disrupt our own ways of thinking about how these systems work, as well as how the ways of working in these systems are beliefs we have internalized about what it means to be human. This work takes time, discernment, and constant, constant practice to stay vigilant and aware of disrupting the status quo.

Begin by Befriending Your Inner Self

When we are very young, part of our subconscious starts picking up messages from our surroundings and internalizing these before it is fully able to process them mentally and emotionally; this part of our subconscious conditioning relates to our inner child. In her newsletter toward the end of 2022, Tarot reader and artist Sarah Gottesdiener described how, if you often find yourself speaking in a baby voice or a childlike voice, this could be a sign that you have not fully integrated your inner child. Now, when I talk about inner child integration, I am referring to incorporating, understanding, knowing, and loving all aspects of yourself – including aspects of yourself that may have been forgotten or neglected in childhood. We all have inner children and while not all of us experience inner child wounding, where these aspects of ourselves are not fully integrated, it is possible that we do feel sometimes like these aspects of ourselves are not cared for.

I spend a lot of time with my inner child, because she tends to make her presence known on a daily basis. When I slip into my child-like voice, which happens when I'm with someone I am comfortable with, or I have an internal discussion with myself about something I simply do not want to do – such as laborious admin or just being upright instead of under the sheets – my inner child lets me know she's right there. When I was younger and more committed to my creative practice (and let's face it, I had more space for it because I didn't have the chores of being an adult), my inner child had more mediums with which to play. Whether it was through thrice-weekly dance classes, sports practice in the afternoons, school hours in the art studio, time on the acting stage, or in band practice with my best friends, I had so many daily creative outlets that I was almost always fulfilled daily. Today, I have to make more of a conscious effort to indulge her and to connect with her needs.

I remember a dear friend of mine explaining a technique her therapist had used to help her explore her own needs. This relates to inner child work, but is more complex, as it involved introducing her to the concept of a community of selves, an approach that allows us to name, put characteristics to, and understand aspects of ourselves that we are not as conscious of. Instead of thinking of ourselves as consisting of our conscious self and our inner child (a binary, which might not be helpful), we can think of ourselves as a community of people who are different ages, have different needs, and behave in different ways. It allows us to see in ourselves the multiplicity of ourselves and complexity of nature, rather than trying to put it down to two aspects of ourselves. The following exercise is therefore something you can do with your inner child in mind, or you can choose to engage with it from the perspective of a community of selves.

A PRACTICE FOR DAYS WHEN YOU FEEL STUCK

I think of creativity as a form of energy that we can play with and are able to access much more easily or unencumbered when we are little. For this next exercise, you are going to work with your creativity to help you loosen up when you feel stuck. This is an exercise you can repeat as many times as you like. You can do this exercise once, or repeat it from the perspective of your inner child or your community of selves.

1. Sit down with some of your favourite things in front of you – this could be a favourite food, an article of clothing, or something else that is meaningful to you. I have asked you to bring together your favourite things because this helps to conjure up and welcome in the spirit of your inner child or hidden self. You do not need to name your inner child, nor do you need to pinpoint the age of your inner child. Especially if this is your first time exploring inner child work, it is important to keep an open mind and not to expect too much.

2. Now, get a piece of paper and something to write with. If you prefer to write using digital means, you are welcome to do so; you should engage in this exercise in whatever way makes you feel comfortable.

3. Take a deep breath and set an intention to know yourself better.

4. Please take the hand you normally write with and put it down next to you, either in your lap, on the table, or down by your side. You will not be using it for this exercise. Switch your focus to writing or typing with your other hand. (If your other hand is unavailable, try putting a writing implement between your toes and doing this exercise with your feet.) If writing does not come easily to you, you can doodle your answers. Using your nondominant hand will allow you to communicate to yourself in a more visceral and direct way, in a way that is not practised and polished. It will also enable you to shift into a different aspect of yourself – one that is rawer and may sometimes be neglected.

5. Next, I would like you to keep a few questions in mind. Then you can begin to add more questions of your own in order to get to know your inner child or inner self. They should be open questions, rather than the yes or no variety. For example:
   - Describe yourself, please?
   - Who are you?
   - What do you like?
   - What do you need?
   - What are you afraid of?

6. Without straining for answers, type, write, or doodle anything that comes to you. Try to stay open to who emerges from the questions you ask. Trust your gut and trust your writing or doodling, even if at first it does not make sense.

7. At the end, look over what you have written or doodled to see if you can learn anything from it. Do you know more about your inner child (or a member of your community of selves)?

8. At the end of this exercise thank yourself, your inner child or your community of selves for appearing to you, being open, and communicating with you.

9. If challenging feelings, ideas, or selves came up in this exercise, take the time to journal about them in a separate space if you have a journalling practice.

10. If you do not have a journalling practice, do a grounding exercise and/or a cleansing ritual. You can take a shower and allow those feelings to wash off from your body energetically. You can go for a walk and

spend some time in nature outdoors. You can also lie down on the floor facing a wall and walk your feet up the wall so that your body is lying in an L-shape that follows the 90° angle between the wall and the floor as a grounding exercise. You can simply take a moment to take a deep breath and feel your feet on the floor.

I have noticed that my handwriting changes depending on the time of day, how long I have been writing, my emotional state, and my overall mood. My energy levels impact this too. Is it possible that this shift in handwriting denotes a shift from one inner self or another? Try this practice at different times of the day and see what emerges. If you are focusing on your inner child then you might find its mood changes and shifts, or indeed you might meet another aspect of yourself at a different point in the day.

If anything comes up that you feel unable to process by yourself, please take this to therapy, to a trusted person who can support you, or to another space where you can process these emotions. This is not guaranteed to happen, but if it does, it is part of the deep work your inner child and community of selves is helping you to do. They are helping you to disrupt yourself.

According to Eden Gray, an authority on the Tarot, the guardian angel shown on the Temperance card "makes the tests and trials that lead us along the path of attainment".[3] Part of these tests and trials may involve the disruption of family relationships as we align ourselves with our true values. But it is important to remember that disrupting what is no longer working can create the space for healthy new growth.

9

REMODELLING AFTER DISRUPTION

We explored the impact of a destabilizing event in chapter 7 and what that can mean in a moment of destruction, but if the catalyst for a destabilizing event is you, and that destruction comes as a result of your disruption, there will be an energetic and emotional fallout you need to be ready for.

It is an incredibly pivotal moment when you choose to disrupt something. Our relationship to that thing, those people, that situation, and the physical place where the disruption takes places changes forever. Call me sensitive (or deeply intuitive), but I believe the "site" of disruption will be forever changed due to your choice to disrupt it. This change is slight. This change is energetic in nature and this change is palpable, but most likely you will be the only one who notices it, at first. Others may have a delayed reaction and their initial response may simply be upset, confusion, annoyance, or resistance.

We have already explored the cycles of grief and how the process of disruption can be mapped onto the grieving process. This can be a useful way for us to understand what happens when we disrupt, but what we need to better understand is the impact that *choosing* to disrupt may have on us. Even if we know the disruption is in alignment with our values, that it was the right thing for us to do and we would not do things any differently if given another chance, we need to be prepared for the mental and psychological impact of choosing to disrupt and be disruptive.

Accountability and Choice

In the Rider–Waite–Smith Tarot, the Lovers card shows an angel looking down and blessing two naked figures who stand apart from each other, with nothing to hide. The card represents love and connection, but it also can represent choice. Letting love in, regardless of what kind of love it is, is a powerful choice. We can choose to receive love in the same ways that we can choose to be accountable in the wider world. We can also choose to accept the aftermath of destruction and the state we may be in when we come through the other side; this is incredibly powerful.

Accountability means making the conscious choice to accept our own role in disruption. This acceptance is a form of awareness; through acceptance of the part we have played in a situation and no longer being in denial, we can start to make the choices we need to process and embrace the work that may be entailed in the aftermath of disruption.

However, taking responsibility for the things that go wrong can often feel unbelievably grating. Conflict is something we may seek to avoid because it is incredibly uncomfortable, but of itself conflict is not wrong. Conflict is most certainly not even bad. In the words of astrologer Jessica Lanyadoo, "Conflict is a motivator for innovation."[1] If we want to truly change the world we live in, in its deepest sense, we need to embrace the fact that conflict is part of that equation. Choose to embrace the chaos and conflict that come with disruptive innovation. This is one of the most powerful choices you can make.

I also want to distinguish once more between *choosing* to disrupt and *being* disruptive, because there is something very distinctive that happens when we deliberately choose to speak up or point out something that others view as inconvenient. When we disrupt a situation and people respond to it, we may gain the confidence to disrupt again. This is an incredibly positive thing and a core tenet of this book, but we also have to think about the impact of potentially being viewed as "disruptive", as this can be a label that people might put on us: because they find the actual disruption inconvenient, they project the process itself onto us.

Throughout history, disruptors have been labelled as such in order to distract attention away from the issue, system, or situation they are disrupting and to put the onus instead on the person who is highlighting the issue. This is a classic defensive tactic that people can use, sometimes unconsciously, to blame rather than to claim responsibility for their part in the perception that something is "wrong". When you come up against someone who does not share a disruptive approach to things and you point out something to them that you think should change, they can take it incredibly personally, which brings us on nicely to the importance of understanding our emotions throughout the process of disruption. How can we remodel things without understanding what we have to work with in the first place?

Understanding Emotions in the Disruption Journey

When it comes to disruption and the art of remodelling afterwards, we need to accept that our relationship to the situation we were in pre-disruption has permanently changed. This does not mean the change is negative; it can be entirely and incredibly positive. Either way, it's about accepting that a change has taken place. What better way to understand this change and our relationship to it than by understanding our emotions?

Robert Plutchik was an American medical professional and psychologist who died in 2006 after writing at least eight books on emotions. Plutchik's theory of emotions postulates ten key rules about emotions, which include a rule of opposites that, "like many things in nature, there is a duality with emotions".[2] He influenced how we talk about emotions today by identifying eight basic emotions and developed a wheel of emotions that is still widely used.[3]

The emotions wheel is based on the eight basic emotions, which are linked to the more intense emotions they can become. For example, anger in its extreme state on the wheel is rage, which can be found at the centre of the wheel. Move in the opposite direction, outward and away from the word anger, and you will find that anger is also linked to annoyance. One version of the wheel is illustrated like a flower with petals that have the names of emotions written on them and have complex connections to the other flower petals. [4]

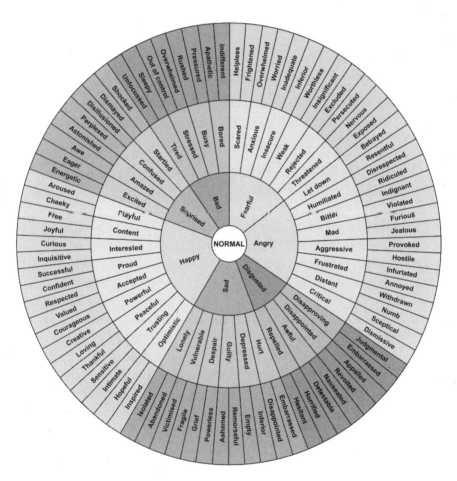

The wheel of emotions by Robert Plutchik.

The first time I encountered Plutchik's wheel of emotions, I remember being floored when I saw how these states connected. I was transformed in my realization that certain emotions I felt could be manifestations of other emotions such as anger, grief, or joy in ways I had never considered before. It has helped me begin to make sense of, for example, a strong emotion that I experienced as a result of explosive disruption: betrayal.

The feeling of betrayal is like nothing else. It is an experience that can flip your world completely upside down. Plutchik's wheel shows how, like other emotions, betrayal is directly linked to a number of others – but in my experience, these can range from feelings around broken loyalty and a breach of trust, to the way it impacts your general sense of safety and belonging. Betrayal also dredges up feelings of shame and guilt, all wrapped up in varying degrees of anger.

Betrayal can impact us on a soul level. It leaves an energetic footprint that is hard to miss and even harder to transmute into something else. It is very difficult to transform betrayal into a positive, inspired action or feeling. In my experience, a deep-seated betrayal that shifts your understanding of yourself and your relationship to other people can be earth-shattering – like a tectonic plate shifting in your internal and external world, your little microverse. All because of all the other emotions wrapped up with it.

As the old adage goes, it is moments of crisis like these, and moments when we stand apart from the crowd to defend what we believe in, that help us to distinguish who is truly in alignment with our values. The people that are not there when you need them, or who choose to believe mistruths about you or the situation, are not doing the work of being good friends. It might be easier for them "not to get involved" or to say that they do not want to pick sides. It may be that they say they find what you are telling them "hard to believe". This is classic evasive behaviour, which might have its roots in anger or it might be coming from a place of the person not having the capacity to engage.

Ultimately, we cannot know what other people are motivated by or why they choose to take action or stay silent, but who is there for you in times of need speaks volumes. It can hurt to find out that the people who you thought supported you or shared your values do not, but it is better to know than not to know. Focusing on your actual support networks and systems will soften the blow. You can also begin to unpick some of the confusion caused by something like betrayal through developing a deeper understanding of the energy of emotions as a whole.

Understanding the Energy of Emotions

In chapter 7, we looked at anger in connection to grief; when we think about how anger can be so overwhelming that it blocks out other emotions or prevents us from accessing them, we can better appreciate the power of this emotion.

According to Plutchik's wheel of emotions, anger can also equate to apathy or indifference, which I had never considered before I saw them next to each other on the wheel. When I thought about it more, it made sense. Anger can push us to a point of no longer caring, and in this respect, apathy is almost like an act of internal defiance. When it comes to betrayal, anger can have a numbing quality to it and manifest in different ways such as unresolved grief or apathy, for example, so the idea that apathy is an extension of anger checks out.

A PRACTICE TO SENSE
THE ENERGY OF EMOTIONS

If you would like to take your understanding of emotions and their energy to a deeper level, you could start by interpreting the energy of emotions as you experience them in your body.

1. Let's begin with one of the emotions that may come up in the aftermath of disruption, which we explored in chapter 7: acceptance, depression, anger, denial, shock, and bargaining. Please take your time to identify the energy signature of each of the stages of grief as you experience these. For example, when you think of it, does anger feel dense, hot, and fast-paced to you, or does it feel thick, immovable, and cold? This signature will be unique to you.

2. Take a few minutes to feel into each stage of grief and describe its energy in this way.

3. After you finish identifying the signature of each of these emotions, make sure to clear them from your body. When reliving a memory, especially a traumatic one, we now know that we are reliving these experiences in our bodies too when we conjure them up. To close this exercise in peace, imagine a fountain of water pouring over your head and think about these emotions being carried by the water down to your feet. Allow yourself to imagine any energetic residue being lifted from your body and drained away.

4. You can now close this exercise by saying, "I allow these emotions to clear themselves from my energy body and I thank myself for allowing them in. This exercise is complete."

We know mind, body, and soul are connected. Schools of thought that sought to separate and rationalize the link between the three most certainly have philosophical merit, but the reality is – especially now that we live in a society with more stress, where the use of technology impacts our adrenal glands and nervous systems, and we have a better understanding of our mental health in relation to brain function – we know that everything in our bodies is connected. The systems within our bodies and the systems of our environment have a direct impact on our health. The macro and micro of our daily lives constantly interact.

Managing Other People's Emotions after Disruption

In the aftermath of disruption, one of the factors you cannot account for relates to how other people will react. Will they get defensive or supportive? Will they believe what you are saying? Will they embrace the change you have catalysed or attempt to build walls around it to prevent it from happening? Will they panic or remain calm? Will they blame you? Will this turn into a scapegoating exercise in which you have to bear the brunt of all the uncertainty, fear, and chaos this moment brings? And is it only fair for you to do so, as the catalyst of this change? Or was this system already failing and you simply put pressure on a weak point that brought it all tumbling down? Though this failure may have been inevitable, will you be applauded or vilified for pointing it out? These are all questions that will be answered via the actions of the people involved in the dynamic of this situation immediately after and in the weeks (or months or years) that follow in its aftermath.

Understanding why people behave the way they do is something we may never fathom, even with Plutchik's wheel of emotions. We can try to read into people's reactions to us and what might be motivating them, but this can be a thankless task. As the spiritual teacher Baba Ram Dass once said, "Emotions are like waves. Watch them disappear in the distance on the vast calm ocean."[5] If emotion are like waves, we simply must learn to ride them or they will engulf us in their crashing crests and pull us into the undercurrent beneath them. We need to remember that no matter how strongly we feel our emotions, they will pass. We are not meant to hold on to them. They are not designed that way. Our emotions are constantly giving us information about our body, our needs, and our reactions to situations. As we saw in chapter 7, anger may be giving us important information about where our boundaries have been crossed; it may be offering us the opportunity to disrupt our own thinking and course-correct.

Disrupting Our Own Thinking

A large part of disrupting our own thinking requires us to understand it in the first place. Like my discovery about the connections between basic emotions and other emotional states when I learned about Plutchik's wheel of emotions, we can sometimes miss wider connections between our thinking and the beliefs that underpin them.

In Theta Energy Healing® we identify and address key thought patterns, beliefs, and thought systems that guide our daily lives. The entire process is about unearthing core beliefs in healing sessions. These beliefs have a massive impact on how we view ourselves, how we view others, and how we interact with the world. It can be very difficult for most of us to understand our worldview until it is questioned or challenged gently. It is likely that there are many things about our own perspective that we have never considered, because we often surround ourselves with people who think similarly to us, or we make assumptions about how other people view the world based on how we view the world. Unless we are asked why we think a certain way – and if we have never considered another way of viewing the world – our perception of the world (and our place in it) may never change.

There are a number of psychological factors that frame the way we see the world: early childhood experiences, our family system, school experiences, class, gender, race, age, and levels of neurodivergence for a start. We might experience the world from a more negative perspective, a more neutral perspective, or experience a more emotionally fluctuating lens on the world, thanks to these factors. Without getting into arguments about nature versus nurture, and the impact of trauma on all of us, or the wider impact of structural trauma such as racism, poverty, and gender-based violence, it is useful for us to take some time to reflect on our view of the world as individuals. Do we generally believe people are good and trustworthy? Or do we feel that people are self-interested, selfish, and untrustworthy? Do we interact with the world in a defensive way, where we try to hide ourselves or project a certain image of ourselves out to the external world? (This can be an image that reads "do not mess with me, I am dangerous", or "I am little, meek, and delicate, so be gentle with me", or anything in between.) When there is a crisis or when something goes awry, what are our initial assumptions? Do we jump to the worst-case scenario or are we more positive about what the cause might be? Or are we neutral?

How we respond to the world is greatly influenced by the energy we have been surrounded by and our reaction to this. Yet it is not simply about energy, as our psychology is impacted by a number of different factors, and once we better understand our worldview we can start to influence and change it, if we want to. It may be that we are content with our view of the world and how we then show up in it.

Being aware of our emotional states, our psychology, and our responses to the world around us is a very important part of having emotional intelligence. It is another way we can learn to develop tools to surf the waves that our own emotions and other people's emotions create.

Chaos Maketh the Muse

When I was younger and first getting into astrology, I used to be obsessed with personality tests. I would take every personality test I could get my hands on. I remember staying up for hours in front of the family computer on weekends and falling asleep, waiting for the dial-up connection if I was bumped offline. I was curious about what these tests could tell me about myself. I was thirsty for information that would allow me to better understand my place in the world and how I could better interact with others. On a superficial level, I just found the tests fun!

Without realizing it, I was also seeking an answer to a question I did not know I had asked: "How can I live in the world with more ease and less discomfort or resistance to the people around me?" This question of living with more easefulness comes back to understanding our values in the world. It was also a deeply energetic question that I couldn't answer with words alone. If we know what is important to us, we can navigate our needs and make better choices for ourselves while minimizing obstacles. If we better understand our needs, we can more easily manage our energy.

Without realizing it, I was trying to unearth a language for, and an understanding of, my values through descriptions of my personality that were pre-programmed by an algorithm. Personality tests were some of the world's first algorithms. Astrology presented me with another framework to navigate why I might be predisposed to certain things or how I might better understand how I interact with the world. However, sometimes it takes difficult experiences for us to truly understand what is important to us and what we truly value.

In 2017, I experienced the worst reality check I had ever had in my life. I was hidden homeless, had survived an abusive relationship, and my visa status in the UK was at risk because of the breakdown of my first serious relationship. I had been with my partner on and off for four and a half years. In the midst of this bottom-of-the barrel situation, I was managing the disintegration of a festival I had been running unsustainably on volunteer hours and precarious arts funding for three years. My health was at its worst, understandably. I was miserable and slowly but surely sifting through what felt like the wreckage of my life. I had hit a low point that touched every aspect of my existence. Nothing was left intact – from my personal life and living situation, to my professional life and professional relationships.

This was all precipitated by a choice I had made a few weeks before this disaster: to disrupt my life – and I was not entirely ready for the outcome. Naïve, maybe, and foolish, most certainly. A few weeks before this car crash of a situation, I had invoked the goddess Kalī by reciting a mantra. The purpose was to clear anything not serving me from my life and, wow, did she deliver. I have detailed this experience in other pieces of writing, so the key thing to revisit here is that I had wilfully and ignorantly welcomed chaos into my life. Little did I know at the time that *chaos maketh the muse*. This became the source of one of the most transformational changes in direction in my life. It pulled what was truly important to me into focus.

I started leaning into my spiritual practice and, given that everything else felt so messy, I seized the opportunity to focus fully on things that had been tinkering away in the background of my mind. I knew I had psychic gifts. I had always been interested in the occult and I had a consistent but unrequited love for astrology. I could not call myself a student of astrology at that point, because I had not committed any time to studying it. But that all this was about to change.

This is when Theta Energy Healing® came into my life. I committed three months to working with an artist, healer, and shaman to start to focus on what I wanted my life to look like. That healer, Eileen, gave me a book to use called a gratitude journal. The format of the *Five-Minute Journal* was simple. Along with inspirational quotes, it had a gratitude practice in the morning, and another gratitude practice at the end of the day. I kept these little notes simple. I was grateful for food, a bed, and a roof over my head. In this period of my life, I was cat sitting, house sitting, couch surfing, and doing anything I could to secure a place to stay. I was still working out if I was going to apply for an extremely competitive visa programme to stay in the UK or call it quits. Though I felt like many things in my life were on hold and some had been a failure, I was still perceived to be incredibly successful in my early career at this point and deep down I knew I had something to build on. I did not want to let it all go.

The combination of Theta Healing® sessions, daily meditations, and the *Five-Minute Journal* was having an impact. I felt myself walking more lightly in the world. I was noticing the small things more, and my dad favourite's saying often echoed in my head: "Don't sweat the small stuff." This man had lived through guerrilla warfare, fighting for independence and living in the deep jungle of Angola. He moved to the UK, where he rose through the ranks of his career in the oil industry, before losing it all, marrying my mother, moving to the US, and starting a new life. He then returned to his country of birth with a cloud hanging over his head based on what happened in his career in London in the 1980s, which massively influenced how he moved through the world. If he could remember not to sweat the small things and simply be happy to be alive, then I could too.

I have a tendency to minimize a lot of the traumatic things that have happened to me. I do not like to give them too much power and I have a high tolerance for trauma (or indeed a low tolerance that requires me not to feel into trauma too much). What I can say about this particular experience, though, is that it was the hardest thing I had lived through up until that point. All of the things around me that had felt like firm foundations crumbled beneath my feet. It was only with the steady practice of identifying the things in my life that were going well and developing the habit of acknowledging them that I could slowly and surely approach the chaos of the rubble of my life.

I had guides, friends, and people who were supporting me on the journey. I knew that the shaky foundations my life was built on would eventually need to crumble. It was only a matter of time. In many ways, choosing when the foundation would crack was a form of protection. I could choose where to go from there, instead of being completely surprised.

Transmutation is a process that feels slow and laborious, then it hits you all at once. I found that the path to rebuild and refocus my life purpose – along with where I was to live, what I would do with my work, and how I would return to a state of good health – required me to take small steps each day. As I started to move out of crisis mode into survival mode and then from survival mode into more stability, I was able to see what was happening as an adventure and a challenge rather than irredeemable destruction.

I share this story because I want you to think about not necessarily just your lowest points, but the points where you feel stuck. Is there a small thing you can do to acknowledge how stuck you feel, but also a way you can give yourself the space to sit in that and make tiny adjustments in the direction you want to go? And if you do not know what direction that is, would you be able to start to explore what that might be?

The Beauty of Chaos

Not everyone is a fan of chaos and crisis. In fact, many people spend their lives doing everything possible to avoid both of these uncertain states, but the truth is that both chaos and crisis are a large part of life. If you are familiar with chaos theory or have engaged with what we know about the Big Bang, everything we know emerged from a moment of chaos. It is the artists and chaos agents out there who find beauty in the noise of chaos. Personally, I sincerely believe that "chaos maketh the muse"; chaos is my muse and I live my life in uncertainty. I am uncertain of who I will be working with at any given point in the future and maybe even where I might be living.

During particularly tumultuous segments of my freelance life in Scotland, I lived out of a suitcase and only knew where I was living as far as the end of the week. However, alongside the anxiety of uncertainty were the excitement and possibility of the future. Literally anything could happen, and I was open to the invitation to move in any direction.

Chaos makes the muse because it is the key ingredient to the next thing that may inspire you. Chaos is also an incredibly necessary step on the path to creating something and bringing it into existence. There is also a period of uncertainty and the energy of fluctuating ideas, methods, and paths forward. It is an energy that, if we do not learn to become comfortable with it, can be extremely overwhelming.

We often think of chaos and uncertainty as two phenomena that are intertwined. However, we may recall the saying that a caterpillar, before it turns into a butterfly, may think it is dying. The uncertainty of turning into mush before it reforms into a butterfly is not only terrifying in its uncertainty, but it can feel chaotic. *What comes next?* the caterpillar might think in this process. Without projecting too much human emotion onto a caterpillar's metamorphosis, we may use this process to think about our own discomfort with uncertainty – and if uncertainty and chaos go hand in hand, our discomfort with chaos.

THE HEARTSONG PRACTICE

The Heartsong is a beautiful practice in the Theta Energy Healing® canon. It can be used to bring balance to the body and create a healing space for emotions. It is a delicate and vulnerable practice that I would suggest we all do regularly. It is a ritual practice, so something that will get easier with time. Each experience of the Heartsong will shift and change, depending on where you are energetically each time you do it. It is something you can do every day if you so choose, and it will allow you to engage with the beautiful and cleansing element of water in a gentle way. You will need the subtlety of your intuition and keen hearing to embark on this exercise.

1. After cleansing yourself either in the tub or the shower, position yourself in a comfortable seated or standing position. It is useful at this point to turn off the water in the shower or remain sitting in the stillness of the bathtub. This ritual entails heart-led warrior work, and it will impact your heart. That is why it is important to support your heart as much as possible throughout this process. Sitting in a body of water, or in an acoustically contained space like a shower, enables you to be fully supported by the vibrations of the space to release the energy trapped in your body. The echo of the space and the ripples in the water created by the echo in your voice, which you can see as ripples in the bath water, magnify the healing process.

2. Now take a deep breath and tune in to your body.

3. Do an energy scan. Is there a particular part of your body that feels like it needs attention? Is there an ache, pain, or simply an unusual feeling? Start with that part of your body. If not, you can simply start at your root chakra, which sits at the root of your body near your pelvic, womb, or tailbone space.

4. Directing your hands to this space, take a deep breath. After taking a deep breath, start to release noise on the exhale. It might sound crackly at first, which is good. The sound will get clearer the more times you practise it. You do not need to open your lips. You can keep them closed and release the sound as a hum. This does not need to be loud, but you need to be able to hear it. It may waver it may sound like a note, or it might be easily broken up.

5. Do this several times and hold the exhale through this sound for as long as you can, until you have no more breath. The idea is to repeat this as many times as possible until you feel the humming sound is clear – uninterrupted, not breathy, and harmonious. This energetic sound clearing will allow you to tap into the energy of that part of your body and clear it of any energetic debris.

6. After doing this humming exercise until the hum sounds clearer, move on to another part of your body. You can choose any part of your body; it doesn't need to correspond to one of the chakra centres.

7. Finally, move to your heart. Put both hands over your heart, take an inhale, and exhale a hum, starting the sound tuning process again. This is why this ritual is called a *Heartsong*. You are tuning in to the song of your heart and releasing any heaviness, stuck energy, emotions, or energy you are carrying in your heart space that is not yours (or that is yours, but needs to be cleared away).

8. When you feel you have completed the ritual, thank your body. Thank yourself for doing the ritual. Gently squeeze your body in an act of physical and embodied love or thanks. Then, if sitting in a bath, drain the water in the tub while thanking the water for the role it played in washing the energy off you.

9. If you wish, you can sit in the tub until all of the water drains out of it. It is important to allow any energetic work to settle, or in healer speak, "integrate". I would therefore suggest not rushing off to do any urgent work

or chores. Make sure you have your own space for at least a little while to do this ritual, even if this means after it is complete you are thrust back into the reality of responsibilities. Give yourself a moment afterwards, if this is the case, to take a few deep breaths before you emerge back into the world.

This is a lovely thing to do at the end of the day before bed as a pre-sleep ritual. You can drink herbal teas afterwards, but nothing too heavy with caffeine or too dense food-wise, unless you feel your body needs it. When I say dense, I mean foods that are not mostly water. Continuing to engage with the water element by drinking water or tea will help the process.

You may find that you have vivid dreams or that ideas, situations, or memories come up in your sleep after a Heartsong ritual. This is because your sleep and dreams help integrate the Heartsong. Be kind and gentle to yourself after this practice.

Rebuilding and Remodelling in a World that Wants Us to Do the Opposite

We live in a world modelled on productivity, which keeps us so tired oiling the systems we live in that we rarely have time to stop and reflect. Reflect on what exactly? Whether or not we like the direction we are moving in and how we might need to readjust things if we are not happy with where the road leads us. Changing course requires time, energy, resources, and a collective willpower on a systemic level. Whether we are dismantling the patriarchy, destroying white supremacist values, or stopping the climate crisis, it is easy to feel overwhelmed and for our efforts to feel minute compared to the problem at hand.

But we know that disruptors have never let this stop them. We know that disruptors have always believed that "Never doubt that a small group of thoughtful, committed citizens can change the world. Indeed, it is the only thing that ever has."[6] Otherwise, they would not have bothered disrupting things. More importantly, we know that these disruptors have enjoyed the work of interrupting the status quo and shaking shit up. That has always been part of the fun! Chaos agents love to bring the chaos. And warriors love to fight. Disruption is an energy that has certain qualities to it that we ought to embrace, much like the figures in the Lovers card can make the conscious choice to reach out to each other in all of their naked honesty and vulnerability.

10

YOUR BODY AND ENERGY IN A DISRUPTIVE WORLD

There are so many things we are continuing to learn about the human body. Have you noticed how, in the last five years, we have become highly focused on gut health and the microbiome – the community of microorganisms that live inside us and on our bodies? This upsurge of interest has seen the rise of intuitive eating – the process of learning to eat intuitively and intentionally when we are hungry rather than dieting – as well as food trends such as eating ketogenic (high fat, medium-protein, low carbohydrate), to an expansion in people's intolerances to gluten and dairy. There is also the growing popularity of kombucha, probiotics, and gut-friendly foods brought on by an awareness of the need to support our microbiomes. We are starting to learn more about the relationship between our gut health and our mental health. We are also developing a greater understanding of the importance of healthy immune function and regulated nervous systems in a world where, increasingly, our bodies are experiencing chronic illness.

We can see our relationships to our bodies as a fluid thing. There is no binary of right and wrong or good and bad. We can view ourselves as inhabiting bodies that energetically need support and restoration, on a spectrum that corresponds to our needs in that moment. Rather than trying to reach a place of perfection or purity, which does not exist, we can approach this journey of healing with compassion.

Understanding Healing in the Context of the Tarot

Just as punitive justice increases harm, so taking a punitive approach to our bodies and to our approach to disruption causes more harm than good. In the Rider–Waite–Smith Tarot, the seated figure of Justice holds an upright sword and a level set of scales, representing cause and effect. Quite often, the first thing we think about, with respect to considering the repercussions of our actions, is punishment for our misdemeanours. In the western world, this is how we also speak about justice. If there has been wrongdoing or harm done, we expect the consequences for these actions to put those involved in one of two categories: a binary of victim and perpetrator. Our language and culture around this are that the perpetrator should be punished, which is a form of punitive justice.

Psychologists, scholars, activists, healers, and researchers have been challenging this approach for centuries. Based on a system that minimizes the complexity of harm and isolates the individuals causing harm, there is an argument for why this approach is rooted in wider beliefs in hierarchy, exceptionalism, and ultimately white supremacy. The for-profit prison industrial complex is predicated on the notion that bodies can be dehumanized and treated as vehicles for profit, which mimics systems of slavery, domination, and exploitation.[1] However, alternative models of harm reduction and restorative justice do exist. Some of them have trialled in Scandinavia and the UK,[2] where humanizing people in order to support their recovery alongside addressing the source of their offending is central to the healing process.

The notion that justice is punitive, vengeful, and retributive, rather than restorative or healing, is similar to the way we have traditionally thought about our bodies. Consider the language we use around keeping our bodies healthy, like "toning our body", or how we maintain our health through measures that require us to punish ourselves if we stray from healthy habits. A more healing, trauma-informed, and compassionate approach to our bodies involves thinking about the relationship between cause and effect as a restorative process, not a punitive one. The potential this has to restore our relationship with our bodies is immense.

Further to this, the standards deemed acceptable in western society are often built in the image of "whiteness" and "thinness". Where these beliefs underpin diet cultures and their punitive approach to our bodies, the legacies of restorative justice and body acceptance are, in contrast, steeped deeply in the cultures of the diasporas of Africa and other indigenous communities. It is no coincidence that other ways of relating to our bodies have originated in cultures which have other ways of organizing – which are not steeped in the cultures and histories of exploitation.

Connections between the Body and the Mind

The body and mind are not separate. We know this. We also know that the impact psychological stress has on our bodies is something that manifests physically. Stress may reveal itself as a racing heartbeat, the sensation of butterflies in your stomach, sweat pooling in your hands and under your armpits, feeling lightheaded, or as the need to vomit. Anxiety can manifest physically as the urge to urinate, heart palpitations, changes in your breathing patterns, and panic attacks that can include a number of these symptoms.

In October 2013, I had a health scare that landed me in A&E. I was lying in bed one morning and my legs went numb. I started to feel a tingling sensation in my lower limbs. I had had a tricky time walking up the stairs to my flat the day before and was feeling very short of breath. As a fit 21-year-old, this was unusual for me. I called for help. Based on my symptoms, I was told not to wait for an ambulance but to get a taxi to hospital urgently.

When I arrived, the medics did an EKG and took an X-ray of my chest. They concluded that nothing was wrong. I probably had a chest infection. I was sent home and told to return if my symptoms didn't improve. Meanwhile, I consulted my doctor in the States, who had been treating me since I was 16, who suggested that I needed a CT scan. She suspected I might have had a mini pulmonary embolism.

I continued to feel confused, light-headed, and incredibly tired. My breathing became laboured even when I walked to the local shop for essentials. I went back to A&E after a few days, as I had been told to do if things didn't improve. I had nearly passed out walking down the street earlier that day due to my light-headedness.

My second trip to A&E was inconclusive and I was treated as more of a nuisance than anything else. A nurse actually shouted at me for telling her my American GP had suggested a CT scan with a d-dimer. She wasn't overly receptive to what she considered to be a back-seat diagnosis. The whole experience was traumatic and I was in a state of utter panic when the consultant came to my room to send me home shortly after, with instructions to rest. I was aware that I hadn't been resting enough. My university life included a lot of extracurricular commitments and I had not yet developed the necessary boundaries to say no. Nevertheless, I was baffled, but I did improve over the next few weeks.

A couple of years later, my American doctor noticed in my annual physical examination that I was experiencing a number of nutrient deficiencies. I'd been having physicals since my first year of life and she had a baseline to compare my current nutrient levels to. My folate, zinc, calcium, and a number of other nutrient levels were very low. I had a high level of thyroid-stimulating hormones, enough to cause her alarm and to suggest I get an ultrasound of my thyroid.

Moreover, my gut health was also the worst it had been in a long time. I had lived with dairy intolerance and irritable bowel syndrome for over 10 years by this point, but the nutrient deficiencies were a new development. My doctor knew there was something amiss. She decided to investigate. In response to this and many other patients' similar symptoms, she began training as a functional medicine specialist. As far as I understand it, the philosophy of functional medicine focuses on treating all parts of the body as a whole. It views all parts of the body as deeply connected to one another and doesn't treat them as separate or disconnected, as is often the case in the practice of modern medicine.

Our investigations into what was causing my ailments began in earnest. Within the year I received a diagnosis that brought everything back to my gut microbiome. Given my experiences of childhood trauma, stress, and anxiety, it appeared that it was all interconnected. While the finding didn't explain the pulmonary episode I'd experienced, it did start to pull together other symptoms I was experiencing.

I was diagnosed with leaky gut syndrome. Leaky gut syndrome is a gradual erosion of the stomach lining, which means food particles and other bacteria leak directly from the gut into the bloodstream, which causes a whole host of inflammation. How this links to food intolerances I am less certain, but the inflammation contributes to a variety of symptoms. Either way, food particles leaking into places they shouldn't is not good. It is only by taking probiotics, changing one's diet, and restoring the lining of the gut, while reducing inflammation over time, that leaky gut syndrome can be managed. Reducing inflammation in the body is central to this process because inflammation contributes to a number of other autoimmune conditions, including rheumatoid arthritis.

I repeated this test a second time a year later to find out if our treatment plan was working and steadily it was. I had lived with chronic fatigue and anxiety for so long that I had almost forgotten what it felt like to feel well. It quickly becomes difficult to understand what health feels like when your baseline for wellness is so low. When the treatment started working I was amazed at how much energy I had in comparison to when I was struggling.

Those of us who live with chronic conditions and illness are often more aware of the changes in our body. We have to be. It gives us the added benefit of being able to pick up on our body's cues over time. If there is any silver lining, it is this.

My story is one example of why it is so important to have a good understanding of your own body, your body's needs, and your body's baseline for stress. It is also important to have a good picture of what wellness feels like for you. Ultimately, I would encourage you to improve your understanding of your energy levels, the subtle changes in your body, to better navigate the impact of the process of disruption. If you do this, you can better prepare for the impact it will have on your physical and mental health.

Another tool that is important for us to use is finding ways to release energy. Shifting energy is one thing, but facilitating the process of getting energy to leave your body is so important. This next exercise will guide us through a method of releasing stuck energy.

A PRACTICE FOR CHANNELLING KALI'S BREATH OR LION'S BREATH

This yoga exercise will enable you to channel and shift stuck energy. It allows you to embody and express repressed emotions. It is incredibly useful if you are feeling angry, highly strung, stuck, frustrated, furious, or a range of these emotions (and others). I find that, particularly when we are in leadership roles, we hold a lot of other people's emotions. These could be the emotions of our team or our own emotions, which we choose not to show our team, our colleagues, and the people we are working with in order to better support them in the work that they do. Our team can be our family, our group of friends, or our communities – any place we feel like we hold a lot of people's needs. This breathing exercise will enable you to experience some relief from this.

1. Position yourself in front of a mirror. It can be any size; the important thing is that you can see your face reflected in it.

2. Next, channelling the goddess Kalī, imagine her fierce pose. As described in chapter 3, Kalī is often depicted with blood-red eyes filled with rage. Her skin is black or blue. Sometimes her tongue hangs out of her mouth. She wears a necklace of human heads and a skirt of human arms. You can imagine the look Kalī has on her face when she is ready for battle. Take a moment to imagine what that might be.

3. Stick out your tongue as far as you can, cross your eyes so that you are looking at opposite sides of your nose, and scrunch up your face so that your mouth reaches the bottom of your nose and you condense the middle of your face. In other words, scrunch up your nose and open your mouth wide so that your top lip is touching the bottom of your nose, or as near as possible. You should see an incredibly fierce look on your face when you uncross your eyes to look in the mirror.

4. Take two shallow breaths. These breaths should be audible and you should take them through your mouth. Remember to huff your throat, making sure to move your shoulders in sync with these short breaths, and also to breathe from deep in your diaphragm or tummy. It is important to inhale and exhale through your mouth for this exercise.

5. On your third inhale, get ready to make some noise by exhaling loudly. This could be accompanied by a scream,

a shout, a loud raspy breathing noise – simply release whatever you need to release and hold that breath as long as possible.

6. Repeat this three to five times. Then allow your tongue to recoil into your mouth, your eyes to uncross, and your face to relax.

You have just channelled the breath of a warrior and allowed your face to reflect your inner world and your inner emotions. And even if this exercise didn't channel your innermost emotions, it has allowed you to express yourself in a way that will enable you to release or shift some of your feelings. This should bring you some relief and it is a practice you can do on your own, in private, whenever you need to relieve the tension of repressing feelings or emotions you feel you cannot show others.

Stress and the Body – A Primer for Disruption

In recent years, our gut has come to be known as our "second brain".[3] We know there is a direct link between our mental state, the signals we send to our gut, and how our digestive system responds in turn. This is why certain conditions we experience as mostly physical symptoms have deep connections to our mental health, which is why there is a growing tendency today to view the body's internal components as being interconnected. Science is beginning to catch up with what spiritual healers have been saying for decades and what traditional medical systems have espoused for centuries. The mind, body, and spirit are deeply connected, which makes sense because they are all part and parcel of the same system.

As our scientific understanding of trauma and its impact on the body has begun to find a language in the physiology of our nervous system health, so specialists who focus on toning the vagus nerve as part of our body's "gut-brain axis" have made inroads into connecting the dots between the gut and brain. The vagus nerve, the longest nerve in our body, is core to our autonomic nervous system and is responsible for transmitting information between our brain, heart, and gut or digestive system. In our parasympathetic nervous system, this nerve controls our immune system, digestive system, and heart rate.

The parasympathetic nervous system is an involuntary system, which means we cannot consciously control it. The parasympathetic and sympathetic nervous systems make up our autonomic nervous system. The parasympathetic system controls the "rest and digest" side of our nervous system, as well as involuntary motor and sensory functions, while the sympathetic nervous system controls the "fight or flight" side of our nervous system, which is responsive to environmental stressors or triggers. Dysregulation of this nerve has therefore been linked to a number of conditions in the body, including general anxiety, acid reflux, irritable bowel syndrome, epilepsy, burnout, and chronic fatigue syndrome.[4] (Quite a few of these are conditions I have suffered with too since my early teenage years. Watching the growth in research on the vagus nerve and gut health has been a salve in my journey to understand and heal my own body.)

The idea of toning the vagus nerve and regulating our nervous systems is not new, but it is becoming more popular. Training programmes such as Jessica Maguire's Nervous System School[5] as well as communities like Science and Nonduality (SAND),[6] which include practitioners, schools of thought, nutritionists, gut specialists, and trauma-informed psychologists, are providing pathways to better understand the nervous system. The vagus nerve's ability to perform its basic functions is central to the body's ability to cope and recover from exposure to trauma and stress, which can lead to chronic conditions that wear on the body in the long term. Our nervous system health is something we can better support and maintain with access to the knowledge, language, and skills that relate to it.

This knowledge of the nervous system, vagus nerve, and gut health coincides with a wider movement that speaks to how we rest, which gets to the core of why we are unwell. Tricia Hersey of The Nap Ministry is a proponent of the healing power of rest as a form of activism, anti-racist learning, and protest against grind culture. Her work as a minister, healer, and researcher has led her to prioritize sleep as a form of healing. With the popularity of books such as Bessel van der Kolk's *The Body Keeps the Score* and Gabor Maté's body of work on trauma and illness, we are collectively gaining a deeper understanding of how grind culture, capitalism, individualism, and hyperproductivity are making us ill. Maté's most recent book, co-written with his son Daniel Maté, *The Myth of Normal*, explores the underlying causes of illness and, you guessed, it is social as much as anything else.

We are living in a time of mental ill-health crises globally. We know that our experience of our health and our bodies is not isolated from our environment. Today, an incredible amount of environmental stressors and factors impact our health   from micro-plastics in the oceans, which contribute to the growth of uterine fibroids,[7] to ecological anxiety impacting the prevalence of anxiety in young people,[8] to the political decisions and current events that have a direct impact on our bodies.

We now know categorically that stress, especially long-term stress, is not good for the body. And we cannot talk about speaking truth to power and disrupting relationships, workplaces, situations, and dynamics without talking about the stress that will be involved. Think of how the tension created in a pulley mechanism by something like a weight can guarantee the perfect harmony necessary for that system to function. However, if the pressure that is holding the weight in place in the pulley system becomes unbalanced, to the extent that the whole system falters and that pressure is suddenly released, this can send everything flying. In a similar way, your moment of disruption will likely create a type of stress that interrupts regularly scheduled programming. Not only will you face resistance from the people involved, but the structure that supports the ways things are (which could be harm or other normalized behaviour) may react like pressure being released explosively from a pulley system – and you find yourself in the line of fire. Regardless of whether it involves a family dynamic, workplace culture, or tight-knit friendship group, the wider dynamics at play in the system will be directly contributing to any stress that is present – precisely because you are trying to change that system. We can experience stress when we experience any type of change, even if it is positive change that we have instigated and which interrupts the regular flow of our lives.

Learning to Listen to Your Body

My experience of poor gut health is directly linked to my extensive experience with anxiety. Anxiety has been my close friend since I was seven years old. I have had nearly three decades to familiarize myself with it and become more comfortable with it. Like any mental state that has an impact on our day-to-day lives, I think anxiety is an emotion that sits on the precipice of the valley of all my other emotions. I have learned to accept that my anxiety is always there to protect me, trying to tell me something; even if it is simply telling me that a situation feels familiar and it is reminding me to take care, given similar situations from my past. I know to take heed of the warning, and not to assume the outcome will be the same as it has been in the past. This takes patience and constant practice. I admit that I am not always good at it, but it is not about perfection.

I have also learned that I may mistake my anxiety for another emotion, because anxiety is such a familiar friend. I am hyperaware of how it looks and feels for me, so my overfamiliarity can cause me to assume it is here for a visit. I may feel anxiety when I am feeling another emotion entirely – like excitement!

There is a fine line between anxiety and excitement. They are close cousins on the wheel of emotion. It is this fine line that is a bit like an adventurer's dream. It is a risky business, but it is an important distinction to be able to make, the difference between anxiety and excitement. As a navigator of your own emotional landscape, you can explore this fine line when you decide to disrupt a situation. Realizing your anxiety is actually excitement could help you navigate the ever-changing waters of your emotions when you choose to disrupt your life. Simply being open to the presence of both emotions during this process may give you some compassion for yourself.

There is a certain amount of adrenaline our body releases when we take a risk and do something that might trigger a fight or flight response. That rush of adrenaline is our body preparing itself to protect itself and do whatever is necessary to survive. Often, after we survive the stressor we will need to learn how to return our body to its window of tolerance. A window of tolerance is an emotional-nervous system safety zone. When we experience stress, depending on its intensity and duration, this can sometimes throw us right out of our window of tolerance. Now, when I have a trauma response, depending on what it is and how activated my body becomes, I am ready to use the tools in my toolbox to bring myself back into my window of tolerance.

Depending on what my baseline stress levels may be, it can nevertheless take me days to get back to my window of tolerance. I can feel agitated, incredibly tired, and frustratingly irritated. I may need to soothe my body with cold water dips or by laying a large, cool crystal on my forehead. I may need to immerse myself in the comfort of nature or move my body in gentle ways outdoors. I may need to watch a familiar TV show that restores a sense of order and regularity, its predictability offering a sense of consistency and balance. I have mentioned earlier that, as an adult survivor of childhood emotional abuse, I have complex PTSD or C-PTSD, which means that states such as hypervigilance, hypoviligance, hyperarousal, hypoarousal, and a number of other fun coping mechanisms are part of my daily life. However, I find these coping mechanisms for my body's responses incredibly useful. I also have a keen intuitive sense of when abuse might be taking place because of my personal history with it in ways that people without this history may not.

For example, I have survived a number of emotionally and psychologically abusive relationships in my adult life because of my childhood history. We sometimes gravitate toward what is familiar, especially if we have lived with that familiarity for a long time. It can be hard to understand what this might feel like if you have never experienced it before. Abuse requires manipulation and concealment to work. Even if it is something we cannot articulate in the moment, I believe it is something we can sense in the body.

Our body is so intelligent. Whether we are aware of it or not, all of these sensations sit in the body. I experience manipulation as a sense of something heavy settling into my upper chest and my throat. I experience its energy as a constricting feeling that makes my throat feel like it is physically closing up. It is a sensation that reminds me of having no voice. Often in these instances, the information I am receiving or the story I am being told does not match up with the reality of the situation, which is the result of manipulation. It feels like wrestling with the reality that the person who is being manipulative is creating and the narrative they are spinning. This in turn warps our ability to express what is happening in the moment and brings us back full circle to the sensation of being unable to speak, which is how I experience manipulation.

A Brief Look at the Chakra System and Auras

According to the concept of the chakras, which originated in the Indian Ayurvedic system, the voice is linked to the throat chakra, a subtle energy centre that is associated with the colour blue and is responsible for self-expression.

Our bodies have several energy centres or chakras in them. The chakra system itself entered mainstream consciousness in the west in the 1970s, when the psychedelic revolution made it ubiquitous. Many aspects of East Asian philosophies made their way to the west through musicians and spiritual seekers who were looking to engage with wisdom traditions to better understand the world around them. The chakra system has remained a permanent part of the spiritual-wellness industries' lexicon.

There are seven chakras that hold our life force energy or *prana* that helps keeps our body's energy regulated. The idea at the heart of the chakras is that our bodies tell us when energy is not moving freely in our system. Our body is made up of energy centres that each chakra sits at the core of. Each chakra relates to aspects of our aura, the field of energy that emanates around us. In the chakra system:

- Your crown or *sahasrara* chakra sits slightly above your head and is purple or violet. This chakra is associated with gold, white, or violet auras. When this chakra is balanced there is a sense of being at peace with the universe and calm in your physical body.
- The third eye or *ajna* is located in the space between your eyeballs and is the indigo chakra. It is also associated with indigo and purple auras. When the third eye is balanced we feel that we are in a state of flow, able to make quick and easy decisions.
- The throat chakra or *vishuddha* is located in the throat, neck, jaw, and mouth region. It is associated with blue auras, and when balanced we can express our desires and thoughts with ease.
- The heart chakra or *anahata* is located at the centre of the chest. It is associated with green or pink auras. When it is balanced we feel compassion for ourselves and others.
- The solar plexus chakra or *manipura* is located at the naval. It is yellow and associated with yellow auras. When this chakra is balanced we feel able to accomplish our goals, set

healthy boundaries, and feel empowered.

- The sacral chakra or *svadhisthana* is located below your belly button. This chakra is associated with intentions and desires is also associated with orange auras. When this chakra is in balance we feel energized about our creativity and able to express our desires.
- The last chakra is the root chakra or *muladhara*, which is located at the base of the spine. It relates to our connection to the earth. It is associated with brown, black, and red auras. When this chakra is balanced we feel emotionally and physically safe, with a sense of being grounded in nature.

As mentioned, the chakra system interacts with the overall energy footprint of your body, your aura, and can influence the colour or appearance of it, depending on how open your chakras are and how balanced your energy is across the different energy centres.

Auras take the form of energy that emanates from our bodies and in many ways maps onto our chakra centres. The aura system has been around for centuries and is referenced in a number of wisdom traditions. Broadly speaking, an aura is a "three-dimensional electromagnetic field that surrounds all living things". [9] We can think of the aura as acting like a fingerprint of light, emotions, and imagery. Some of us are naturally gifted and can read auras from birth. Others study auras to strengthen their ability to pick up on them. As with other clairsenses, people can read or "sense" auras in many different ways – they can even be photographed using Kirlian photography – but the most common way to describe them is through colour, like the chakras are.

Human auras are made up of seven separate layers with distinctive purposes and meanings. An aura is part of your emotional body and wider energy system, which mirrors what is going on inside your body and mind. Therefore, things like imbalances, illness, and stress can impact your aura. Understanding your aura is another way of understanding your energy and learning to cultivate a practice of protecting it. It can also offer an insight into your personality and the personalities of the people around you.

Like the chakra system, each of the seven layers in the aura has its own specific meaning and purpose. Every layer is associated with one of the seven chakras and the more balanced a chakra is, the more the corresponding layer will glow:

- The layer closest to the body is the etheric layer, which corresponds to the root chakra. It presents as grey, white, or light blue in colour.
- Next is the emotional body layer, which corresponds to the sacral chakra. It is the most colourful and can change depending on your mood.
- The third is the mental body layer, which corresponds to the solar plexus chakra. It appears brighter in those who are mentally active.
- The fourth layer is the astral body layer, which corresponds to the heart chakra. It is the layer most connected to the spirit realm and most likely to connect with other people's auras.
- The fifth layer is the etheric template layer, which corresponds to the throat chakra. This layer contains all of the information about your physical body and can be accessible through healing modalities such as sound healing.
- The celestial body layer is the sixth layer and it corresponds to the third eye chakra. It is where you can access your subconscious mind through meditation.
- The etheric template layer is the last layer and it corresponds to the crown chakra. It is said to contain information about your past, your past lives, and your life purpose in this lifetime. It can be accessed through deep meditation.

A number of healing modalities use the chakra system and aura as a means to practise healing and address energy imbalances within the body. By tapping into these energy centres, healing can help shift blocked energy that may be contributing to aches, pains, diseases, and mental illness. Issues with your thyroid, acid reflux, tonsils, and sore throats can indicate a throat chakra imbalance, for example. As a practice at home, you can meditate on the colour related to the chakra (such as blue in the case of the throat chakra) to help shift stuck energy.

Engaging in energy healing work with an experienced healer, using mantras guided by a guru or other spiritual leader of a tradition that utilizes mantras, practising yoga, or doing other somatic (body-based) healing work are other ways to balance the flow of your energy, or chi. In Chinese healing and wisdom traditions, chi or *qi* is the energy of the universe or life force energy that is also inside us. These traditions have their own maps of life force energy for balancing or working with meridian lines, the energy lines that traverse the entire body and connect to energy centres within us.

Working with your chakras, aura, and meridian lines are important ways to bring your body back into balance when you choose to make good trouble. Inevitably, energy disruption interrupts, shifts, and impacts the flow of energies in our own body, too. After all, our own energy bodies are part of the wider energy of our world. They interact constantly with the energy around us. This is why an important part of maintaining our body's health involves maintaining and supporting the flow of our body's energy. You can do this by working with a body worker, exploring meditations that help with chakra energy flow, or engaging in physical movement that helps you keep your chakra centres in balance.

Other Methods of Coping with Tension

During the first UK lockdown in the Covid pandemic, I had a session with a Theta Healer® whom I had trained with and worked with over the years. She is a voice specialist and embodied movement coach, among other things. As well as her special focus on the voice and the throat chakra – which is an area I have been particularly focused on working with to release tension, trauma, generational blocks, and personal blocks about expressing myself or being seen – she also focuses on sensuality and sexuality.

Ironically, a large part of my career has involved public speaking. From my early days at nursery to my first full-time job as President of my students' association, I have always been loquacious. I have never had trouble speaking my mind. However, I internalized messages that limited my self-expression. From a young age, it did not always feel like it was safe for me to voice my needs, be direct, and state the truth – though it was always my instinct. While speaking comes easily to me and I have been known to speak easily off the cuff – I weave narratives quickly, adeptly, and comfortably – I have still had to do a lot of work around my throat chakra.

I mentioned earlier how I used to be in a rock band as a teenager. However, though I loved to sing, I was repeatedly told by a family member that I was tone-deaf and I needed to stop singing. That one comment had a big impact on my self-esteem and relationship to my voice. No matter how often I wrote lyrics for our songs or notes for our music, I would rarely feel comfortable enough to sing outside of band practice. Singing became a point of shame and embarrassment rather than a natural way of expressing myself.

In 2018, I worked closely with the Theta Energy Healer® I mentioned before to gain confidence around my voice. We worked on singing exercises, breathing exercises, and natural movement. All the while, this healer used Theta Healing® techniques to heal my old beliefs systems, generational patterns, and past-life experiences around my voice. I experienced a profound memory of myself in a past life being punished for using my voice to speak up. This past-life memory aligned very closely with my current life experiences. We also explored some traumatic experiences and associations I had growing up that related to my need to perform for others – messages I'd picked up, received, and internalized that I had to perform well in order to have my needs met. I realized that I had learned to put my own needs second. It was by working with theta energy and focusing directly on the body that I was able to resolve some of this. As we have seen, our bodies keep hold of the memory of these events because we experience our psychological world in the physical. We store these memory events in our bodies in ways that are not always in our conscious awareness.

This healer would encourage me to sing in order to channel energy and emotions. But most importantly, because I did a lot of public speaking in my own language, which is as familiar to me as breathing, we practised singing in a language I did not know as well. Portuguese is the native language of my dad's side of the family. Singing in a different language like Portuguese gave me the space to make noises and sounds that I did not associate such a visceral meaning to. When we are open to experiencing our body in ways we would not in our daily lives, when it is making sounds that are unfamiliar to it, or moving in a way it does not traditionally, we can unlock and move energy in ways that are healing.

Our Global Systems and Our Physical Health

We are living in a society that encourages us to overwork. We measure every moment of productivity, and we are required to constantly be switched "on" via the technology we engage with. Scrolling on our devices late into the night is negatively impacting our sleep. The blue light our screens emit is literally messing with our melatonin production, which is negatively impacting our sleep cycles[10] – and we know it, but we all do it anyway. We are constantly striving for more, bigger and better. Many people have been questioning for decades this need to grow constantly and we have plenty of examples of how our societies were organized before the industrial revolution that enabled us to live more slowly.

Lots of us are no longer interested in living in a state of constant burnout, exhaustion, and overwhelm. The growing interest in the gut microbiome, the increase in food intolerances, and the concern about mental health crises that particularly impact men and young people all allude to the evidence that our current ill health is intrinsically linked to the way we now live. We can only opt out of the way we live to a certain extent, because we are of this world, even though in this individualistic society we are encouraged to see ourselves as islands, rather than as part of an interconnected web of relationships, networks, and landmasses that contribute to our collective well-being.

This approach to how we live is entirely cultural and not universal. This individualistic belief system is incredibly modern, incredibly western, and incredibly white. Indigenous people, communities, and belief systems are and always have been deeply interlinked. They work in ways that acknowledge the individual as part of a collective that is whole. This perspective exists in most wisdom traditions across the world. It is as old as time. The cult of individualism that is our current object of obsession is, however, useful to encourage in a society that thrives off competition over collaboration and the notion that some of us can be winners while most of us are losers. This sense of exceptionalism of the few has contributed to so many forms of inequality in our world and it does not seem to be slowing down. In my opinion, this is an entire belief system that we need to disrupt. Will you disrupt it with me for the sake of our collective well-being?

If you seek to disrupt or interrupt a way of being, you need to understand the systems you live within, how they are structured, how the people within them think, and also what the general beliefs are that uphold that system. A system will work to protect itself. It will fight like hell when it is being challenged. As with any organization, family system, group of friends, or romantic partnership, it is important to see this system as a living, breathing organism and entity. It is an animated thing. It has its own energy and it will move in ways to protect itself. That is why when you initially seek to disrupt a system it will act to preserve itself and rid itself of the disruption attempting to change it. Like any other organism, it works to ensure its own survival. So, how do you ensure your own survival in a process that may be acting against you or acting to rid itself of you? You stay grounded, centred, and vigilant.

Self-Care and Community Care

We spend so much time these days talking about self-care that it has become an overused and diluted term or hashtag. The fact is that we all know that we cannot heal or care for ourselves without others. Despite the isolating impact of technology in some respects, we do not live on our own islands. Without the presence of others – others to speak to, others to ask for guidance, and others to hold space for us physically or emotionally – we may have no real way of caring for ourselves. Where would we be without experts who provide services to heal us when we need it, from medical professionals to body workers? We have always lived in community and anything that tries to convince us otherwise is simply an illusion.

Whether we want to admit it or not, we are always living in relationship to others. It could be our animal friends, our neighbours, the person at the local shop selling us our favourite drink, or the person we walk past on a wander down the street. We may not always actively engage with community, and we may find it easier when a community exists around us in such a way that we do not have to go to lengths seek it out – like school or a workplace. But our relationship to community is in our control and we can choose to have community around us, one that we support and nurture in the same way that it supports and nurtures us, in a state of symbiosis.

Over the years, I have been part of and helped shape many communities. I have relied on all kinds of communities in all kinds of settings. These include creative networks, which have enabled me to meet people who have given me work, through to voluntary groups and charities that have created the space for me to experience deep friendship – the kind that only comes when a friendship group has been through some serious "stuff" together. When I was younger, these community groups extended to church nativities and sandwich-making sessions on Friday night as part of a volunteer delivery service to people experiencing homelessness in the city – still one of my favourite things to do. At times, my communities have included groups of friends gathering for "book clubs", which turned into two-hour-long therapy sessions. Other times, community has taken the shape of spiritual groups that I have leaned on in times of deep change. The latter have given me the life-altering experience of connecting with my ancestors. Sometimes, the groups have been formed for specific and temporary purposes, as when I have gathered with people to organize an event. All types of communities apply here. What is important is the camaraderie, mutual understanding, care, and friendship lasted well beyond the moments we came together.

It is our choice to cultivate these spaces by making them happen regularly and holding space for others to gather, being open to meeting new people, or supporting someone else regularly by holding them accountable to their own journey with their care and yours.

Friction as a Pathway to Healing Our Bodies and Minds

Like many people, I have an incredibly complicated relationship with my body. I find it difficult to take my own advice at the best of times. The tension between what we know we should do and what we actually do is a constant point of friction.

When we are in the process of healing, which is a lifelong journey, our trauma is constantly interacting with our healing journey, as well as other people's healing journeys. Sometimes, it is friction that causes change, like the friction used to start a fire or create a spark. It is uncomfortable, and it is not always a successful firestarter, but if we allow the friction to energize the space between how we want to be and how we are, we can move toward an acceptance of what we need. We can also learn to use moments of friction as indicators of what our bodies need.

We know that a complex range of emotions, physical reactions, and psychic reactions can make us feel overwhelmed, as well as the act of disruption itself. By using coping mechanisms that allow us to channel that tension and release it, we can start to learn to accept it as part of being alive. Our ability to hold space for this extreme discomfort allows us to move through tense moments in our lives and enables us to avoid simply absorbing these moments in ways that they get stuck in our bodies. We have the tools we need to cleanse, move, shift, and release this tension. We can apply these to ourselves, our minds and bodies, and to the societies we move in, to rebalance the scales of Justice in ways that are restorative rather than harmful.

11

STANDING IN YOUR INTEGRITY IN THE FACE OF RESISTANCE

Our approach to disruption may change over time depending on our experience with it. For some of us, the more we disrupt the harder it may get, because the stakes can feel higher. We can be more aware of the consequences of our disruption and as a result we may be more hesitant or more intentional when we next disrupt, because we now know what to expect from the process. On the other hand, we may get used to being disruptive and find it easier with time, precisely because we do know what to expect. The process may be clearer, including how to approach it, how people may react, how we may time and word it, and when we decide it is or isn't worth it.

When we become more aware of the shape disruption can take, we begin to realize that we may be disruptive in little ways in many aspects of our lives. It might be that disruption becomes second nature to us, or a large part of our approach to life, because it is more integrated into our worldview as we gain a deeper understanding of our values and what honouring those values regularly looks like.

Standing in our integrity in a world that wants us to stay silent can feel like a daunting task. I often find that when I have been direct with someone about how they are treating me, or have been honest about a manipulative situation, I have to stay strong. There are ways to stay strong gently, with kindness, and with love. I find that setting these intentions when we need to be honest helps direct our energy to be open to whatever comes from our honesty.

Often, my first instinct is to question my experience and my directness, or to allow someone's apology to overshadow how I feel about their behaviour. This is learned behaviour that comes from people-pleasing and the urge to overempathize. Your feelings are always valid, even if they shift once you receive an apology or hear the other person's perspective on what happened.

It is very easy for us to get wrapped up in the shame of a situation or in the shame that somebody else is feeling about how they behaved, particularly if we are very empathetic people. This is where our boundaries come into play. We need to separate out what is ours and what is theirs in terms of what we are picking up energetically from their emotional landscape and what part of this experience is our own emotional response. We have to remember that when people treat us poorly, it is a reflection of how they feel about themselves – because, as we know, we are all mirrors for each other. Also, how somebody interacts with us very likely mirrors how they interact with lots of other people in the world. Our experience may not be unique. Quite often someone's response has very little to do with us, even when it has a direct impact on us.

Very few people are able to admit when they have behaved badly, because of the shame they feel about their behaviour. The idea that they have done so may go completely against their view of themselves. Their perception of themselves as good might be so embedded in their psyche, they cannot admit that – even though they are generally a good person – they have caused harm or behaved badly. Admitting even that tiny amount of wrongdoing to themselves is something they cannot do without imbuing their entire view of themselves with those feelings of shame. Being open to that reality confirms their deep fears of rejection or of being flawed, which can hurl them into a sea of terrible self-talk and nasty self-criticism, so they would rather avoid the risk of this consequence altogether. Taking responsibility for harm you have caused can be deeply unsettling and activate such deep-seated wounds from past experiences that many people will do everything in their power to avoid experiencing those negative feelings again. Often this is automatic and subconscious, so they are not even aware they are doing it.

There will also always be humans who have a different worldview and values system to yours. It is possible that this gives them a feeling of superiority or a special status. Their beliefs may enable them to ignore easily how others experience the ways in which their beliefs impact their general behaviour. They may operate in the world in a manner that means manipulating others to suit their needs seems normal to them. It could be fundamental to their values – for example, success at any cost or ambitions to hack hustle culture. They might undermine the people around them and try to control them. They may talk down to you and the people they surround themselves with, because that is just the way they show up in the world.

And they may see absolutely nothing wrong with this. Their belief systems may enforce their perspective that this is a competitive world and everyone must do what it takes to get ahead. The ends may justify the means for them. They may not be interested in the process or what happens along the way to achieving their goals. They might not realize there is any other way to be. It may be that they have always done whatever is necessary to get ahead. They may not see the casualties of their self-focused behaviour as anything but that: a fallout that is not their responsibility.

This is a way of being that goes against my very being on a cellular level. It is one I have never understood, but it is a way of being that I am intimately familiar with because of the community I grew up in, which was in the midst of the politicos of Washington, DC. Even a city as beautiful and multi-faceted as Washington, DC, is the seat of so much power that it is an environment which breeds this type of behaviour.

Standing in Our Integrity and the Archetype of the Fool

Standing in our integrity requires us to ride the waves of our emotions and those of others, while we use the tools we have worked with in these pages to understand what lies within our control and what is not. As we have seen, it is important to use discernment to cultivate the energy that is ours and to step away from energy that isn't. Can you remember my request for you to cultivate the energy of the Fool at the beginning of this book?

The Fool in the Tarot is the central protagonist in the story of the Major Arcana. The character in this card makes the decision to embark on a journey, acknowledging that they know very little about what lies ahead of them. Their willingness to embark on the journey anyway is represented by the image on the card. The image shows the Fool approaching the edge of the cliff in full knowledge that they are about to walk off of it. This figure has full faith and trust that even if they walk off the cliff they will be ok. It is not even a leap of faith, it is a walk of faith. In other words, this archetype's story suggests that being a fool will enable you take a walk of faith – to be fully present in the choice to embark on a journey that could lead you anywhere. When it comes to walking with integrity, especially after engaging in an act of disruption, having the presence of mind to remain grounded in your choice to journey into the unknown is incredibly empowering.

Learning to Let Others' Foolishness Wash over You

Part of the purpose of this book is to prepare you for the reality of making good trouble. Much of this is about accepting that you will be at the receiving end of many people's feelings. What I mean by this is that a range of emotions could be directed at you as a result of your audacity to challenge things. You might experience the full spectrum of emotions that come with resentment and blame, which include other fun emotions such as shame, embarrassment, anger, rage, and denial. You might be on the receiving end of these emotions, because people will do anything to absolve themselves of responsibility and maintain their sense of reality/safety through self-delusion.

The important thing to remember at all times is that truth is on your side. It may be that you do not experience the justice of truth being revealed in your lifetime, but the people in your working life or relationships who act in ways to cover up their wrongdoings will nevertheless know the truth of the situation. I would like to think that the energetic impact of doing wrong and trying to hide it leaves its mark, because we know the impact harm has on our bodies, our energy, and our relationships.

I am no expert in trauma nor in psychological analysis. Nor am I a spiritual teacher who can comment on the nature of karma and dharma. These conditions of living, life, and the universe have been studied by gurus, lamas, spiritual teachers, and referenced in the teachings of wisdom traditions ranging from Zen koans to yoga sutras. But in my experience, the collective energy of harm does not simply impact a small group of people. If there is toxicity within a relationship, a family unit, a friendship group, a place of work, or a society, we will start to see the impact of it outside of those circles. That toxicity will seep out in the form of dis-ease, un-wellness, and behaviours or belief systems that cause us to deny our humanity. We see this in the nature of our conversations about the state of the world on a regular basis, and we witness the impact of this on our interpersonal relationships, based on the amount of violence that takes place in them.

It is important that we adapt a certain mindset around harm and use tools to return to a place of grounding when harm emerges. The more violent the reaction you receive to naming harm or abuse, the more likely it is that the harm is real, tangible, and that it is being concealed. The harm and abuse become energetically animated as a reaction to your audacity to uncover it. You are experiencing an energetic reaction. This may feel horrible, but remember that this reaction is a way for you to confirm and validate the harm's existence.

A particularly useful way to prepare yourself for dealing with abuse tactics is through learning what the acronym DARVO stands for. It is an acronym you may be familiar with if you have already explored or experienced gaslighting, a form of psychological manipulation in which someone plants the seeds of doubt in another person's mind to avoid their own accountability. "Gaslighting" was the *Merriam-Webster Dictionary* word of the year for 2022, after all.[1]

DARVO stands for Deny, Attack, Reverse Victim and Offender. This sequence describes a common reaction that perpetrators of wrongdoing display "in response to being held accountable for their behaviour".[2] It is also a tactic used by psychological abusers. The embarrassment, shame, or sense of being exposed that an individual may have in relation to the harm they have caused – especially if they feel these uncomfortable emotions are justified – can result in this sequence of behaviour. This acronym is self-explanatory, as these are signs you can look out for when someone is attempting to manipulate you and cast doubt over a situation. Do they deny what they have done? Do they attack you for raising and highlighting it, and do they reverse who is the offender in the situation by making themselves the victim?

An incredibly useful means to combat DARVO is with the grey-rock method. I have only come across this technique recently, but it is a method I have been intuitively using for several years now. (It's fascinating how the mind and body intuitively knows how to respond when under threat.) As the name suggests, in these situations, the idea is to become as uninteresting and disengaged as you possibly can in order to de-escalate the situation. Do not just channel the energy of a grey rock, become a grey rock. This involves showing little emotion, giving noncommittal or one-word responses, showing little vulnerability, keeping your personal information private, and my all-time favourite, minimizing contact.[3] Ultimately, the aim is for the other party to lose interest and mind their own business. It is not always effective, but that has less to do with the method and more to do with the person you are employing it on. Which takes us on to our next exercise – of learning to mind our own energy, like these abusers should.

Minding Your Own

I have mentioned before that I am a recovering people-pleaser and perfectionist. I was raised in a world where love was conditional and the only way I could receive what I needed from an early age was by being hypersensitive to pleasing others. Whether by being agreeable or behaving in other ways that were expected of me, I was constantly on the alert for possible criticism if I did not do exactly as I was told.

This is often a gendered experience for many women and non-binary people growing up in a world dominated by men. Our existence is often only desired for, and validated by, our ability to serve and please. In abusive or harmful dynamics, being pleasing and pleasing your abusers – especially when they are your caregivers or you are reliant on them – becomes a form of survival. You learn to do this on such a subconscious level that sometimes you may not even realize that people-pleasing is, or has been, your modus operandi.

When you are living with constant gaslighting, you begin to question your own reality. This also impacts and can become enmeshed with your self-esteem or how you see yourself. When you are forced to care what others think in order to ensure your basic survival, it is unsurprising that you might become hypervigilant about the opinions of people around you. It takes time to unlearn this. This process of unlearning and learning to care less about what other people think can be a powerful, long, and daunting but liberating process. It provides you with much-needed perspective. Tending to your self and your own life is a very important part of this process. This is where affirmations can be very helpful. A mantra that I love to return to is this one:

What others think about me is not my business.

This isn't about cutting yourself off – we saw in chapter 10 how we cannot live in isolation – but about reclaiming your sense of self.

A PRACTICE FOR SELF-AFFIRMATION

This exercise is about using a set of affirmations that will allow you to counteract gaslighting and affirm your own being and existence, especially when your integrity is being called into question for doing the right thing. If you find yourself doubting whether or not standing up to an abuse of power was worth it, this exercise is definitely for you. You can do these affirmations on your own when the outer world gets quiet and your inner critic gets loud.

1. Take yourself to a quiet place where you can be alone. It might be useful to choose a location where you can make some noise, such as a spot tucked away outdoors where you feel comfortable and won't be overheard. Or this could be as simple as closing your eyes and focusing inward, once you have familiarized yourself with the affirmations that I am going to be sharing with you.

2. I want you to repeat some phrases to yourself. You can repeat them silently or out loud. It is important to say these phrases to yourself, not just skim-read them. Let yourself savour and absorb every word to quiet your inner critic and affirm these statements. This is how they work their magic.

3. Repeat these phrases as many times as you wish:

I am standing in my integrity and power.

I speak out when I witness or experience harm.

I know that the path to healing is addressing harm and hurt.

I am standing in the power of truth.

I am a facilitator of justice.

What others think of me is not my business.

I am my own and my opinion of myself is what matters.

I live by my values and I make choices that help me live my values out loud.

I am grateful for the support the universe gives me for doing what I feel is right.

The universe is on my side and has my back.

If I need help, I will ask for it.

If I need support, I will seek it.

I am not alone and I am held up by the many people who came before me and who were not silent when they witnessed injustice.

I believe that what I have done is right.

I continue to stand in my integrity and stand by my word.

I focus on what is in my power and how that power has the ability to transmute anything for positive change.

I know the power of making good trouble.

My energy will protect me.

I am always protected.

Once you are familiar with them, you could make it a daily or weekly practice to recite these affirmations just before or shortly after a nap. (I find I am either crankiest or the most hopeful about my life choices just after a good nap in the middle of the day. It depends on which side of the bed I wake up on!) Or you can practise them when you have just woken up in the morning; choose a time when you are feeling refreshed.

Trusting the Path of the Fool

In the Tarot, the Fool is known as a character courageous enough to follow their own path and, when called for, to break the rules. Rules can be tricky for us to challenge because they are made to be followed. Our understanding of rules may vary, based on our relationship to them throughout our lives. I grew up with a mother who often told me rules were made to be broken, but she also told me to do what she said, not what she did. I have only ever followed rules if I believed they were justified or made sense, and I would also follow rules that had been made collectively and agreed upon by whatever group I was part of. While I have always followed rules intended to keep me and others safe, I have struggled with those authority figures who expected me to follow them blindly, even if they were my seniors or somehow responsible for guiding me. If they did not seem trustworthy, or they demanded my compliance, or did not earn my trust, I would find it very difficult to respect them. Moreover, if they didn't have an ability to engage with the questions I had about whatever we were doing together, I would have trouble listening to them at all.

My relationship to rules was cultivated at a young age thanks to the philosophy of Maria Montessori, which I touched on earlier in chapter 8. Montessori's philosophy for schooling and engaging with the world was based on critical thinking and curiosity. We were taught to question everything and form our own opinions about the world. Rules were there to be understood, challenged, and questioned. They were not always static, they could change and be renegotiated for good reason. We were taught that a rule should never be followed blindly or simply because it exists. We should always ask ourselves, "What is this rule's purpose?" Is it to separate or protect? Is it there to maintain order or provide guidance? Is it fair or based on harmful assumptions? What does this rule seek to achieve?

If we never questioned rules in society nor questioned our relationship to rules in general, then we would be abandoning one of our best skills – to engage in critical thinking to order to make decisions for ourselves. What is your own relationship to rules? Do you feel you can break them, bend them, adapt them, or do you always follow them to the letter?

The whole notion of being a fool for life – that is, being willing to experience life like a fool, with the openness that naïveté brings and hopefulness that ignorance breeds – is that we are then able to try anything with very few qualms, reservations, or inhibitions. Ideas of what is right, proper, socially acceptable, and how we are supposed to behave are things we do not stop to consider. The unformed nature of a fool is like a mound of clay ready to be formed, ready to be influenced; the fool is ready to take risks that might have permanent consequences.

To use another metaphor that fits with the image of the wandering Fool – it's like a new pair of shoes, made to be worn and to tread through dirt. The knowledge that the shoes may be permanently marked, scuffed, or ruined makes their newness all the more exciting. The possibility that they will be damaged only brings an anticipation of what is to come – for the shoes are about to serve their purpose, and be marked in the process of memory-making. The mark-making itself is part of the journey and part of the beauty of wearing them. This is what they are made for. (Unless, of course, you are a sneakerhead and the shoe's aesthetics are more important; in which case their purpose is to be admired and maintained.)

Finding Your Own Way by Channelling the Energy of the Fool

As I mentioned, finding our own way was a big part of the Montessori journey for me as a child. Being encouraged to be kind and care for the world was a significant part of the worldview cultivated at my Montessori school. Bugs were never killed, they were simply let outside. We kept many pets indoors too. We learned American Sign Language and we learned to plant things in the garden. We learned to share and to address conflict head-on when there was any friction with other students. We were also supported to cultivate our own inner worlds.

Montessori School is based on a set of core principles. I am not a specialist in educational pedagogy, but I can comment on the impact those principles had on me. First off, I learned the lesson to be kind and, second, the lesson to question everything. We were sent off to explore the world on our own, albeit within safe boundaries and within our community. I remember my shoelace coming undone and instead of my teacher tying it for me, she gave me a diagram showing me how to tie my own laces. There were some rules like the golden rule of treating others how you want to be treated. There was also some structure; there was a time to eat and a time to go outside to move our bodies. We would come together for certain group activities, but otherwise you were encouraged to go at your own pace and in your own time.

It may be that my inner world already included a set of values that aligned with Montessori School teachings or it could be that my values were informed by those early years. Either way, these values have followed me through my life and influenced my interactions with my parents, my neighbours, and how I grew up. However I acquired them, they have continued to serve me – although, like any values, they are flexible and have grown with me. If you look at where you are in your own life now, it may seem obvious that some of your values have similarly diverged from where you first set out – and that is ok.

Trusting that we are on our own paths and letting our paths guide us is fundamental to the path of a disruptor. A path that enables us to support the achievement of justice that rebalances abuses of power, that questions authority that does not have any legitimacy, that holds others accountable for their poor behaviour, and that seeks to be restorative rather than punitive is a righteous path. A path that seeks to create space for complexity, healing, and imagination – that allows us to dream up an image of the world that is a safer, more sustainable place – requires us to believe that very world exists. The path to this future requires us to do some difficult things. We need the courage to face what lies ahead of us.

Jessica Dore talks about the journey of the Fool in relation to rule-governed behaviour, which she describes as behaviour we choose and the actions we take as a result. This is not about behaviour based on what is right, but based on things like social reinforcement and an avoidance of discomfort. She talks about how rules followed without question can trap us and how we need to question more often why we do the things we do. We need to question our desire for things to feel good all of the time, for example. The Fool has the courage to ask the questions needed, even if the questions they ask are seen as foolish. We can all be fools for the sake of satisfying our curiosity – and our curiosity is a great tool for resistance.

We can be fools in our choices and also in who we associate with. We can be led by the false gods of likeability. When we are so wrapped up in our environment, rather than questioning the principles of that environment, it is easy for us to act out of our integrity. Is being liked more important to you than treating others with care and challenging systems that harm? If that is the case then this is not the path for you.

It is very easy for us to choose to be included, to be liked, and not to stand out in order to be accepted by the people around us. We are social beings and more often than not we want to be included. Otherwise, life can feel like a long and lonely journey. However, although the path of the disruptor can involve frequent rejection, it allows us to create space for fellow disruptors or people who align with our values. It has the capacity to help us create space for deep acceptance, love, and support. When we understand which environments are not for us and let go of trying to be included in them, we make space for this. I believe that by understanding what is not for us, we better understand who is for us. The people who genuinely align with our values are seeking us, too, and the world we want to live in, in the future. This journey takes courage and involves the risk of walking alone, but rest assured that you will not walk alone forever.

12

UNDERSTANDING WHAT IT MEANS TO TAKE A STAND

It would be disingenuous of me to start rattling off a list of famous activists and whistle-blowers who I believe have had a massive impact on the world as we know it. We can thank the labour movement for eight-hour work days, vacation days or holiday leave, sick days, and weekends, for example. We can acknowledge the suffragettes for their tireless work in fighting for women's suffrage and the right to vote, which women in many countries only got surprisingly recently. It was the Unionists and suffragettes in the north of England who paid for Frederick Douglass's freedom from slavery. Later, Ida B Wells worked in the north of England to help the abolitionist movement all over the world. It was freedom fighters and activists who fought the horrible rule of Jim Crow in the American South alongside activists such as Martin Luther King Jr. and Malcolm X, who pushed for civil rights in the United States. Today, it is activists such as the members of Extinction Rebellion who have highlighted to the mainstream media the urgency of reducing our global temperature rise to at least 1.5°C to prevent human extinction. There have been countless movements all over the world – from the Zapatistas in Mexico to multiple waves of feminist revolution, the most recent occurring in Iran – that signify our world is and has always been ready for change, change through the energetics of disruption.

Disruption and the World

In the Tarot, the World card represents a number of things. Traditionally, it is a card that portrays absolute reality. In other words, it represents the nature of the universe and the cycle of life. It is mercurial in nature, erratic, and shifts quickly. The Rider–Waite–Smith image depicts a woman surrounded by a wreath, which in some decks is an ouroboros (or snake swallowing its tail) and symbolizes infinity among other things. She is watched by four creatures – the heads of an eagle, an ox, a lion, and a man – which represent the natural world. Another way of thinking about this card is that it represents the acceptance and the complexity of "conflicted truths", which is a useful concept to unpack if we are to become effective disruptors.[1]

It can be incredibly challenging to live in a world that is constantly changing and constantly in flux. Yet those of us that are comfortable with uncertainty, change, and the fluidity of things know that there is no ultimate truth. Commentators have suggested that we live in a post-truth society – that no information can be trusted because it cannot be easily verified. We also hear the phrase "speak your truth" regularly. The nature of "truth" and "reality" is subject to who is experiencing it.

As an example, let's say we all experience an event. It could even be a film we see at the same time. If you were to ask anyone else what they thought of the film, what it was about, and what they noticed, you might receive as many different answers as the number of people you approach. It is the same principle as the Indian parable of the group of blind men who encounter an elephant. When they are asked to describe it through touch, they all give different responses. They are all correct. They are each describing the elephant, they are just describing different parts of it. They are describing several aspects of the whole.

If we are to zoom out, keeping the World card in mind, how can we apply this principle to our experience of the truth – to our various lived experiences? Like the three Cs (which I talk about later, on page 217), the truth is often uncomfortable, unclean, and inconvenient, because it is not always consistent, especially when we are seeking the truth from many different perspectives. We need to be prepared for this in our journey with disruption. Having your own truth does not rule out, overshadow, or negate another account of the truth. These truths can all exist at once.

Disruption is Not Easy – But It is Worth It

It can be easy to understand disruption on this sort of global scale and to think of disruption as a necessary part of social change; however, when we think of disrupting our own lives by having difficult conversations, being honest with ourselves, and honing our intuition to be able to tap into our needs, values, and the subtle messages given at any moment from our bodies – this is not so easy. It takes courage and it takes knowing ourselves. It also takes a willingness for things to be messy and to invite chaos into our lives.

It also takes awareness and discernment. It is one thing to support the #MeToo Movement, which was started by American activist Tarana Burke – and made popular by white Hollywood actresses, who appropriated the hashtag to pull focus on a movement they still get credit for today, but which Tarana is barely credited for. It is another to actively encourage protestors to put themselves in harm's way through taking direct action, like Extinction Rebellion do, without necessarily thinking through the implications of how some people risk facing police brutality more than others do. Following that kind of directive, Black people or people of colour could take risks that result in the loss of their lives. It is even easier to repost the horrible story about the disappearance of Sarah Everard without thinking twice about reposting pleas to find the many lesser-known young Black or indigenous women who disappear daily in the UK, North America, and all over the world. These women are literally never found again, because their cases are not prioritized by the police nor by our own public interest, resulting in unsolved cases and non-existent media attention.

What I am getting at is that it is easy to be disruptive when it is not too inconvenient for us to be so – and it is even easier when it is trendy. When there is a collective interest in being disruptive, it becomes about going along with the flow of the status quo. It can be easier to do things en masse, because there is little to no resistance. The hard part is doing things when no one else is speaking up and when the risk you take requires you to go against the grain of the collective consciousness. The stakes are higher because you are one of the few people taking that risk.

It is much harder to speak up when no one else dares to, when no one else believes you, and when you believe the abuse you have experienced has only happened to you. Chances are that you are not alone, because it is statistically more likely that you are not the first nor the only person to experience this. Yet harm continues to be perpetuated in environments where it is normalized and where people choose to ignore it, either out of fear or because they simply cannot be bothered to intervene. It takes them too far away from their comfort zone to do anything about it. They think it is simply not their problem. We have seen this phenomenon manifest itself as bystander syndrome – when a number of people witness a crime from a safe distance, and everyone else believes another witness will do something about it, so ultimately nothing is done to stop the harm from continuing, nor does anyone report the crime.

It can be even more challenging to disrupt your life when what you are disrupting is the terrible behaviour, bad habits, and the harmful silence you experience from the people closest to you. This may involve a family member who is respected by the wider family unit, but who rules by fear. Their power grows because they isolate each member of the family at whom the harm is directed. They continue to get away with it because everyone lives in fear and in silence, turning a blind eye to the abuser's behaviour. The reason no one speaks out may be justified in the moment. It is a form of self-protection. But once it is safe to intervene, do other members of the family unit try to stop the harm? This type of silence from witnesses to harm is a form of complicity: even if their reasons are complex, they are enabling the harm to continue because they are taking no steps to name it, stop it, or interrupt it.

It is always worth disrupting harm, because harm thrives in silence and it heals out in the open, writ large, for everyone to see. Even if those causing harm refuse to acknowledge it and refuse to redress the harm they have caused, acknowledging it by speaking about it is a healing balm. It helps right the path of the energy being misdirected to hurt and it helps the healing process begin.

It has only ever been through speaking about the things I never wanted to speak about, nor thought to speak about, that I have found validation, love, support, and healing in a shared experience of surviving harm. We humans are social beings. This is not news. We exist in community; even if we feel isolated and think we should stay away, we heal better together. We cannot do things in complete isolation, especially the hard things – if we try to go it alone, we will not make it.

Disruption and Lessons in Love

I had a neighbour called Earl when I was growing up. He lived directly across the street with his wife, whom I rarely saw beyond a wave here or there as she was going into her house. She was polite, but distant. I spent many a day in Earl's driveway, listening to him talk about the weather, the car he was restoring, and just telling jokes. As a little one, I could barely see over the hood of the car he was working on.

I lived across the road from him from the time I was born until I was about 11 years old. Earl was someone I loved dearly. I still do. It was not until years later that I learned Earl and his wife, Eva, had a daughter also named Brianna who passed away at a very young age. It was too difficult for his wife to interact with me and to spend time with her little neighbour, who was not only her daughter's namesake, but was about the same age as her own little one would have been if she were alive. I did not know this at the time, nor did I take her distance personally; she was nice enough to me, but I did sense that my time with Earl was precious to him for a reason I could not quite name.

I did not know about or understand their grief until I was invited into their house for the first time for a glass of lemonade. Before I went inside their house, I dutifully walked back across the street to ask my parents if it was ok, and they told me to go ahead as long as I didn't impose myself on the couple for too long. I remember walking into the house and immediately seeing photos of their daughter on the fireplace mantel. I could feel a thickness in the air and a steadiness to it that I had never experienced in a house before. It was grief I was feeling in the air – like the energy around them did not move. It was almost stagnant, and somewhere deep inside my little heart I suspected what had happened, though I was not able to speak a word of my suspicions or process any of this information until I was older. I made sure not to stay too long and continued to spend time with Earl in the front yard. I could sense that maybe my presence in their house, which was once the abode of their little one, may have been too much.

Nevertheless, this type of disruption to Earl and Eva's life was positive. It was unexpected. It took making choices and it was intentional. It required interrupting the status quo of their lives, the routines they had created to protect themselves, and it required them to choose to be curious – to choose once again to love (or to show it, as I am convinced it is not something they ever stopped doing). It required them to be brave in their grief and to choose the uncertainty of opening their home and their lives to their young neighbour across the road. It is a form of disruption that I will always be grateful for and a relationship that not only taught me the importance of knowing your neighbours, but showing them your love and care.

Part of allowing ourselves to disrupt others and be disruptive is about allowing ourselves to dream, to imagine, and to work toward building a vision for the world we want to live in. We also have to envision who we will be in that future world and future place; which version of ourselves, if not the person we are already.

I believe that artists and creative people are among the world's most positive disruptors. I've mentioned them before, in the context of getting comfortable with grey areas, as they are the visionaries who are most comfortable with being uncomfortable and most familiar with being uncertain. I am not saying it is any easier for them than it is for anyone else, but they continue to put themselves into uncertain spaces, with unfamiliar paths to the future. They experiment with different ways to tell stories; they use their art to process their emotions; and they live and understand the world through their work. They show us what we need to pay attention to and hold up a mirror to the details of our lives that we are missing or the details that we may take for granted. They dare to ask the question "why?" again and again. An artist is always asking why in an infinite number of ways. Artists hold on to their need to feel this world, rather than constantly think their way logically through it.

An artist is not motivated to work to make money. For some, that might be part of their artistic process, they have to eat and live like everyone else, but they are making work for many reasons – sometimes it is just for the sake of it. They have to make it. They cannot ignore their need, their urge, to create as a fundamental part of their existence. It is an urge they do not deny. If we all approached life with the same amount of curiosity, wonder, acceptance of uncertainty, and a willingness to disrupt ourselves – to change course, to start again, and to see nothing as a failure (unless it is valuable to see it that way), but rather as a redirection – then we would be enjoying much more fulfilling, true-to-our-desires lives.

Disruption and the Three Cs of Behaviour Change

An academic who specializes in pro-environmental behaviour, Elizabeth Shove published a journal article that later became a book called *Comfort, Cleanliness and Convenience* in 2003, in which she considers the conditions that prevent people from changing their behaviour to be more positive toward their environment.[2] This is a work I have never forgotten and I quote regularly. When I was a sustainable development student, Shove's research helped me put into words something I had suspected: the existence of a resistance to change, which I did not know how to work against in the fight to stop the climate crisis. It was deeply frustrating. Her work gave me some hope and the language to explore this by affording me a deeper understanding of the psychology of the human condition.

In her book, she introduces us to the concept of the three Cs: comfort, cleanliness, and convenience. Her theory is that if something is not comfortable, clean, or convenient, we simply will not do it. Why would you inconvenience yourself recycling an object when it is more convenient just to throw it away? For example, why would you choose to refill your laundry detergent if you have to take the old laundry detergent bottle, wash the sticky solution off it, carry it to a refill shop and risk getting the sticky liquid all over your hands as you refill it, and then wipe off the bottle, which might leak while you're carting it home? It is a messy process. It's inconvenient and uncomfortable. It requires more effort, more time, more thought, and more planning to execute this more sustainable way of buying laundry detergent than simply going to the shop and purchasing a new, dry, clean, full plastic bottle on the way home. For Shove, the three Cs were the answer.

When we think about the three Cs in relation to our avoidance of disruption, we can apply them here, too. It is incredibly uncomfortable to speak up about a harm or injustice you have experienced or witnessed. It may create conflict. It might be extremely challenging to do on your own, because you have to draw attention to yourself in a way that you would not normally do. The outcome of you raising this issue might result in some very uncomfortable discussions at best and extreme consequences at worst. When you think about how messy all of it could be – when you could be simply getting on with life without any added complications – the second C might reinforce why you do not want to do this.

When it comes to convenience, disruption takes effort. It takes research. It takes planning and it takes biding your time. Occasionally, it might be spontaneous or instantaneous. It all depends on the situation, but sometimes the most sinister and difficult harm to interrupt is the harm that is steady, systematic, consistent, and regular. It is harm that goes unnoticed. It is barely perceptible and sits under the radar. Disrupting this form of harm requires us to trust our gut and our intuition. It requires us to hone our psychic senses. It requires us to follow a trail of information that may not be fully formed, nor readily available. It requires us to wade through the muck and messiness of our relationships to try to get to the truth. It requires us to be uncomfortable, inconvenienced, and to get messy.

Understanding Conflicting Truths While Honouring Your Own

When it comes to the notion of conflicting truths and the nature of reality, we must honour our own truth without discounting another. It is important that we practise standing in the integrity of our truth and making choices to honour this reality. This notion of integrity can feel quite inaccessible, lofty even – as if integrity is a word uttered by an action hero, rather than something we can work toward maintaining. But when we are out of our integrity, we often cause ourselves harm. We make ourselves smaller by compromising our values to accommodate someone else. There is nothing inherently wrong with accommodating others, but as we discussed earlier, where we do not feel emotionally safe around them, or they impose themselves or their values on us, we risk compromising in ways that take us out of our integrity. They might not be aware of what they are doing, but it is our job to make them aware. Saying what needs to be said, in order to act as a living embodiment of our values and what we feel is right, is fundamental to living a life with integrity. Also, how often do we need to remind ourselves that heroes are not infallible and that perfection is unattainable? We should not hold ourselves to unachievable standards, but we can aspire to model good intentions.

It goes without saying that our own truth may be in conflict with, in contrast to, and diametrically different from that of the people we are around. We live in in a world where it is easier for us to stay in our own bubble of the truth, with our own preferences on food, music, and what we watch. We can curate everything to our own tastes. It might feel like our truth is one of many in a collective pool of lived experiences.

What do those different truths mean for our energetic interactions with other people? It is incredibly important to remember to attune ourselves and our clairsenses to pick up on any information that may not be expressed physically, but communicated to us psychically. When we are learning how to receive this information, it is also important to remember those who have come before us. They did this, so it is possible. We have archetypal messages to model from figures we revere which exist in many wisdom traditions.

The courage to do what we believe is right and the courage not to be liked are two important virtues to cultivate. When we remember what true leadership looks like, we can remind ourselves what it is not. We can be inspired by all of the examples of leadership we do not want to aspire to – and choose the opposite. We can remind ourselves to let go of our creations when it is time and to understand where our skills lie, while we appreciate where others might be better placed to support our visions for the future.

We must always be led by our values and take the time to remind ourselves constantly of what those values are. By creating space to check in with ourselves frequently on what our values are, while allowing the room for them to shape-shift in the future, we build a better and more authentic relationship with our self. We can then make informed choices about when we disrupt and when we choose to walk away from a situation, or when we would rather provide support to others navigating the depths of their own disruption. When we feel we must interrupt the status quo to help build a fairer and more just world for the communities of which we are part, we know that disruption is the way forward.

By understanding the true impact of disruption and how this can affect our relationships, our sense of self, and our relationship to our life more widely, we can be better prepared for the impact of choosing to disrupt our lives. We can then think about and make choices about anything else we need to disrupt in our lives, such as if we are living out of alignment with our values in our relationships, interactions, and the various spaces where we spend our time. We also understand how to rebuild after the inevitable change that disruption brings and how to minimize the impact on our bodies in the aftermath of choosing to disrupt our world. We remember that we always heal in community and we can make choices to support our body, our nervous system, and all aspects of our health while we go through this transformation process.

Last, we begin to cultivate a relationship to what standing in our integrity feels like and the choices we need to make to maintain it. This enables us to continue to build on an ethic that, in turn, allows us to support others to live ethically, and, even more importantly, cultivate a world that our future self will thank us for.

A PRACTICE FOR
INSIGHT AND DECISION-MAKING

Part of the process of understanding what it means to take a stand involves envisioning the world you want your future self to live in. To that end, the first part of this exercise invites you to envision your future self and make decisions on their behalf. However, if thinking about your future self is not how you would like to approach this sort of work, you could try the second version of this exercise instead, in Part 2 below. This second part of the exercise will hopefully allow you to meet your higher self. Unlike your future self, this self is your spiritual self, the part of you that is eternal and infinite. Your higher self has the wisdom of multiple lifetimes and an infinite relationship to the divine and the universe.

Part 1

1. Sit or stand where you will not be disturbed. Take a moment to breathe deeply. Take three deep breaths and allow your inhale to be as long as your exhale. If you like, you can count to six or eight on the inhale, hold your breath for a moment, exhale and then hold your breath for the same amount of time.

2. Once you have grounded your breath, if you can, please remove your shoes and socks. Take a moment to plant your feet on the ground and imagine them deeply rooted in the earth. This moment of touch – connecting your body to the ground – is an important rooting process. Even if you are not outside or able to touch the ground with your feet, you can imagine the coolness or the heat of the floor beneath you, whatever you prefer. Feel or imagine its smooth or textured surface. Allow

yourself to feel held by the ground and reassured by the surface underneath your feet.

3. Next, I want you to imagine your future self. I know this might feel like a tall order, but I hope the practices we have been exploring throughout this book will make this process a little bit easier. You can choose a future self that is five years away, ten years away, or just a few months away (especially if you find yourself in a situation that makes it difficult to visualize what might be in your future – that is ok too).

4. Can you envision a few things that this future self might be doing? If you were to imagine what your life might be like, who might be around you, and what this future you might be like – what would the world around you look like, feel like, taste like, smell like, and sound like?

5. Imagine making a decision from your future self's perspective; use the next few prompts to explore what might . . .
   – inspire your future self
   – embolden your future self
   – make your future self feel hopeful
   – protect your future self
   – support your future self
   – enable your future self to look back with the certainty that you did what was right.

6. Taking your answers to these prompts or any other future visioning, dreaming, or imagining you have done with your future self in mind, think about how you might create a future that helps you move toward the version of yourself that you have just been exploring.

Part 2

7. Take a deep breath and imagine yourself outdoors in an environment you love. You can see yourself in a forest, on a snowy peak, near a waterfall, on a beach or anywhere else that comes to mind. Do not overthink this; let you mind guide you to where you want to be in the natural world.

8. Clear your mind and allow yourself to take deep breaths, then invite your higher self to show itself. You may see your higher self as a beam of light, you may experience your higher self as a feeling, or you may see a full figure in front of you that is your higher self.

9. Invite your higher self to make itself known to you. You can ask it to appear in front of you or ask it specific questions (or both).

10. As you breathe deeply, notice different aspects of your higher self. If it presents itself to you as a certain colour, take note of that colour. If it engenders a certain feeling, remember the feeling. If it has certain physical characteristics or is holding particular items, pay attention to those. If it is embodied in human form, is it wearing certain clothes?

11. Your higher self is a part of you that you can access at any point for wisdom, insights, and comfort. If you create space to revisit this place in your mind, sit in a meditative state, and welcome your higher self in, you will always be able to access this wisdom.

12. Thank your higher self, and come out of your visualization.

13. Take a moment now to think about what you encountered during your visualization exercise. It is very useful to reflect on any colours, object, textures, clothing, feels, sounds, and smells you encountered. If you are curious, it may be worth looking up the meaning of some of these objects and items. Do they have special meaning to you? Is there something you encountered during this visualization that you have encountered before, or that you are curious about? It is always valuable to look up the meaning of certain colours or imagery you may have encountered, like animals or plant-life, and also to think about any messages that your higher self passed on to you during this visualization.

14. If you have a journal or a space in which you like to take notes, please spend a few minutes writing down everything you remember from the visualization. It can be useful to return to these notes to reflect on any messages you've received. Sleeping on this experience may also reveal further information, as our minds take time to process whatever appears in our psyches. It is also important to drink plenty of water afterwards, as this will help you process the experience, too.

This practice is a space you can always return to and as you develop a relationship to your higher self, as well as beginning to form a picture of your future self, you can begin to make clearer decisions. These decisions will help you take baby steps toward the future you want to shape for yourself. When you need more clarity on a situation or a decision, you can take a deep breath and return to this visualization space. Here, you can ask your higher self questions directly to help you discern what to do. Listen gently and give your higher self enough time to respond to you. The response may come in the form of symbolism, colours, and dreams rather than as fully formed sentences. If you are in doubt or you want some support, you can always ask your higher self and then check if this decision allows you to move toward the future you want for yourself.

Flowing with Change

Like our higher self, the nature of disruption is mercurial – it can be hard to define and difficult to describe. Though the essence and deep truth of who we are may stay the same throughout our lives, the details may shift. Just as we can use our discernment to identify the deep truths behind people's intentions, we need to continue to practise discernment to pick up on the subtleties of the changes in our environment. In order to know who intends to cause harm and who seeks to prevent harm, we have to use discernment to know the difference between what is truth and what is deception. It is important for us to pay attention, because it can all be a little hazy.

In ancient Roman mythology, Mercury is a winged messenger who can often wreak havoc on communication. The originator of the term mercurial, Mercury is a planet in the astrological lexicon that is in retrograde a few times a year. During this, we can experience breakdowns in communication, disruptions in short-term travel, mistakes in our diaries, glitches in our technology, and lapses in communication. But, at the same time, this retrograde helps us pull focus on what needs our attention. Are we communicating clearly? Are we overscheduling our diaries, have we backed up our devices to the server, and are we trying to move too much too often? This time can remind us that we need to hone the skills that allow us to manage mercury-ruled aspects of our lives, which include our words and how we communicate, and the small but important details of our lives.

We start to ignore the finer details of our life to avoid making the changes we need to make to them. We may stay in relationships, friendship groups, family dynamics, and in jobs, because this seems easier than leaving them. It is the path of least resistance, but ultimately, by choosing to avoid resistance we risk building a life that becomes so bolstered by the decisions we do not want to make that we end up resisting the life we do want, by default. We must pay attention to who around us is reinforcing this behaviour because it benefits them for us to stay the same and our decision to make a change threatens their sense of security. Are they are working toward creating a world that reflects the world you want to live in? A world that favours justice, collaboration, harm reduction, and fairness, or are they simply serving themselves?

It is always the choices we make that define our lives. By choosing a life that allows us to take a path of least resistance, we may trick ourselves into thinking we are living a life of peace. But nothing is less peaceful than living a life that requires you to be dishonest with yourself, about yourself and to others. When we suppress our greatest needs and desires by trying to accommodate everyone around us – taking less of a risk to be seen, heard, respected, and loved – we lose the opportunity to truly connect with the people around us. Our desires for happiness, satisfaction, and genuine ease come with taking risks to truly give ourselves a chance to be fulfilled.

Ultimately, you choose your life. You may try to convince yourself that it is easier to live a life with as little disruption as possible, but the fact is that you might choose to disrupt your life precisely to minimize drama, harm, and guarantee peace. If this is the path you choose after reading this book, then I am so grateful to you. Take a chance, embrace everything that life has to offer, and remember in the process to make good trouble.

NOTES

Preface

1 Nicholas, Chani, "Week of October 31st", Astrology of the Week Reading/Podcast, CHANI App.

2 In astrology, the South and North Nodes (also known as the Lunar Points or Nodes of Destiny) are celestial points that relate to the gifts we bring with us into this lifetime and the new directions in which we take these. The North Node is often related to skills or themes we are cultivating in our lives, while the South Node relates to things we want to release. Our South Node often sits in a zodiac sign whose traits we have mastered or aim to master in this life. In other words, the North Node is where you are "insatiable" and the South Node is a point of "surrender". Read more online at: https://chaninicholas.com/north-node-and-south-node-placements-in-chani-app/

Introduction

1 Dore, Jessica, *Tarot for Change: Using the Cards for Self-Care, Acceptance, and Growth*, Hay House, Carlsbad, 2021, p.36.

2 Greene, Liz, foreword in A E Waite, *The Original Rider Waite: Key to the Tarot*, Rider Books, London, 1993, p.ix.

3 Waite, *Key to the Tarot*, p.38.

4 Dore, pp.3–4.

5 Waite, *Key to the Tarot*, pp.6–7.

6 Dore, p.10.

7 It is worth noting as an aside that the Tarot cards also exist independently from one another, and the Fool has nothing to do per se with the querent, i.e. the person receiving a reading.

8 Waite, A E, *The Original Rider Waite: The Pictorial Key to the Tarot, An Illustrated Guide,* Rider Books, London, 2021, p.125.

9 Dore, p.23.

10 Waite, *Pictorial Key to the Tarot,* p.125.

11 Ibid, p.124.

12 Dore, p.22.

13 Waite, *Key to the Tarot,* p.152.

14 Waite, *Pictorial Key to the Tarot,* p.121.

15 Waite, *Key to the Tarot,* p.119. Note: the Strength card, whose order A E Waite switched without explanation with the Justice card, normally the eighth card in a Tarot deck, is a card meaning fortitude. To Waite, this card signifies a "connection with the Divine Mystery of Union" in one of its most "exalted aspects". (See Waite, *Pictorial Key to the Tarot,* p.121.)

16 Dore, p.23.

17 Ibid, p.115.

18 Waite, *Key to the Tarot,* p.77.

19 Ibid, p.121.

20 Waite, *Pictorial Key to the Tarot,* p.159.

21 Dore, p.23.

22 Waite, *Key to the Tarot,* p xiv.

23 Waite, *Pictorial Key to the Tarot,* p.145.

24 Waite, *Key to the Tarot,* p.22.

25 Waite, *Pictorial Key to the Tarot,* p.139.

26 Ibid, p.140.

27 Ibid.

28 *Oxford English Dictionary,* available at: www.oed.com, 2022.

29 Waite, *Key to the Tarot,* p.119.

30 Waite, *Pictorial Key to the Tarot,* p.130.

31 Nicholas.

32 Waite, *Key to the Tarot,* p.30.

33 Ibid, p.119.

34 hooks, bell, *All About Love,* HarperCollins, New York, 2001, p. 87.

35 Ibid.

36 Ibid, p.90.

37 Ibid, p.93.
38 Ibid, p.233.

Chapter 1

1 Dore, p.36.

Chapter 2

1 Waite, *Key to the Tarot*, pp.124–5.
2 Dore, p.92.

Chapter 3

1 Dore, pp.55–7.
2 You can find out more about Kalī in the following titles: *Kalī Puja* by Swami Satyananada Saraswait; in the works of the Hindu Shakta poet and 18th-century saint Ramprasad Sen; Shanmukha Anantha Natha and Shri Ma Kristina Baird's *Divine Initiation*; the *Dictionary of Hindu Lore and Legend* by Anna L Dallapiccola; *The Rise of the Goddess in Hindu Tradition* by Tracy Pintchman; *The Goddess of Kalī of Kolkata* by Shoma A Chatterji; and "Kalī the Dark Mother" by Irina Kuzminsky. It is always important to consult source texts where you can, so reading the *Mahabharata* and beginning with Hindu mythology would be a good way to begin, before moving on to Hindu scholars' analysis of Kalī as a goddess figure.
3 Hylton, Ethosheia and Gharavi, Tina, *African Queens*: "Njinga", Netflix, episodes 1 and 2. Released 15 Feb 2023. Available at: www.netflix.com/watch/81459060?trackId=155573560
4 Robertson, J, "Power Masterclass", NUS UK Conference for New Sabbatical Officers, 2014.
5 See: www.nusconnect.org.uk/resources/democracy-is-dead-long-live-democracies/
6 Robertson. (This theory was also borrowed from VeneKlasen, L., Miller, V., "Power and empowerment", PLA Notes, 2002, 43: 39–41)

Chapter 4

1 Dore, p.69.
2 Ibid.
3 Ra Uru Hu, *The Human Design System*, 1992, CreateSpace, Scotts Valley, CA, p. 4.
4 Sinek, Simon, *Start with Why*, Penguin Books, London, 2009.
5 The online Oxford Dictionaries definition of crisis.

Chapter 5

1 These questions have been adapted from their original format, shared with me by Mel Harris, an Edinburgh-based executive, coach, and management consultant who introduced me to the values compass exercise in 2015. In the format given here, the questions are less heteronormative, single-partner based, and colonialist in their wording to reflect more modern, inclusive perspectives on relating, living, and being.
2 Rilke, Rainer Maria, *Letters to a Young Poet*, Penguin Books, London, 1929 (first translated edition) and 2011, p.18.
3 See: www.hubofallthings.com
4 Robinson, Sir Ken (narrator), "Changing Education Paradigms", RSAnimate, Royal Society of Arts, 2011. Available at: www.youtube.com/watch?v=zDZFcDGpL4U&ab_channel=RSA
5 Inglehart, Ronald F, "Why is Religion Suddenly Declining?", Oxford University Press website, 7 Dec 2020. Available at: https://blog.oup.com/2020/12/why-is-religion-suddenly-declining/

Chapter 6

1 "Quiet quitting" is when an employee puts in the bare minimum of effort at work. For further reading, see: www.bbc.com/worklife/article/20230828-workers-are-quiet-quitting-and-only-employers-can-stop-it
2 The "Great Shift" refers to the move to remote working in some companies, but also applies to the wider change in attitude during

the early years of the pandemic, when people began to make major life changes as soon as they were out of lockdown – like cross-country moves, getting pets, leaving jobs, and ending friendships. This suggested a wider shift in people's priorities as they began to assess what was important to them. For more information, see this Refinery 29 article: www.refinery29.com/en-gb/pandemic-changed-priorities-career-moving

3 The Gottman Institute takes a research-based approach to relationships. The institute is the culmination of the work of doctors John and Julie Gottman, who famously came up with "The Four Horsemen of the Apocalypse" of relationships that indicate relationship failure or a pathway to relationship decline; these are Contempt, Criticism, Stonewalling, and Defensiveness. See also Lisita, E, "The Four Horsemen: Criticism, Contempt, Defensiveness, and Stonewalling", Gottman Institute website, 23 Apr 2023. Available at: www.gottman.com/blog/the-four-horsemen-recognizing-criticism-contempt-defensiveness-and-stonewalling/

4 McDriguez, Santana, "Misunderstood Sayings . . . and Books that Prove the Counterparts True", Anythinklibraries.org, 1 Mar 2021. Available at: www.anythinklibraries.org/blog/misunderstood-sayings#:~:text=%E2%80%9CThe%20blood%20of%20the%20covenant,that%20you%20don't%20choose.

Chapter 7

1 Waite, *Key to the Tarot*, p.xiv.
2 See the *Britannica* definition: https://www.britannica.com/science/chaos-theory

Chapter 8

1 Dore, pp.35–7.
2 Lanyadoo, Jessica, *Ghost of a Podcast*, episode 287, 2022. Available at: www.lovelanyadoo.com/ghost-of-a-podcast/2022/11/27/287-acceptance-horoscope

3 Gray, Eden, *A Complete Guide to the Tarot*, Bantam, New York, p.46.

Chapter 9

1 Lanyadoo.
2 Karimova, H, "The Emotion Wheel: What It is and How to Use It [+PDF]", Positive Psychology.com, 24 Dec 2017. Available at: https://positivepsychology.com/emotion-wheel/
3 Staff writer, "Robert Plutchik's Wheel of Emotions", Study.com, 2023. Available at: https://study.com/academy/lesson/robert-plutchiks-wheel-of-emotions-lesson-quiz.html
4 Dhuka, Faruz, "How to Use 'Wheel of Emotions' to Express Better Emotions", Medium website, 24 May 2020. Available at: https://medium.com/age-of-awareness/how-to-use-wheel-of-emotions-to-express-better-emotions-8037255aa661
5 Dass, Ram, *Remember, Now Be Here, Now Here Be*, Lama Foundation, San Cristobal, NM, 1971, p.12.
6 Staff Writer, "Margaret Mead", Good Reads website, 2023. Available at: www.goodreads.com/quotes/1071-never-doubt-that-a-small-group-of thoughtful-committed-citizens

Chapter 10

1 See Alexander, M, *The New Jim Crow: Mass Incarceration in the Age of Colourblindness*, The New Press, New York, 2010.
2 Gash, T, *Criminal: Why People Do Bad Things*, Allen Lane, London, 2016.
3 Bradley Ruder, D, "The Enteric Nervous System that Regulates Our Gut is Often Called the Body's 'Second Brain'", *The Gut and Brain*, Harvard Medical School, Winter 2017. Available at: https://hms.harvard.edu/news-events/publications-archive/brain/gut-brain#:~:text=The%20enteric%20nervous%20system%20that,brain%20when%20something%20is%20amiss

4 Cleveland Clinic, "Vagus Nerve", Cleveland Clinic website, 11 Jan 2022. Available at: https://my.clevelandclinic.org/health/body/22279-vagus-nerve.

5 Macguire, J, "When You Change Your Nervous System, You Change Your Life", Nervous System School website, Jun 2023. Available at: www.nervoussystemschool.com

6 Science and Nonduality, Jun 2023. Available at: www.scienceandnonduality.com

7 Lang, K, "How Phthalates Accelerate the Growth of Uterine Fibroids", Medical News Today website, 18 Nov 2022. Available at: www.medicalnewstoday.com/articles/how-phthalates-accelerate-the-growth-of-uterine-fibroids

8 Léger-Goodes, T, Malboeuf-Hurtubise, C, Mastine, T, Généreux, M, Paradis, P O and Camden, C, "Eco-Anxiety in Children: A Scoping Review of the Mental Health Impacts of the Awareness of Climate Change", *Frontiers of Psychology*, 25 Jul 2022, National Library of Medicine, National Institute of Health. Available at: www.ncbi.nlm.nih.gov/pmc/articles/PMC9359205

9 Anon, *Aura Reading Cards*, Gift Republic, London, 2023.

10 Newson, R and Singh, A, "How Blue Light Affects Sleep", Sleep Foundation website, 17 Mar 2023. Available at: www.sleepfoundation.org/bedroom-environment/blue-light#:~:text=Inversely%2C%20exposure%20to%20blue%20light,we%20are%20trying%20to%20sleep

Chapter 11

1 Staff writer, "'Gaslighting' Named *Merriam-Webster*'s 2022 Word of the Year", Psychiatrist.com website, 29 Nov 2022. Available at: www.psychiatrist.com/news/gaslighting-named-merriam-websters-2022-word-of-the-year/#:~:text='Gaslighting'%20Named%20Merriam%2DWebster's,of%20The%20Year%20%7C%20Psychiatrist.com

2 Definition of DARVO, University of Oregon website. Available at: https://dynamic.uoregon.edu/jjf/defineDARVO.html

3 Villines, Z, "What is Gray Rocking?", reviewed by Marney White, Medical News Today website, 10 Jan 2023. Available at: www.medicalnewstoday.com/articles/grey-rock.

Chapter 12

1 Dore, p.120.
2 Shove, Elizabeth, *Comfort, Cleanliness and Convenience: The Social Organization of Normality*, Berg, New York, 2003.

SELECT BIBLIOGRAPHY

Alexander, M, *The New Jim Crow: Mass Incarceration in the Age of Colourblindness*, The New Press, New York, 2010

Allende, S C, *Be More Pirate: Or, How to Take on the World and Win*, Penguin, London, 2018

Askew, C and Tarbuck, A (eds), *The Modern Craft: Powerful Voices on Witchcraft Ethics*, Watkins Publishing, London, 2022

Bradley, R D, "The Enteric Nervous System that Regulates Our Gut is Often Called the Body's 'Second Brain'", *The Gut and Brain*, Harvard Medical School, Winter 2017. Available at: https://hms.harvard.edu/news-events/publications-archive/brain/gut-brain#:~:text=The%20enteric%20nervous%20system%20that,brain%20when%20something%20is%20amiss

Brown, A M, *Pleasure Activism: The Politics of Feeling Good*, AK Press, Edinburgh, 2019

Campbell, J, *The Hero with a Thousand Faces*, Fontana Press, London, 1993

Chatterji, S A, *Goddess Kalī of Kolkata*, UBS Publishers' Distributors, New Delhi, 2006

Cleghorn, E, *Unwell Women: A Journey Through Medicine and Myth in a Man-Made World*, Weidenfeld & Nicolson, London, 2021

Cleveland Clinic staff writer, "Vagus Nerve", Cleveland Clinic website, 11 Jan 2022. Available at: https://my.clevelandclinic.org/health/body/22279-vagus-nerve.

Dallapiccola, A L, *Dictionary of Hindu Lore and Legend*, Thames & Hudson, London, 2004

Dhuka, F, "How to Use 'Wheel of Emotions' to Express Better Emotions", Medium website, 24 May 2020. Available at:

https://medium.com/age-of-awareness/how-to-use-wheel-of-emotions-to-express-better-emotions-8037255aa661

Dore, J, *Tarot for Change: Using the Cards for Self-Care, Acceptance, and Growth*, Hay House, Carlsbad, 2021

Fleming, P, *Resisting Work: The Corporatization of Life and Its Discontents*, Temple University Press, Philadelphia, 2015

Francis, G, *Recovery: The Lost Art of Convalescence*, Profile Books, London, 2022

Freyd, J, "What is DARVO?", Centre for Institutional Courage, University of Oregon, 2023. Available at: https://dynamic.uoregon.edu/jjf/defineDARVO.html

Gallagher, A M, *Inner Magic: A Guide to Modern Witchcraft*, Octopus Books, London, 2001

Gash, T, *Criminal: Why People Do Bad Things*, Allen Lane, London, 2016

Gaventa, J, *Power and Powerlessness: Quiescence and Rebellion in an Appalachian Valley*, University of Illinois Press, Chicago, 1980

Gift Republic, *Aura Reading Cards*, London, 2023

Gray, E, *A Complete Guide to the Tarot*, Bantam, New York, 1992

Herstik, G, *Craft: How to be a Modern Witch*, Ebury Press, London, 2018

Hodges, K, *Warriors, Witches, Women: Mythology's Fiercest Females*, White Lion Publishing, London, 2020

hooks, b, *All About Love: New Visions*, William Morrow and Company, New York, 2001

Hsiao, A and Lim, A (eds), *Book of Dissent*, Verso, London, 2010

Hylton, E and Gharavi, T, *African Queens*: "Njinga", episodes 1 and 2, Netflix. Released: 15 Feb 2023. Available at: www.netflix.com/watch/81459060?trackId=155573560

Inglehart, R F, "Why is Religion Suddenly Declining?", Oxford University Press website, 7 Dec 2020. Available at: https://blog.oup.com/2020/12/why-is-religion-suddenly-declining/

Karimova, H, "The Emotion Wheel: What It is and How to Use It [+PDF]", Positive Psychology.com, 24 Dec 2017. Available at: https://positivepsychology.com/emotion-wheel/

Kimmerer, R W, *Braiding Sweetgrass: Indigenous Wisdom, Scientific Knowledge and the Teachings of Plants*, Penguin, London, 2013

Kuzminsky, Irina, "Kalī the Dark Mother", *Esoteric Quarterly*, 15(1), 2019, pp.31–54

Lang, K, "How Phthalates Accelerate the growth of Uterine Fibroids", Medical News Today website, 18 Nov 2022. Available at: www.medicalnewstoday.com/articles/how-phthalates-accelerate-the-growth-of-uterine-fibroids

Lanyadoo, J and Greenaway, T, *Astrology for Real Relationships: Understanding You, Me, and How We All Get Along*, Ten Speed Press, Berkeley, 2020

Léger-Goodes, T, Malboeuf-Hurtubise, C, Mastine, T, Généreux, M, Paradis, P O and Camden, C, "Eco-Anxiety in Children: A Scoping Review of the Mental Health Impacts of the Awareness of Climate Change", *Frontiers of Psychology*, National Library of Medicine, National Institute of Health, 25 Jul 2022. Available at: www.ncbi.nlm.nih.gov/pmc/articles/PMC9359205/

Lisita, E, "The Four Horsemen: Criticism, Contempt, Defensiveness, and Stonewalling", Gottman Institute website, 23 Apr 2023. Available at: www.gottman.com/blog/the-four-horsemen-recognizing-criticism-contempt-defensiveness-and-stonewalling/

Macguire, J, "When You Change Your Nervous System, You Change Your Life", Nervous System School, Jun 2023. Available at: www.nervoussystemschool.com

Mandybur, J, *Rainbow Power: Manifest Your Dream Life with the Creative Magic of Colour*, Hardie Grant, London, 2022

Maté, G, and Maté, D, *The Myth of Normal: Trauma, Illness and Healing in a Toxic Culture*, Vermilion, London, 2022

McDriguez, Santana, "Misunderstood Sayings . . . and Books that Prove the Counterparts True", Anythinklibraries.org, 1 Mar 2021. Available at: www.anythinklibraries.org/blog/misunderstood-sayings#:~:text=%E2%80%9CThe%20

blood%20of%20the%20covenant,that%20you%20 don't%20choose

Natha, S A, *Divine Initiation,* Shri Kali, Sadolxem, 2001

Newson, R, and Singh, A, "How Blue Light Affects Sleep", Sleep Foundation website, 17 Mar 2023. Available at: www. sleepfoundation.org/bedroom-environment/blue-light#:~: text=Inversely%2C%20exposure%20to%20blue%20light, we%20are%20trying%20to%20sleep

Nicholas, C, *You Were Born for This: Astrology for Radical Self-Acceptance,* Yellow Kite, London, 2020

Nicholas, C, "Week of October 31st", Astrology of the Week Reading/Podcast, CHANI App

NUS staff writer, "Democracy is Dead! Long Live Democracies!", National Union of Students website, 18 Feb 2018, Available at: www.nusconnect.org.uk/resources/democracy-is-dead-long-live-democracies/

Odell, J, *How to Do Nothing,* Melville House Publishing, New York, 2019

Oxford Dictionaries staff writer, "Crisis", Oxford Dictionaries website, 2023. Available at: www.oed.com/dictionary/ crisis_n?tab=meaning_and_use#7813670

Pintchman, T, *The Rise of the Goddess in Hindu Tradition,* State University of New York Press, New York, 1994

Psychiatrist.com staff writer, "'Gaslighting' Named *Merriam-Webster*'s 2022 Word of the Year", Psychiatrist.com website, 29 Nov 2022. Available at: www.psychiatrist. com/news/gaslighting-named-merriam-websters-2022-word-of-the-year/#:~:text='Gaslighting'%20Named%20 Merriam%2DWebster's,of%20The%20Year%20%7C%20 Psychiatrist.com

Ra Uru Hu, "Introduction to the Human Design System", Jovian Archive, 2010, p.4. Available at: www.jovianarchive. com/Stories/10/Introduction_to_the_Human_Design_ System

Rilke, R M, *Letters to a Young Poet,* Penguin Classics, London, 2011

Robinson, K (narrator), "Changing Education Paradigms", RSAnimate, Royal Society of Arts, 2011. Available at: www. youtube.com/watch?v=zDZFcDGpL4U&ab_channel=RSA

Robinson, K and Aronica, L, *The Element: How Finding Your Passion Changes Everything*, Penguin, London, 2009

Saraswati, S S, *Kalī Puja*, Sunstar Publishing, Iowa, 1999

Science and Nonduality website, 2023. Available at: www. scienceandnonduality.com

Science Direct staff writer, "Chaos Theory", Science Direct, 2011. Available at: www.sciencedirect.com/topics/earth-and-planetary-sciences/chaos-theory

Sheridan, L, *The Comparison Cure: How to be Less "Them" and More You*, Orion Spring, London, 2019

Shove, E, *Comfort, Cleanliness and Convenience: The Social Organization of Normality*, Berg, New York, 2003. Available at: https://scholar.google.co.uk/citations?view_op=view_citat ion&hl=en&user=w-t6aYYAAAAJ&citation_for_view=w-t6aYYAAAAJ:u5HHmVD_uO8C or www.homepages.ucl. ac.uk/~ucessjb/S3%20Reading/shove%2003.pdf

Stardust, L, *Saturn Return Survival Guide*, Hardie Grant, London, 2021

Stibal, V, *Theta Healing®: Introducing an Extraordinary Energy Healing Modality*, Hay House, London, 2006

———, *Advanced Theta Healing®: Harnessing the Power of All That Is*, Hay House, London, 2009

Study.com staff writer, "Robert Plutchik's Wheel of Emotions", Study.com, 2023. Available at: https://study.com/academy/ lesson/robert-plutchiks-wheel-of-emotions-lesson-quiz.html

Tarbuck, A, *A Spell in the Wild: A Year (and Six Centuries) of Magic*, Two Roads, London, 2020

Van der Kolk, B, *The Body Keeps the Score: Mind, Brain and Body in the Transformation of Trauma*, Penguin, London, 2014

Villines, Z, "What is Gray Rocking?", Medical News Today website, 10 Jan 2023. Available at: www.medicalnewstoday. com/articles/grey-rock

Waite, A E, *The Key to the Tarot: The Official Companion to the World Famous Original Rider Waite Tarot Deck*, Rider Books, London, 1910

——, *The Pictorial Key to the Tarot: A Visual Companion to the Rider Waite Tarot*, Rider Books, London, 1910

ACKNOWLEDGEMENTS

This book would not exist without the support of Alice Tarbuck and Claire Askew, who invited me to contribute a chapter *The Modern Craft: Powerful Voices on Witchcraft Ethics*. That chapter provided the spark for me to write this book and prompted Watkins to publish it.

As I have been on my own journey with healing and energy, I have encountered many teachers and guides. From shamans and artist healers to Theta and movement healers, I have only been made more grounded and aware by your presence. Thank you all for your guidance, love, care, and support. You know who you are, but a few names I must mention are Eileen Hall, Jennifer Main, and Emily Phillips. To the coaches that have held me so beautifully Nadia and Dawn Thompson. To Jason who has been a large part of this journey in sharing my voice and keeping me accountable.

For the readers that I return to for their guidance from the tarot, astrology, and the Akashic Records, Amelia Amber-Lee (Carnelian Keep Tarot), Kalem Turner (Fortune by Kalem), Daya Parvati, and Marina Oswald (talk with marina). To the people that have created community for so many like Brook Mackay-Brock (Black Moon Botanica).

To the readers, mediums, astrologers, and healers that hold us in virtual community, like Chani Nicholas, Jessica Lanyadoo, Jerico Mandybur, Chris Corsini, Colin Bedell, Matthew Oliver, Bri Luna, and Jill Wintersteen.

To the yogis that have created beautiful space for me to transmute energy over the years, Anna Hodgart, Paula Radziszewska, and Rebecca Duncan.

To my teachers in faith like Ali Newell and Harriet Harris in Edinburgh, Matthew Hanisian, Erin Hensley, Wendy Stengel, George, and the Barbaras in Washington, D.C. Thank you to those at Grace Episcopal, Maret, and the University of Edinburgh to enabled me to explore wisdom traditions with a hunger and voracity that was always encouraged. To Mr Wills for demonstrating how religion can be understood with a fluidity of interpretations. To my teachers in life at Barrie and Newport who were not afraid to bring themselves into the classroom, including the wonderful Ms Jones.

To the landscapes and places on this earth that have brought so much healing and so many predestined encounters, from the deserts of Sedona to the jungles of Bali; from the cobbled streets of Washington, D.C. to the coastline of Cancun; from the tan cliffs of the Algarve and the caverns of Paradise Valley and Taghazout. I extend my gratitude to the terrain that has brought me so many insights and unlocked so much of my consciousness in ways I never imagined.

To my therapists, Candace and Gabriella, whom have both had a profound effect on my life and to whom I will be forever grateful. To all of the people that taught me how not to be. I am forever appreciative for the lessons you taught, me even if they came to pass the hard way.

To my incredible editor Ella Chappell who created the perfect container for me to write this book and who supported me at every stage of this process with grace, calm, and fire. To copyeditor Sue Lascelles and to the entire team at Watkins who have been beautiful advocates for this book.

To Pai and Grandma. You are no longer with us, but I carry your spirits with me always. To my ancestors who continue to guide me and watch over me.

To my partner Paul, who has held these words with love and care. To Clélia, who sits and watches from her favourite perches in the house or keeps me company while she slumbers.

And last to Bella Caledonia and the Auld Reekie. Getting distance from you was the only way this volume could pour itself out of me. The mystery and magic of this city never ages. The layers of beauty never cease to unearth what the darkness allows us to discover.

ABOUT THE AUTHOR

BRIANA PEGADO FRSA is a fellow of the Royal Society of Arts. She is a trained ThetaHealer, a psychic intuitive, a student of astrology and an artist. She was named one of Scotland's 30 Under 30 Inspiring Young Women in 2017 and has won a number of awards for her work as a social entrepreneur in the creative industries. Currently, she is an anti-racism and governance consultant working across the third and public sector. She is a data-driven innovation ambassador for the Edinburgh Futures Institute.